MBO II

A SYSTEM OF MANAGERIAL LEADERSHIP FOR THE 80s

George S. Odiorne

Fearon Pitman Publishers, Inc.
Belmont, California

Illustrations: Carl Brown

Jacket design: Russell Leong

ISBN–0–8224–0977–1
Library of Congress Catalog Card Number: 78–72336
Printed in the United States of America.

2.9 8 7 6 5 4 3 2 1

Contents

PART **4** MBO in Operation:
The Subsystems Affected   177

PART **5** The Hard Part of MBO:
Making It Work   269

Preface

When *Management by Objectives* was published in 1965, the system of management by objectives (MBO) was considered a new idea and the book was the first to be published by that title. Even though others (such as Peter Drucker and Ed Schleh) had written about MBO, and there had been articles and speeches about it, it certainly wasn't management orthodoxy. As we enter the 1980s, however, it can be said that MBO is *the* dominant form of management in large corporations and in government. Studies have shown the extent of its adoption.

In 1965 MBO was still considered a rather original and useful form of management performance appraisal. Indeed, its major proponents, notably Douglas McGregor and Rensis Likert, treated it almost entirely as such a system. In the original edition of this book I proposed a new interpretation—that it was a *system of management*. This proved to be prophetic, for indeed it has evolved into such a system. The present edition of the book reflects the evolution and growth of MBO. It spells out the fundamental nature of MBO as a managerial system: it is not an addition to the manager's job but rather a way of managing.

In 1965 there was very little research into MBO to report. Here more research is included. There is also more on applications and implementation in this edition because there is more experience to describe.

In the past, the system of management by objectives has sometimes been interpreted as a simple approach to conducting the "annual performance review" required by the personnel department. Such a view was usually symptomatic of a clash between a system for measuring and controlling performance, and a highly personalized, normally chaotic, mode of operation. This book views MBO in a larger context than that of a mere appraisal procedure and regards appraisal as only one of the several subsystems operating within the larger system of goal-oriented management.

This book also posits that *any* system of management is better than no system at all. In defense of the social and political values system described here, let us hastily add that it incorporates most of the accepted major principles of management. Among its many advantages is vastly better appraisal of performance.

In the 1960s one often heard the question: "Is management by objectives really a *system*?" Purists in systems design would ask: "Where are the networks? Where are the 'three time estimates' of PERT? Where does probability analysis come in?" The answer is that there is nothing in management by objectives that excludes such subsystems if the circumstances call for their use. However, a general system of management—if it is actually to be used by the majority of working managers to improve results—should not employ special subsystems merely for the sake of being "systematic." That is, a management system:

- Shouldn't overcomplicate and oversophisticate the function of being a manager but should try to simplify as much as possible a job that has become laden with data, methods, and procedures.
- Shouldn't be dominated by its mechanics or by recipes to be followed slavishly.
- Shouldn't be so philosophical and speculative that its effects are beyond measurement. Measurement of results is imperative because, ultimately, the economy itself imposes a crude but effective measure: something of value must be produced.
- Should allow line managers to use it without having to lean on staff specialists every step of the way.
- Should be reasonably self-regulating and self-operating rather than requiring heavy inputs of fear, control, or direction by a few top managers.

Management by objectives is, in itself, not a complex system. Indeed its first requirement is that it *simplify* and add meaning to overwhelming masses of information. How necessary this is for today's managers is all too evident. Jargon assaults them on all sides—human relations, operations research, delegation, PERT, supportive management, discipline, linear programming, control organization, job evaluation, responsibility accounting, motivation, methods analysis, communications, value engineering, Theory X, Theory Y, and all the rest. Without a system that classifies and shows input and output effects, it is impossible to make sense, let alone practical use, of all these terms.

The major premises of MBO can be stated as follows:

1. Business management takes place within an economic system that provides the environmental situation for the individual firm. This environment which has changed drastically over the past forty-five years imposes new requirements on companies and on individual managers.

2. As a way of managing aimed at meeting these new requirements, MBO presumes that the first step in management is to identify by one means or another the *goals* of the organization. All other management methods and subsystems follow this preliminary step.

3. Once organizational goals have been identified, responsibility is distributed among individual managers in such a way that their combined efforts are directed toward achieving those goals.

4. Managerial behavior is assumed to be more important than personality, and this behavior should be defined in terms of results measured against established goals, rather than in terms of common goals for all managers or common methods of managing.

5. While participation is highly desirable in goal setting and decision making, its principal merit lies in its social and political value rather than in its effect on production, though even here it may have a favorable impact, and in any case seldom hurts.

6. The successful manager is a manager of situations, most of which are best defined by identifying the purpose of the organization and the managerial behavior best calculated to achieve that purpose. This means that there is no one best pattern of management, since all management behavior is discriminatory, related to specific goals and shaped by the larger economic system within which it operates.

During the past twenty-four years I have personally observed MBO in operation in many different organizations, have studied literally thousands of statements of objectives set by operating managers, and have assisted in subsequent evaluations of the effects. At General Mills, a pioneer in the formal installation of this system, I obtained many valuable insights while serving as a member of the company's executive team. In various forms, MBO has long been used by General Motors, DuPont, General Electric, and numerous other leading corporations.

Many thanks are due the many practitioners who developed the basic ideas of MBO in use. A great deal of scholarly research into the applications of MBO has been done on campus and in behavioral science and organizational development departments of corporations and government agencies. While it is not possible to note all of these sources, credit is given wherever possible in the notes, which have been moved to the back of the book in order to make the flow of the text smoother. Readers who wish to study further and to check sources may use these notes to assist them.

Appreciation is extended to many generations of students at the University of Michigan, the University of Utah, and the Amherst Campus of the University of Massachusetts who have studied MBO under me and given me the advantage of their best critical thinking. Numerous other colleagues have made a heavy impact upon the development of the ideas in this book. Peter Drucker (my original professor who introduced me to MBO many years ago), Earl Brooks of Cornell University, and others such as George Morrisey, Al Schrader, Geary Rummler, John Humble, Bill Reddin, Dale McConkey, and many, many industrial leaders have helped me shape the concepts and procedures into their present form.

George S. Odiorne

PART 1

Management by Objectives as a Philosophy and General Theory of Management

What began twenty-five years ago as a simple technique for managers doing the annual performance review has blossomed into a general theory of management. The three chapters in this first part spell out three facets of that growth:

Chapter 1. The Simple World of MBO and How It Became So Sophisticated
Chapter 2. MBO as a Style for Managers
Chapter 3. Stemming the Decline of Risk Taking and Innovation

CHAPTER 1

The Simple World of MBO and How It Became So Sophisticated

For every complex problem in the world there exists a simple solution which is always wrong. . . .

—H. L. Mencken

When management by objectives (MBO) started getting popular, it was grabbed up by everyone in sight as a simple solution to a whole batch of complicated problems.

All you had to do, it was thought, was sit down with each subordinate at the beginning of each year and talk with him or her about objectives and—Shazam! . . . MBO would solve every problem. People would be motivated, committed, responsible, productive, happy. The boss would get terrific productivity, lower costs, higher profits. The method would produce participative management suggested Doug McGregor, and it would produce management planning and control said Peter Drucker. It was almost as though people who managed by objectives had 22 percent fewer cavities than people who managed by other systems.

In just enough instances to attract favorable attention, many of these benefits were realized. But in a lot of others, gaining these advantages turned out to be more of a hard, long haul involving tough follow-up. Thus, along about 1970 it began to dawn on people that MBO was a lot more complex and required a lot more skill and attention than simply having a folksy little chat with the help at the start of each year.

MBO is complicated, but it is deceptively simple in its underlying theory, which is: *the first step in managing anything is to define your*

2

objective before you release any resources or spend any time trying to achieve it.

Though hard to practice competently, MBO is easy to explain and it has the advantage of being both *systematic* (logical, orderly, rational, and conscious) and *humanistic* (people-improving, equitable, developmental, therapeutic, and caring).

Once MBO became widespread, people began to make all sorts of discoveries about it:

- "We've always done things that way."
- "History shows that the basic idea has been embedded into leadership practices for centuries."
- "It is really applied common sense."

Because MBO has become orthodoxy, it seems worthwhile (at least to me) to review briefly the way it got started and how it developed. If you disagree and don't care a darn about such background stuff, simply turn now to Part 2 and get going on how to use and apply MBO. I really think, however, you'll find it invaluable to get the answers to three questions about MBO before you start applying it:

1. Who constructed the whole idea to begin with and how did it grow?
2. Has anybody ever really tested it with rigorous research, and, if so, what did they find out?
3. Are there people who still oppose it, and, if so, why do they feel that way?

Who Constructed MBO?

One of the more popular pastimes among some academics is discovering the origins of the MBO idea. Such quests have unearthed a plethora of originators.[1] Old Testament quotations and examples, including Abraham's covenant with God and Moses' search for the Promised Land, have been cited. One wag has suggested that the goal "Promised Land" was without criteria, and that's why it took forty years to reach and then proved to be the only place in the Middle East without oil. The Koran is cited: "If you don't know where you are going, any road will get you there." Several Greeks, including Aristotle, noted the importance of *purposes* to success. In modern times, Disraeli declaimed that "success is a product of unremitting attention to purpose." Systems expert C. West Churchman, who was trained as a philosopher, has noted that the earliest constructions of the systems approach are readily found in Plato, Aristotle, St. Thomas Aquinas, Nietzsche, Descartes, Hobbes, Leibniz, Bentham, Kant, Marx, and others.[2]

The idea of goals being defined as a preliminary step to all subsequent management actions seems to have permeated most management theory. It would be easy to construct an underlying management theory of goal-and-result-centered management from the histories of organizers of great corporations, such as Andrew Carnegie or Pierre du Pont.

For instance, when young du Pont joined his family business at the turn of the century, he came under the tutelage of Arthur Moxham who not only taught him the virtues of cost accounting but also profoundly impressed du Pont with analytical management. Moxham's balance sheets told at a glance which parts of the company made money and which did not, making it possible to have a rational basis for investment decisions. This attention to accounting and its development through statistical analysis was already in its formative stages before the turn of the century and comprised a set of lessons du Pont was to carry to other places and times to the advantage of his business. When he became president of General Motors in 1920, one of du Pont's first moves was to reorganize GM into divisional form and initiate the development of impersonal statistical and financial controls. As Chandler and Salsbury observe, "Only a constant flow of information on divisional activities and performance in terms of sales, output, and above all, return on investment could permit the division general managers to operate without constant personal supervision."[3]

When du Pont resigned from GM in 1923, he left a management system in which clear targets in inventory, return on investment (ROI), sales, output, and other important aspects of the business were in place. But despite a well-developed system for measuring ROI, GM had no well-defined governing objective against which to measure its results until 1925, as Alfred P. Sloan has pointed out. In 1925, the corporation adopted a concept created by Donaldson Brown which related a definite long-term return on investment objective to average or standard volume expectations over a number of years. These goals were broken down into volume, costs, prices, and rates of return on capital. Every car contained a standard amount of steel and also contained an engine, wheels, a battery, and so on. Standard cost hours, amounts paid for each purchased part, and the hours of labor required for each function followed. These were only in part accounting techniques, for they included statistical data, ratios, rates, and amounts for every business purpose.

"The guiding principle," Sloan says, "was to make our standards difficult to achieve, but possible to attain, which I believe is the most effective way of capitalizing on the initiative, resourcefulness, and capabilities of operating personnel."[4] This concept, Sloan points out, makes profit residual for most managers and also makes it possible to estimate very closely what profit will be at various volumes. Profit was tied to the Executive Bonus Plan, which in turn was based upon rewarding performance as it related to standards. It seems reasonable to suggest that it was Sloan, with his associates Donaldson Brown and Albert Bradley, who perfected the major elements of modern MBO. Indeed, Peter Drucker, who many years later conducted a study of GM's management system, reported to John Tarrant, his biographer, that he first heard the term *management by objectives* used by Alfred P. Sloan. Accordingly, both the detailed configuration of method and the language of MBO should properly be attributed to Sloan.[5]

In the marketing field, it was not du Pont or Sloan who developed the first rudimentary examples of MBO but John Henry Patterson of National Cash Register. Patterson had acquired a sagging company known as National Manufacturing Company and changed its name. After overhauling the design of the cash register so that it could be manufactured economically, he turned his attention to launching a selling and sales training program of unmatched effectiveness. He established a quota system and guaranteed territory instead of pitting one salesperson against another in the same circumscribed area. The quota system ran contrary to all selling concepts of that time and led Patterson to market domination in the field with 94 percent of the market.

It was the quota system under which Thomas Watson, Sr., learned his trade as a marketer, and in 1914 he transferred the idea to his own firm, the International Business Machines Corporation. By 1924, Watson had made it clear that his style of management was unique and astonishingly successful. The creation of the One Hundred Percent Club, open to those who had achieved their quota, was supplemented by an evangelical enthusiasm for success.

Part of the new IBM spirit was that no one was to think of himself or herself as a boss. "The farther we keep away from the boss proposition," Watson said in 1925, "the more successful we are going to be." On the other hand, one could be leader mainly on a one-to-one basis, with one person giving guidance to another by helping to do the job instead of just saying "do this." Thus, the supportive aspects of management that are so highly regarded in modern MBO—setting tough goals, showing great enthusiasm, and helping the subordinate achieve — were commonplace at IBM under Watson. In 1927 he told members of the One Hundred Percent Club, "It is a shame for any man, if he is in good health, to put in twelve months in a territory in our business and not come through with 100 percent of quota."[6] Watson demonstrated with unremitting energy that he would set high goals and exhorted everyone to attain those goals. If top management support is an essential ingredient of MBO, then Watson was living proof of its effectiveness. By 1930, goals-centered management was spreading.

Quite independently at Standard Oil of New Jersey, president Walter Teagle faced up to growing administrative problems in that giant, worldwide firm; and in 1933 he issued a memorandum that effected a basic MBO program, though it was not known by that name. The memo ended the era of the entrepreneurial genius method of management and provided for a complete delegation of operating authority to independent operating units, making each unit responsible for its operations in a given territory. At the corporate level, a coordinating committee defined goals and policies and approved operating and capital budgets and operating indicators proposed by the units. Annual meetings were held in which previously secret information was widely shared, and a strong program of training for younger managers was instituted.[7]

By 1940, this model of decentralization of operating authority, with commitments to a top-level policy control group, was recognized as a necessary form of organization in most corporate giants; and lessened control over means of operating was coupled with rising attention to outputs and results.[8]

Peter Drucker: The Theoretician of Divisionalization

In the late thirties, Peter Drucker, an Austrian by birth and an immigrant to the United States, was invited to consult with the management of General Motors. As an economist and an outsider, he brought to his study the observational skills of a Tocqueville or a Darwin. Without using questionnaires or statistical techniques, Drucker walked about conducting reportorial interviews, making notes, and drawing conclusions from common sense and systematic observations, which he then presented to GM in skillfully written reports.[9]

In analyzing the significance of decentralization and divisional forms of corporate organization, Drucker provided a distinction between *federal* and *functional* decentralization which was widely copied. The fact that he saw goals and objectives as secondary, a natural product of that key concept, is often missed. In his lectures at New York University in later years, it was the importance of decentralization as a route to greater industrial democracy, the personalization of large bureaucratic corporations, and the pushing down—or delegation—of decisions that he pressed upon his graduate classes. *A cogent case could be made that decentralization and divisionalization produced MBO, rather than any personal genius of an inventor*. Thus, necessity once again gives birth to invention.

The major limit of MBO as a means of making divisionalization work is its tendency to confine itself to financial goals. Yet with divisional organization it becomes apparent that no other concept of management will work at all. General Foods with 17 divisions, General Electric with 70 divisions, or ITT with 300 divisions could not be controlled by the most capable individual except by control over outputs and resources. The variety and sheer volume of activity makes the idea of close control of processes unthinkable.

It is not surprising, therefore, that in 1954 General Mills changed from a functional to a divisional form of organization prior to adopting MBO as its management style. The Drucker refinement of *organizational planning*, defined also by Holden, Fish, and Smith (1948) and Louis A. Allen's NICB study (1952), supplanted the previous "principles of organizations" approach. MBO made decentralization work! This development came in the nick of time, for corporate giants were beginning to demonstrate evidence of unmanageability in their functional form of organization.

Public concern over the size of corporations was widespread during the thirties. In his 1937 charge to the Temporary National Economic Committee (TNEC), President Franklin D. Roosevelt requested that the Congress address the question of whether the concentration of great power in private hands, "greater than that of the democratic government itself," was in the public interest.[10] It is plausible to speculate that without decentralization and divisionalization greater pressure for antitrust legislation or other laws to break up large corporations might have been a *fait accompli* today. Certainly, without divisionalization and the management processes to make it viable, conglomerates could not exist.

Drucker was undoubtedly forced into paying attention to MBO as a natural product of decentralization if we are to judge by the response of his audience to his lectures and books. The fact that Drucker is a political scientist at heart, and a management scientist by request only, is often overlooked. For him, MBO was a simple technique brought about and made necessary and logical by the need for political reform inside the modern corporation. His structures for management behavior did not grow out of any efficiency-engineer motives but out of the deeply held assumption that the preservation of the capitalist system required some basic structural changes within the corporate system. Thus, he was probably closer to those other Austrians Hayek and Von Mises than he was to McGregor, Maslow, or Likert. Accordingly, divisionalization was an end and MBO a means.

Drucker's first major report on General Motors was published in 1946 in his *Concept of the Corporation* which is totally devoid of any mention of management by objectives. The book described for the first time his concept of GM's plan of decentralization which Sloan had firmly put in place and skillfully operated. It was this decentralization, which Drucker described as a kind of *federalism,* that occupied his attention, but he did note that the relationship between central management and the respective divisions was achieved "through the power of the central management to set the goals for each division" and through setting limits on authority, checking progress, offering help, and relieving divisions of any work not related to goal attainment.

However, it was in his 1954 book, *The Practice of Management,* that Drucker first used the expressions *management by objectives* and *self-control,* which struck such a popular chord.[11] In part, management by objectives caught on as a concept that might be copied and applied by other large firms because of Drucker's extensive speaking schedule before management groups. It was during this period, when he was a professor at the graduate school of business at NYU, that Drucker moved the MBO concept to the center of his thinking rather than as a sideline to the major theme of decentralization.

Management Science and the Systems Approach

If there is a theoretical basis for MBO, perhaps it might be found in the evolution of management science, operations research, and the *systems approach.* Originating in the operations research movement during World War II, the systems approach emerged when physical scientists were drafted into duty to help solve complex strategic problems for the British Navy. By applying mathematical programming and modeling, they brought rigorous methods of analysis to social as well as military problems. From this came a more comprehensive approach to management known as the systems approach. This approach is commonly identified by Churchman's almost universally accepted 1968 definition: "A system is a set of parts coordinated to accomplish a set of goals."[12]

The techniques of the systems approach are mathematical and more sophisticated than most managers are accustomed to employing, but the basic stages are as follows:

1. Total system objectives are defined.
2. The system's environment, the fixed constraints, is defined.
3. The resources of the system are defined.
4. The activities of each component of the system are spelled out.
5. A method of managing to attain the goals is charted.

The most common elements in the systems approach are inputs, activities (processes), and outputs. The first step is to define the objectives in terms of hoped-for outputs. The choice of objectives is, of course, the first step in all variations of the systems approach, and without objectives, operations research is pointless. In the years since 1946, this field has been known sometimes as management science, sometimes as operations research and sometimes, in college and university curricula, as quantitative methods. For decision making, it is the definition of objectives (sometimes called the objectives function) that dominates the theoretical work. Operations research is the scientific approach to managing by objectives.

The effect of MBO has turned attention to the systems approach, and the training of thousands of managers and technical specialists in management science has perhaps had a more important effect upon current decision making than is ordinarily appreciated by more traditional managers and MBO devotees. The growing use of the systems approach in the many management decisions that affect marketing, plant location, inventory control, cash management, and investment has, in fact, substantially altered the ways complex management decisions are made.

1. The tools of mathematics were turned loose on tough management problems. Usually these problems were financial or were obscured by a rash of large numbers. Millions of dollars, thousands of products, and thousands of customers all created confusion. Management science, operations research, and the growing use of large computers made the systems approach a practical tool of management. All such management-science methods began with a definition of the systems *objectives*.

2. Concurrently with this rising complexity in decision making at the quantitative level came an ever larger array of management problems which called for a knowledge of behavioral science. The increasing number of engineers as employees produced a rising level of expectations of management. At the same time, minorities and women who had previously been left behind began to demand equal opportunity. A new generation of young people seeking a more participatory style of leadership from their elders surged into the colleges—occasionally rioting and overturning old leadership styles.

These two influences together produced a demand that management be *functional* (get the job done efficiently) and *developmental* (meet the human needs of organizations and people in them). The first edition of this book, written in 1965 and subtitled *A System of Managerial Leadership,* implied that MBO would solve both sets of problems at once.[13] The idea that a common thread ran between the two major problem areas—the rational and the human—was heartily welcomed. Such a marriage of two apparently discordant ideas around objectives had previously been tried by consultant Walter Mahler, and his success in help-ing clients solve this dual problem through MBO was considerable.

The Standards-of-Performance Movement

Before MBO as a philosophy could gain acceptance in corporate head-quarters and administrative offices, some deeply held attachments had to be supplanted. For one thing, performance appraisal was strongly tied to personality-assessment and trait-rating systems. The early human re-lations movement had made amateur psychologists of many managers, and so appraisal systems were often composed of lists of such personal-ity traits as initiative, drive, integrity, and loyalty. Managers were re-quired to rate subordinates against these traits, and their amateur clini-cal judgments became a part of their employees' permanent personnel files.

By 1950 there were widespread attacks upon this personality-based management by both academic and business groups. William H. Whyte, for instance, in his widely read book *The Organization Man,* said such personality-assessment methods were an invasion of privacy and repre-sented false scienticism.[14] And in industrial psychology there was in-creasing evidence that the concept of the occupational personality was not to be found, no matter how hard people searched. Then the Ameri-can Management Association, which became the leader in the educating of executives, came down hard in favor of more objective standards based upon agreed-upon goals and targets. Hundreds of thousands of managers from leading firms attended seminars, conferences, and courses where they were admonished to avoid personality-based assess-ments and instead define standards of managerial performance.[15]

The standards-of-performance movement of the fifties can be cred-ited with the decline of personality-based assessment systems, but the movement had its own problems. For one thing, standards of perfor-mance required reams of paper and inordinate amounts of time. Secondly, standards of performance were almost entirely oriented toward activities and duties rather than toward outputs. The standards-of-performance movement, then, reversed the way people thought about managerial per-formance (although the standards were unsystematic) and paved the way for the MBO movement, which emerged in the late fifties and blos-somed in the sixties.

The Original Adopters of MBO

With the appearance of Drucker's *The Practice of Management* in 1954 and a book and several articles by another consultant, Edward Schleh, a number of companies began to consider applying MBO.[16] These were not companies like GM that were already following the basic MBO idea without calling it that but companies turning toward decentralization or seeking improved managerial-appraisal plans.

Among the earliest was General Mills which had set up a division system under president Charles Bell in 1954. In 1955 Durward Balch, Vice-President of Personnel, conducted an extensive study of the MBO idea, and Professor Earl Brooks of Cornell, an early pioneer in designing and installing MBO programs, became a major consultant in implementation at General Mills. The creation of twelve new divisions in 1954 called not only for the selection, development, and appraisal of new division general managers but also for new group vice-presidents with profit responsibility who had some clear ideas as to what they expected and how their executives' bonuses would be administered.[17]

During this period Howard Johnson, who later at MIT became director of the Sloan program, dean, and then president, was employed at General Mills as Balch's assistant. Johnson's influence was undoubtedly great, and perhaps he was one of the earliest to note the important behavioral aspects of MBO, as well as its functional and profitable aspects. It was Johnson, when he joined MIT, who told Douglas McGregor about the General Mills appraisal system, and this became the basis of McGregor's classic article, "An Uneasy Look at Performance Appraisal," which appeared in the *Harvard Business Review* in 1959. McGregor was unabashedly a humanist and a strong advocate of participative management, and he urged the use of MBO as a vehicle for participative management.

At this time General Mills organized an executive development course jointly with three other Minneapolis companies, Honeywell, Dayton's, and the Northwest Bancorporation. In ensuing years, all top managers in the four companies were trained with a strong results-centered emphasis through this course. The course, which is now multi-company, started with top executives of the four companies and went through the officer ranks, and it became the first example of a formal implementation of what other corporations had slipped into their pro-in a more tentative fashion following decentralization.[18] From the course emerged a generation of executives for whom the basic management style was clearly MBO.

By 1960 it was established that if you didn't have an MBO system, you could acquire it by training your managers, starting at the top and working down through the organization. In 1959 the University of Michigan initiated the first monthly seminar to train managers in MBO, leading to a rash of similar university and association seminars, conferences, and courses.

Has MBO Really Been Tested by Research?

During the sixties there was a floodtide of MBO plans, but there was a notable lack of books on the subject. The first book with the title *Management by Objectives* was written by me in 1962 and published in 1965, after considerable testing in the Michigan Seminar. After that the literature grew rapidly.

One of the most important researchers in the field was E. A. Locke of the University of Maryland. His research was crucial to the acceptance of MBO on a widespread basis in corporations staffed with sophisticated human resource people. Locke produced an astonishing twenty-one articles, mainly in psychological journals, which probed and defined the effects of MBO. His first rigorous research examined such basic questions as "Does MBO Change Behavior?" He found that having goals improves performance results and motivates people to work and that when people set goals and achieve much, they enjoy their work more.

Locke demonstrated that MBO really works, and without his research there might not have followed the host of other scholarly research studies that, in effect, shaped the conditions by which MBO must abide in order to succeed.[19] This spate of rigorous study, in turn, generated further studies in refinements of Locke's work. For instance, Henry Tosi and Stephen Carroll of Michigan State University researched the kinds of people with whom goal setting would work and more generally defined the kinds of responses that could be predicted from MBO programs when various kinds of implementation techniques were tried.[20] At least ten doctoral dissertations in MBO, its extent of use, conditions for success, and special applications were produced during this period. The journals in which this literature appeared spanned the fields of psychology, management, education, and public and hospital administration. Locke, Latham of the Weyerhaeuser Company, Anthony Raia of U.C.L.A., Tosi, William Reddin, consultant Heinz Weihrich, William Reif of Arizona State University, Carroll, Marlow, and Bruce Kirchoff of the University of Nebraska produced a great volume of psychological research about MBO and its effects.

In the management literature, I have personally published some thirty-five books, articles, and publications; and John Humble, Dale McConkey of Wisconsin, George Morrisey, Peter Drucker, Charles Hughes, and Glenn Varney are among the major writers. The division of labor between the psychological and management contributions has been most productive. The management journal writers were refiners and wrote about MBO based upon field experience and "by construction." Almost always they were advocates. It was during this period that major developments in the field took place, and the management writers, often fresh from successes or failures with client companies, described new areas of application and new techniques in design and implementation. The application of MBO to such chronic management problems as selection, discipline, collective bargaining, compensation, marketing, and purchasing were described in case-study form and prescriptive articles. At every step the academic researcher probed and tested, drawing up lines of reservation and constraint, questioning assumptions, pricking bubbles, and refining techniques. The management professors and consultants initiated, designed, constructed, theorized, and speculated; and the behavioral researchers followed closely, deflating overly ambitious claims and clarifying the requirements of MBO in theory. In sum, without doubt, MBO is one of the best tested, most thoroughly researched techniques of management of recent times.

The MBO Haters

The ranks of those who detest the entire system of MBO are actually small, but their vehemence has been real and their motives understandable.

In one category, there are those who must be defined as journalistic needlers, such as the editor who assigns writers to "find a popular idea and stick a pin in it." The cover of *Purchasing Magazine* once showed a tombstone with the epitaph, MBO—R.I.P., and the story inside began by suggesting that MBO had indeed expired and that the article would comprise its obituary. Actually the article (which was based on interviews with some leading corporate purchasing directors) hedged considerably, for most of the stories stated conditions that *could* cause MBO to falter but then proceeded to describe how purchasing departments had overcome these defects. Not really dead but capable of failure seemed to be the substance of the article.

Professor Ed Wrapp of the University of Chicago attracted considerable attention in the business press with a 1966 article in *Harvard Business Review* by proposing that top management does not really set objectives but actually wheels and deals without much attention to goals, strategies, performance measures, and the like.

However, Dr. Harry Levinson's 1970 article, "Management by Whose Objectives?" in the same journal was a more fundamental attack upon the MBO idea. Levinson, one-time staff psychologist at the Menninger Clinic and long interested in the mental health of managers, expressed deep concern over the suppressive and top-down effects of MBO programs. These effects were a barrier to people seeking their *ego ideal* at work, a matter of considerable importance in Levinson's scheme of things. While the article did not bar MBO in all its forms, it did propose some serious limitations upon its top-down character.[21]

Many other critical articles about MBO cannot be included in the hater category, for they were written in a research vein. Such articles were more apt to describe the kinds of MBO practices that would cause the system to demotivate people and to fail. Tosi, Carroll, Raia, Ivancevich, Kirchoff, and Locke certainly were not blind in their acceptance of the idea of MBO, but they defined the conditions necessary to its effectiveness.

The National Education Assocation, strongly advocating opposition to MBO in the appraisal of teacher performance, expressed strong distaste for the whole idea, at least as it would apply to teachers. Teachers unions, it suggested, should come out against MBO-based rating systems because school boards and superintendents might use them to crack down on teachers and bust their unions. However, the NEA did concede that MBO might be satisfactory for administrators and principals rating one another.[22] I suspect that this objection grew more from a basic mistrust of any kind of administrative control of teachers than to the unique character of MBO. Indeed, this has been the exact way in which some school systems have employed MBO, and perhaps the rationale of the unions, considering their actual experience, is plausible. One school superintendent, for instance, announced the introduction of citywide MBO as follows: "We have adopted a new and modern management system known as MBO this fall. Every teacher will be required to submit their MBOs in September. If they are failing to achieve these MBOs by January, in detail, they will be warned. If they are still failing to achieve their MBOs at the year's end, their employment will be terminated for cause." It is not surprising that with a single memo he had created an ample complement of fearful MBO haters.

Similar applications in firms and government agencies have likewise produced coteries of mistrustful and angry MBO haters. The pervasive use of MBO in government at federal, state, and local levels has met with several types of opposition.

The *antiplanners* are a common type of manager in both business and government, and Churchman has identified several categories. One is the *adherent of practical approaches* that grow out of experience coupled with sound intuitions, solid leadership, and a brilliant mind. A second is the *skeptic* who believes that life and the world are so complicated that nobody could possibly understand them well enough to control or predict them. The skeptic is reluctant to try any planning method and hostile toward those who insist otherwise. Objectives, thinks the skeptic, should be "It all depends" and "We do things informally." Wrapp falls into this category and has ample company.[23]

A more serious kind of antiplanner is the *determinist* who believes that human choices are not in the hands of responsible people but in the hands of immutable social or physical forces that will produce outcomes in spite of human intervention. Evidence and analysis are pointless, for "What will be, will be." Governmental administrators who favor political maneuvering and incremental budgeting are often violently opposed to program planning and MBO. They believe that the determinism of changing political tastes and trends will determine goals and that these goals in turn will determine budgets, which will inevitably rise. Religious determinists reject the idea of defining human plans for the

Almighty has already chosen what will be. Mystical religions are more apt to adhere to such a belief than those that are strongly institutional. The Catholic and LDS (Mormon) churches operate by excellent MBO methods.

The fourth category of antiplanners is concerned almost wholly with the *integrity of the self* and with individual differences. The major purpose of life for these people is to know oneself, be oneself, and like oneself, and any formal system that would diminish that purpose should be banned. This view perhaps best expresses the rationale behind Levinson's opposition. While it might also be characteristic of other behavioral scientists, it would not include the "third force" group of psychologists such as McGregor, Maslow, or Herzberg. They place work and its fruits high in the scheme of things by which individuals find their self-expression and identity.

A final category of anti-MBO groups is that of the *existentialist*. This group adheres to a philosophical system that detests system. As Albert Camus expressed it, "If you lack character, you need a system." The world and human personality, it is felt, are rooted in existence and determined by luck, guilt, situationality, and death; all else is futile. Existence precedes essence, and we make ourselves by our choices. Yet even here, a close study of existentialism shows that purposes comprise an important part of this philosophy's scheme of things.

Summary

From its history, it is apparent that MBO is much more than a set of cookbook rules for managing a business. It consists of a philosophy that suggests that purposes and aims are important in determining the quality and style of life. It is also a concept that supplants other concepts such as personality-based management, or class- and cult-based management. In addition, MBO is a system that begins with hoped-for outputs, and measures the quality of effort and the effectiveness of resource utilization against these hoped-for outputs. It subsequently becomes a set of forms and procedures, its least important aspects. The future impact of MBO on such areas as personnel and training, governmental budgeting, and behavioral applications in supervisory management looks promising.

CHAPTER 2

MBO as a Style for Managers

If we can know where we are and something about how we got there, we might see where we are trending—and if the outcomes which lie naturally in our course are unacceptable, to make timely change.

—Abraham Lincoln

Like styles in clothing and office buildings, styles in management change. Management by objectives, in addition to being a somewhat scientific system and a humanistic mode of managing, is a *style* of managing. That style is one that is *situational*. That is, we adapt our behavior and *our goals* to suit the environment, the culture, and the milieu in which we are operating. As one behavioral scientist suggests, you sing hymns in church and bawdy songs at a party and never mix the two, or you'll be thrown out of both places. Therefore, it is important to look ahead and try to assess what kind of managerial style will be prevalent during the coming ten or fifteen years.

The dominant style will be a performance-based system and not one of caste, class, personality, or ancestry. This style is already apparent in legal and administrative rulings, such as those having to do with affirmative action, equal employment, and the strong attention to due process. We have opted in favor of rules and laws that look at achievement rather than personality, physique, or background.

Toward a Management Style Change for the Eighties

Management styles seem to last for ten-year periods. It is possible to spot the distinctive styles of the leadership in the workaday world of the

18

past three decades, and in looking at them we might be able to perceive what the managerial style of the eighties will be. For one thing, the social and cultural climates of each decade were distinctive.

The Fifties

Many people look back with nostalgia to the Good Old Days of the fifties. It was an age of personality, with Eisenhower the father of us all. There was Korea and the cold war. The space age came in with Sputnik. There was the growth of the welfare state, the emergence of the behavioral sciences, and the beginning of the important role of high-talent manpower. Permissiveness in the schools was part of an era of peace and prosperity, containing within it the seeds of a social explosion to follow.

The Sixties

A man on the moon, the revolutions of the college-age young people, the rise of the counterculture, the springing up of alienated blocs of people, and the decline in respect for authority all emerged during the decade of the sixties. This period taught organizations that minorities were willing to work, to organize, to fight for opportunities to get jobs, and to compete for the advantages held by the white middle class.

The Seventies

In this managerial climate, government became the partner of every executive. OSHA, ERISA, and hundreds of environmental and consumer-oriented laws and other regulations represented the intervention of Washington into the corporate decision-making process. Changes in laws on equal employment opportunity sparked the women's revolution. Due process in the work place and the presence of signs of a more informal life-style, as reflected in attire, hair length, and personal morality, became ordinary. An energy crunch made lasting changes in the way companies viewed growth and resource management.

Cultural Lag?

The leadership style of management is often as much a function of a situational background as it is of individual managers' initiative or taste. Managers influence the environment and are in turn influenced by it. Very often they are still responding to the culture of the past decade when the new one lands upon them, in part because problems and solutions require some lead time and such time appears to be collapsing on management. The management of the fifties seemed to be responding to the militant labor climate of the thirties, while the labor-market climate was filled with concerns of managing engineers and scientists. The management of the sixties responded well to the needs of the fifties in managing high-talent employees such as engineers and scientists, while outside their offices a racial revolution was going on. In the seventies, management was responding admirably to the racial pressures of the sixties at a time when the feminist pressures of the seventies were ringing about them. The management of the seventies was also busily responding to the counterculture of the sixties, wearing long sideburns and more casual clothes, as the generation of the seventies — more square and work oriented than ever before — came along out of college.

All of this, of course, isn't evidence of some special slow-wittedness but the common phenomenon of cultural lag that afflicts all parts of society and not just business. In fact, a pretty good case could be made that business seems to have a better speed of response than many other institutions in our society, such as education, the church, or the municipal government.

Unless responsible managers are able to see, however dimly, the major contours of the future, they are doomed to respond forever to the past and its faded problems. Perhaps the rise of delphi panels, long-range planning, strategic planning, and the study of the future with scenarios, Club of Rome computer forecasts, and the like are attributable to this need to look ahead.

What, then, is the basis of one having the temerity to forecast? Some rely upon statistical data, making computer forecasts. "If we don't change our ways there will be fifty persons per square foot on earth by the year 3000," one seer predicts. Others are less precise but nonetheless rely upon extrapolation combined with an active imagination. Mark Twain once projected, tongue in cheek, that since the Mississippi River had been shortened by floods by 150 miles between Cairo, Illinois and New Orleans, Louisiana during the eighteenth century, it was safe to conclude that the Mississippi would continue to shorten 1.5 miles per year indefinitely. Therefore, in 800 years, he said, Cairo and New Orleans would become a single municipality, with a single city council and common utility company. It's amazing how one can speculate based on very little information.

This chapter tries quite modestly, late in the seventies, to forecast what management styles will be required for the eighties, for most of the influences are already present which will shape the eighties. It is impossible to predict droughts, wars, energy crises, scientific breakthroughs, effects of terrorism, or similar major social and physical upheavals. However, it is probably safe to bet that some upheaval of large proportion will occur and that we will not fully respond to it until the nineties. But other events are already emerging that make preparation more possible for management. Such informed armchair prognostication is not wholly without value. Our purpose here is to make you a bit more future minded and to prompt you to do your own futuristic speculating.

By seeing "where we are trending," in Lincoln's phrase, we might be able to anticipate and avert some of the less desirable events that appear to lie naturally in our path or perhaps exploit opportunities that might otherwise be missed.

Ten Elements of Management Style for the Eighties

There are ten rather discernible elements of a management style for the eighties. They are as follows:

1. Old Shoe Will Be In

There will be less emphasis on reducing bureaucratic procedure and more on personal differences. When President Jimmy Carter in 1977 walked down the middle of Pennsylvania Avenue at his inauguration, wore a sweater to talk to the nation about energy, and carried his own briefcase on his travels, it was both a symptom and a signal. The trend has been to move away from status symbols, limousines, procedures, red tape, and rank exerting its privileges. Partly a reaction to Watergate and partly a carryover from the counterculture, the casual style has been manifested in the soft conversational speech, the one-liner instead of the long joke, denims in the executive suite, and trail bikes instead of limousines. A very human and down-to-earth style will become the accepted manner of behaving and of relating to people. Hortatory and inspirational speechifying is out. Listening carefully to others, responding with changes when confronted by the opposition without giving up basic strategies, and keeping pipelines open to the grass roots will be the executive way of the eighties.[1] The president of the corporation may want to hold on to friends from the early days in the plant, for example. Language will probably be more a "shucks" than the expletive-deleted style that followed the dirty speech movement on campus in the sixties. In its most extreme forms, this old-shoe style might even be an antiintellectual style.

2. Management Will Be More Systematic

It may seem paradoxical, but the leader of the eighties, shuffling about in old-shoe style, will also be considerably more systematic than any generation of managers before this decade.[2] This means that the systems approach will become more ordinary. There will be more computers in use, especially more mini- and microcomputers, which will have a devastating effect on many established practices. The manager of a small business will be able to use these powerful and very inexpensive devices for all kinds of managerial problems: handling receivables, inventories, reordering, payroll, payables, sales analysis, and follow up. This practice will probably be the death knell of the small certified public accountant who has not been keeping up with the computer. The minicomputers, with their large storage and computing capabilities, will erode some of the huge data processing empires that have grown up around the main-frame computers. More decentralization of decisions will be possible as the giant central computing facilities become obsolete and uneconomic. Lower-level managers will be forced to become more computer centered, not through remote terminals but with units standing in place in their own shops.

There will be more attention to objectives, input-output relationships, and achievement motivation. The MBA degree or the knowledge contained in its curriculum will become the ordinary skills of the manager. Even the oversupply of MBAs which is forecast as every college in the country offers the degree won't come true. More than likely, MBAs will dominate management by the end of the eighties not because of their diplomas but because of their behavior. Systems language, models, and rational decision making will prevail more widely than they do now. People will be using words such as *throughput, scenario, activity trap, cost benefit, zero-based budgets* and *MBO* as the language of management.

3. Managers Will Be More Developmental Centered

During the seventies the training revolution and human-resources development movement caught on; they will become even more pronounced in the eighties. IBM's heavy commitment to education as a way of running a business, well established during the seventies, will become more common in the eighties for large firms. Xerox's learning center, Eastman Kodak's giant training and development center, the GM Institute in Flint, and similar company schools that flowered during the seventies will be copied widely, expanded, and made more innovative. Adult education, so widely touted as their future growth area by today's colleges and universities, will probably see its full flowering in the private sector rather than in the universities. For one thing, the universities are responding defensively to a loss of undergraduates and graduate students rather than aggressively building up adult education. For another, the universities are so bound up in academic constraints, including a generally ineffective organizational model known as the extension division, that they are most unlikely to respond actively and intelligently to the situation. The corporation, the trade association, and the trade union will do most of the creative and continuing education, and only the overflow from those programs will appear on the campuses, which will be rented out as ivy-covered hotels for corporate clients during the summer to help pay off the dormitory bonds. Educational, training, and developmental managers will undoubtedly rise in stature, rank, and pay in business during the eighties as they meet the challenge of developing and retaining qualified personnel in the face of job- and career-change statistics. Some of the traditional functions of personnel managers will decline proportionately, as these people do more pedantic bureaucratic chores in connection with personnel administration.[3] The successful personnel department will become strategy centered rather than obsessed with procedures.

4. There Will Be an Increase in Situational Management

The manager of the eighties will probably be hearing about and applying more situational management methods than ever before. This idea has been around for many years, starting with Mary Parker Follet, a pioneering management consultant. Pigors and Myers's *Personnel* text of the fifties was based upon this idea. On the campus among the management faculty this idea is sweeping the field, with a rash of articles and Ph.D. dissertations appearing under the label *contingency management*. This idea is to define goals and targets clearly and then allow for more variety in the ways people may get there. Orders are more apt to be of the kind that are *situational;* that is, they will be orders that explain ("This is the job that must be done") rather than orders that dictate ("Do this.").

Giving more attention to arranging the situation so a desired behavior will be apt to occur is another facet of this rapidly growing style of management.[4] Future managers will manage the entire situation—physical environment, group working teams, information flows, and opportunity for face-to-face discussions between people—and the policies, rules, and regulations to get things going in the right direction. Situational management will call for a corresponding decline in traditional charismatic and directive styles of leadership. One of the reasons for this somewhat more complex method of managing will be avoidance of the possibilities for interpersonal conflict and confrontation as groups of people such as minorities and women move up the managerial ladder.

The supervisor who posts the seniority list on the bulletin board along with the work and job assignments is presenting the situation in such a way that people can see that no personal bias, favoritism, or arbitrary bossiness has been involved in the decisions made. "Here is the situation and here is the task to be done" will preface the directives about who will do what.

5. Management by Commitment Will Increase

If managers are to loosen personal control over people doing their work, they must move toward an even better form of control—self-control. Self-control requires that responsible people make commitments in advance to the boss, customers, colleagues, or government officials. They are then held accountable for delivering the commitments they have made. Getting people to internalize those commitments, of course, means that people must have a thorough understanding and acceptance of the situation and the task. The most widely promulgated way to achieve acceptance is to let people participate in decisions that affect them and for which commitment is sought. The alternative is to overpay people and let their rewards be monetary, which is pretty expensive but nonetheless workable in many situations.

6. There Will Be a Rapid Spread of Achievement Motivation

Studies by David McClelland of Harvard and other behavioral scientists show some tangible effects on output and growth where there is a high level of achievement motivation in the people involved.[5] This means that the major motivational influence in the work force is the internal pressure to achieve that is present in successful organizations. This achievement motivation, in its simplest explanation, is brought about by having high goals, speaking the language of success rather than the language of failure, instituting systems that reward and reinforce achievement of goals, and building teams of people jointly working toward achievement. Evidence shows that organizations, teams, companies, and even nations whose leaders have a high level of achievement motivation become high achievers. There is also evidence that achievement motivation can be affected by the training aimed at producing it, and this new style of management can predictably be forecast as having an important effect on executive and supervisory development programs in companies and nonprofit organizations.

7. There Will Be More and Better Uses of Group Management Processes

Good group management starts with the board of directors, where outsiders and special-interest groups, including public-interest representation, audit committees, and minority members, will become more common. The emphasis upon team building will call for the more creative use of task forces, matrix management configurations of organization, project management systems in research and development, and a diminishing of the huge smear of committees, which go on and on without ever coming to a conclusion that anyone can notice. Good management in the eighties is more likely to be characterized by an assertive but patient use of group processes, with perhaps some lamentable diminishing of personal risk-bearing and plunging-ahead behavior in individual executives.[6] As in the past, the exception to the rule will probably occur in new enterprises where the founder-owner is still around running things with a firm hand. Larger organizations, with ever-enlarging publics to be served or considered, will require that more people have a hand in the decision process in order to avoid the hassles that follow decisions that omit somebody's interest.

8. There Will Be More Due Process in Personnel Decisions

Starting with the campus rebellions of the sixties, rising rapidly in government, and moving from there to industry, there has been a sharp increase in the demand for due process. Such properties or entitlements as a right to a job, a promotion, a benefit, or a merit increase and the right to grievances over decisions has followed a classical pattern of due process. Under law, people now have a right to be protected against anonymous statements about them in their personnel files, credit folders, and governmental files. They have more of an interest in confronting any accusers, having a full hearing of their case, and feeling freedom from being deprived of their rights without due process of law. While it may seem harder and harder to fire people for incompetence during the eighties, that will only mean that the processes are expanding to allow for the full working out of due process. The expansion of due process will call for some revisions of rules of working, penalties for violation, and a clear procedure for handling cases where penalties of any kind are to be assessed.

The genius of the U.S. Constitution will be extended more and more into the workplace, especially as charges and protestations of discrimination for various reasons such as sex, age, race, national origin, and religion are stated more and more emphatically. This pressure will require personnel policies and procedures with due process built into them at every step. Legal processes will become more common in the workplace, and possibly more law school graduates, already in oversupply for ordinary legal practice jobs, will appear in labor relations, arbitration, personnel administration, and consumer and public affairs. To offset this, lay managers will become considerably more familiar with the legal characteristics of the due-process system than they have in the past.

9. There Will Be More Management by Information

It is probably especially true for the eighties that (as the IBM advertisement puts it) "management means handling information." People in charge must know what is expected, how resources are being employed, how well they are performing, how well they have done in the past compared with standards of performance, and what things are impending. Accurate information must go rapidly to the right place at the right time if managers are to predict what lies ahead. Here again, the minicomputer, perhaps tied together in new kinds of networks, will come into widespread use during the eighties in response to this demand.[7] Word processing, data retrieval, more group sharing of information, and more one-to-one dialogue and other knowledge and skills in the communication process will be required of managers. What used to be called the communication gap in management will be subsumed under the new rubric of the *information revolution,* which is already pretty well underway.

10. The Physical Aspects of the Workplace Will Change

The workplace will undergo some important changes to achieve many of the style changes noted above. For one thing, occupational health and safety will assume heightened significance as OSHA moves away from being a trivial enforcement agency and moves closer to dealing with important causes of fatalities and long-run occupational health hazards. Thus, capital budgets of the eighties will entail spending for more secure working conditions and more concern for the health, safety, and fitness of people at work. It is now widely accepted that people should not be required to donate a thumb, a lung, or their central nervous system to the firm in order to earn a weekly paycheck. Nor will people consent to live at the bottom of a cesspool of polluted air to earn their daily bread.

Beyond this security-level physical factor, there will be more concern for the motivational effects of physical plant design and layout. The traditional concern for amenities will be supplemented by concern for motivational influences at work. Too often the job has in effect told the worker, "Don't do me." Engineering departments that used to cluster all their professionals into a giant room, with drafting boards lined up in great rows, will be broken into more manageable and human clusters. The precepts of orthodox job enrichment promulgated first by Frederick Herzberg will become more a concern of industrial engineers, personnel managers, and technical engineers. These layouts will follow changes in planned work flow which will give people more control over their own work content, more of a client relationship with other people, more information about the effects of their efforts, and more information about how others relate to their tasks.[8] Not all of this technology is in hand, nor in place.

A Cheerful Note

All of these style changes will not come along quietly. Some will require considerable management education. All will demand that managers change their behavior, either willingly or with considerable kicking and screaming. For some people the situation will only be resolved by acquiring enough points in their retirement plan to allow them to retreat to places like Sun City or Leisure World where things are more stable. Good golf courses, shuffleboard, and a security system that forbids anyone to enter the grounds under the age of thirty unless driving a liquor truck will be required to solve some companies' management problems. Fortunately there seems to be emerging from our campuses a replacement corps of bright-eyed youngsters who, strangely enough, view all of this change and the prospect of tough problems with considerable zeal. The graduating classes of 1980 are already juniors as this is written. For the first time in more than a decade college students seem to be interested in jobs, assuming responsibility, earning money, and living the good life. They will have until the year 2025 to show their stuff. If they don't solve the problems during the eighties, they will have ample opportunity to try again in the nineties and beyond.

CHAPTER 3

Stemming the Decline of Risk Taking and Innovation

Slowly—or perhaps not so slowly—the industrial United States is moving toward a form of economic republic without historical precedent.

—Adolph A. Berle

Joseph Schumpeter had a mind that constantly dismayed those who most would have liked to agree with him. Though he wrote in the forties and fifties, he is refreshingly modern—and enjoying a resurgence in the late seventies. Schumpeter often straddled issues in seemingly paradoxical fashion. In one breath he said, "Can capitalism survive? No, I don't think it can." And in the next he demolished the critics of capitalism in the most ultra-conservative manner. An admirer of Marx as a theorist, he also held that "in capitalism somebody must get hurt" and proposed that occasional unemployment was a cheap price to pay for gains in economic growth.

Schumpeter saw his "march into socialism" as a migration of the people's economic power from the private into the public sphere and cited four major trends in the recent economic history of the United States as the reasons for believing that this march would not halt.[1]

In the first place, the very success of business in creating a new high standard of living for society bred its ultimate control by political forces through its own bureaucratization.

Secondly, the *rational* nature of capitalism spreads rational habits of mind, and free contacts between superior and subordinate tend to destroy a system based solely upon satisfying individual short-run utilitarian interests.

30

Furthermore, because business managers concentrated on the technology of managing plants and offices, there sprang into being a political system and an intellectual class independent of, and hostile to, the interests of corporate business.

And finally, the value system of capitalism has bred counter values of security, equality, and regulation which must ultimately overwhelm it.

The civilization of inequality and the family fortune were, so Schumpeter declared, basic to the capitalistic system. However, capitalism might still provide economic growth, so long as capitalists behaved like capitalists—that is, so long as they showed the innovative temperament, the daring, and the spirited willingness to stake their personal fortunes on the chance of great gains through new ideas, breakthroughs, and innovations. Such people, Schumpeter suggested, have become rarer and rarer as capitalism itself has created corps of administrators, pale, gray-clad, and gray-spirited people who listen too closely to the intellectuals who surround them and to the dictates of their own fears—all this in an environment that their predecessors daringly created.

Productivity and Innovation

With the same voice as he predicted socialism, Schumpeter also defended capitalism. His theme was no simple, soothing apologia for the system of the consumer vote but was a more unflinching, occasionally even truculent, defense of pure capitalism—capitalism the supreme producer. Citing the growth of production through good times and bad for sixty years prior to 1928, he noted that, measured in real terms, the distribution of this constant gain of production of 2 percent per year had substantially changed in favor of the low-income groups:

> This follows from the fact that the capitalist engine is first and last an engine of mass production, which unavoidably means also production for the masses.

Schumpeter then went on to explode the idea that the rich get richer and the poor get poorer under capitalism. Noting that the higher-income groups spend more of their money for services, he pointed out that it is the cheap cloth, boots, and cars that are the typical achievements of capitalism and not, as a rule, the kind of improvements that would mean much to a rich man. "The capitalist achievement," he declared, "does not consist in providing silk stockings for queens but in bringing them within the reach of factory girls in return for steadily decreasing amounts of effort."

The risks in the process, he went on, are tied to the gains and can be summarized in two aspects of capitalism: the business cycle and attendant unemployment. Unemployment, he frankly conceded, was "among those evils which, like poverty, capitalist evolution could never eliminate of itself."

A second risk is to the personal prosperity of the risk taker, formerly the owner, today the manager. But in eradicating the former, we've erased the latter.

How, then, should we cope with such evils?

For one thing, it is evident that the rate of unemployment for the sixty years prior to World War I showed a horizontal trend. Bad as this may have been, it was an inescapable condition of capitalism but not one that feeds on itself and worsens. Moreover, the unemployment rate was counterbalanced by the constantly increasing production that accompanied capitalism. If the system had had another run like the sixty years before World War I, it would have met all the desiderata of the social reformers—including most of the cranks—without any interference with the capitalist process. From such a rising production and its increasing tendency to distribute its output widely among the lower-income groups, "ample provision for the unemployed, in particular, would then be not only a tolerable but a light burden."

But from the viewpoint of its implications for managerial style, Schumpeter's theory of business cycles is more pertinent than his defense of capitalism. The theory of cycles centers on the entrepreneur as the initiator of action that disturbs economic equilibrium and ultimately raises productive levels. It is the risk-taking manager in quest of profits or personal prosperity who makes innovations in business. Expansion does not come about simply through stealing customers from others, or playing what modern game theorists would call a *zero-sum, two-person game* in a specific market. The entrepreneur invents and innovates, then persuades bankers to extend credit, bidding up interest rates and paying higher wages to entice labor into vacant positions. Wages and prices rise. This has a weakening effect on profits, and a general period of inactivity and falling-off in innovation occurs. The expansion period of the cycle depends upon the time required for the invention to be introduced into the economic system through the installation of new processes and equipment. Thus it is that through innovation and disruption originating with risk-minded business leaders the capitalistic system expands, economic growth occurs, and capitalism raises the standard of living for all.

At the heart of Schumpeter's theory are the innovators, the tradition breakers, the disrupters of the status quo in the garb of bourgeois economic royalty. Their dissatisfaction with things as they are, coupled with their personal initiative in introducing change, underlies all economic growth and also accounts for periodic slumps. The two, Schumpeter implied, are related; one is the price that must be paid for the other. Economic growth demands innovation, and innovation requires compelling business leadership to make it happen. The hope of gain lies in the prospect of increased productivity so that interest can be earned. The alternative, Schumpeter suggested, is a state of equilibrium in which saving and investment in the past are balanced by the consumption of the present.

Furthermore, Schumpeter argued, capitalism attracts the best brains to business. Spectacular prizes bring forth people of "ability and energy and supernormal capacity for work" far more than an equal distribution of rewards would do. Such individual risk-taking leaders are selected not by management development programs or performance appraisal forms but by the system itself to which individuals are chained by the bourgeois value systems that accompany capitalism. Thus, obsolete methods and incompetent managers are swept away. Failure also threatens the able manager, thus whipping the leadership into more productive effort than a more just system of penalties or a more logical system of selection could ever do.

The Taming of Risk

Despite his strenuous arguments for the capitalist system, Schumpeter predicted its decline on the grounds of the decline of risk taking and the dwindling possibility of spectacular gain. The very fruits of productivity that capitalism generated had bred a social system that was obstructive to the entrepreneur. Where Marx had envisioned the end of capitalism in violent capture of the machinery of production by the masses, Schumpeter saw its demise implicit in "administered capitalism." In socialist eyes, corporate enterprise is an economic system that will not function except on capitalist lines. No alternative exists for the central planner except to run it according to its own logic, but in the interests of its proletarian constituency. Public and private collectivism and bureaucracy are the result.

Even while Schumpeter was writing, evidence was accumulating that bore out his case. Adolph Berle and Gardiner Means focused the microscope of economic research on the growth of corporations as dominant social institutions and concluded, "Corporations have ceased to be merely legal devices through which the private business transactions of individuals may be carried on." The corporation, owning the dominant share of productive property in society though its owners comprised only a minuscule fraction of the population, was both a method of property tenure and a means of organizing economic life. The effect of this increasing size would be the disappearance of private enterprise. In fact, Berle and Means concluded that the corporate enterprise was taking on the dimensions of a system just as feudalism had been a system. Moreover, they noted:

> Only to the extent that any worker seeks advancement within an organization is there room for initiative—an initiative that can be exercised within the narrow range of function he is called upon to perform.[2]

Here was clearly a denial that capitalism, as Adam Smith had described it, even existed any more. Under his classical schema, the motive for production was conceived to be self-interest, "but the guidance of this motive, so that it conduces to the interest of all concerned, is brought about by the mechanism of the market and the force of competition." This whole concept was now considered dead.

Eight years after Schumpeter's book appeared, prominent business leaders were calling for a better description than Adam Smith's of modern corporate capitalism, on the ground that classical economics had "lost touch with the colossal developments of the last forty years."

Businessman Oswald Knauth calmly declared that in meeting the exigencies of the modern world, business leaders had fashioned a new form of economy.

How had this affected the role of the risk bearer and rambunctious destroyer of the status quo? According to Knauth, a major effect was the rise of *impersonal* leadership. "Decisions are made by groups," he said, "and not by individuals." Only the chief executive can express his personality, said Knauth, "and he does so by putting his imprint on the system rather than determining particular policies." Employees, presumably including the leaders in the corporate system, surrendered their personal liberty voluntarily, and the hero or superstar of the capitalist society was extinct.[3]

The upshot was the rise of managerial enterprise, a new system that supplanted risk and tamed it but lacked a clear definition of its own nature and had no codes or natural forces to guide it. Essentially, this system was defenseless against the charges of recklessness and irresponsibility which had been accepted as part and parcel of capitalist risk taking.

In a sense, though, there was perhaps one code by which the new system could abide. By common agreement the impact of any individual was held to be insignificant. But this seemed to be the limit of the system's logic. Beyond this, it was surrounded by an ice cap of managerial skills, tools, and philosophies centered in group decision making and in the eradication of the zest, innovation, and change that spring from the hope of great personal gain.

Today every large corporation has its department of stockholder relations, testifying to the need to insulate chief executives from pressures that might stimulate excessive interest in larger gains at risk to the owners. The major airlines assist one another by sharing profits during a national strike, thus eliminating the risk emanating from strong collective bargaining.

Among the fastest-growing industries these days are those financial and banking institutions that sell what John R. Commons called risk-prevention services, assuring bureaucrats of the eradication of actuarially determinable hazards. The areas of uninsurable risks in business are constantly being reduced, and for sound economic reasons. The administrator is a preserver rather than an innovator.

Inside the corporation, there has been a marked proliferation of risk-reduction departments. Armed with the tools of modern mathematics, these departments have introduced a more rational concept of risk than was heretofore possible. By devising predictive models rooted in empirical studies of the past, management produces self-fulfilling prophecies of risk management in the future. The true significance of these developments lies less in their rationality than in their general proposition that risk itself can be removed from the area of uncertainty and turned into statistical and mathematical certainty.

The Creative-Destructive Hypothesis

Though there was some similarity between the views of Berle and Means and those of Schumpeter, there were also sharp differences. The Berle and Means studies of concentration in industry led them to the conclusion that competition was dead. Schumpeter scoffed at this idea, holding that mutations in the form of capitalism were necessary, but this did not mean that competition was extinct or that the corporation was no longer subject to the mechanism of the market. The new capitalism of the corporate society was an evolutionary phase from which capitalism could emerge stronger and more socially useful than before. This would be achieved by a process of *creative destruction,* Schumpeter said, because capitalism is "by nature a form of method of economic change" and not only "never was but never can be stationary."

Competition emerging from pure price bases naturally evolved through this process into monopolistic competition, whose *modus operandi* was to discipline before it attacked. The large-scale production required to achieve economies does not call for despair over the system but understanding of it. On the record, Schumpeter stoutly insisted, monopolistic competition or oligopoly led in the long run not to price increases but exactly the reverse. The steady increase in output through innovation and the creative destruction of existing business by better ones was so prevalent in modern corporate society that if large firms attempted to fix extortionate prices (as most would do, according to classical theory), they would find the ground slipping from beneath their feet. No company becomes so large or so secure in its market position that it can ignore the possibility of another introducing change through innovation and wiping it out. In the large corporate entity, survival was as real a problem as of old, requiring as much attention to innovation and vitality as it ever had done.

Schumpeter's stand was not without its critics, however. Polanyi, pointing to the great transformation that had overtaken us, concluded "nineteenth-century civilization has collapsed." Stretching his horizons beyond pure economics, he surmised that this collapse had come about through the failure of the balance-of-power system, the international gold standard, the liberal state, and the self-regulatory market. It was the latter that drew his sharpest fire. Polanyi further declared that the main failure of capitalism had been in its inability to understand the problem of change. The self-adjusting market was "stark utopia" which couldn't exist for any length of time without "annihilating the human and natural substance of society." Had it continued, in the end it would have physically destroyed men and "transformed its surroundings into a wilderness." Hence Polanyi denounced what he termed "a mystical readiness to accept the social consequences of economic improvements, whatever they might be."[4]

Bureaucratic Leadership

Obviously the preservation of capitalism in its mutated form called for different styles of leadership from those that had characterized the actions of the old merchant prince or the early capitalist manufacturer. To make creative destruction work forcibly for the preservation of capitalism, innovation and the sweeping away of less effective enterprises had to be rampant. But the executive of this most necessary process was blocked by the internal forces of self-generated bureaucracy.

The vast wastelands of passive and dependent people in middle-management positions and the concept of the administrator as the person who by situation and temperament *prevents* things from happening bore within them the seeds of capitalism's downfall. Far more deleterious than the ranting of radicals, or the conspiracies of bomb-throwing Marxists, were the blockers on the corporate payroll, the security-minded managers.

The reduction of administration to a science was undoubtedly another contributing factor. In such an environment, natural innovators or visionaries found themselves up against a value system in which there was no more unnerving form of behavior than "rocking the boat."

While the new industrial society went beyond the capitalism of classical economics, it failed to follow the path predicted by Marx, who envisioned capitalist competition leading to gluts of commodities that would bring about business crises in which small firms would go under and large firms would grow larger. This, Marx said, would lead in turn to an increase in the number of working-class people whose misery would grow with their enlarging numbers. Thus, the rich would get richer and the poor would get poorer, and the inevitable end would be upheavals during which the masses would finally take over. The spectacular failure of this prediction does not mean, however, that the new industrial society does not have some hefty problems of its own.

The major blocks to the creation of a society of high production and rising standards of living lie not so much in our institutional forms and economic organization as in the suppression of risk taking, which the industrial society has built into its very fiber. Concern over equitable distribution and the alleviation of discontent growing out of people's personal and social needs have diverted our attention from the fact that our physical needs can be satisfied. They will remain so if we retain the basically productive orientation of our system. Overattention to equitable distribution of the existing product can only have the inevitable effect of expanding bureaucracy inside business, blunting its growth, and stemming innovation.

One effect of bureaucratic leadership is the decline of innovation. If there is one thing administrators in a bureaucracy cannot abide, it is chance taking or individuals being held accountable for results. Their value system revolves around the preservation of the status quo, especially their own. In the eyes of bureaucracy, the triple goals of organization, planning, and control, which comprise the bulk of most executive development courses, are perfectly suitable and practical methods of achieving this objective. Administrative practices and human relations, as they studiously pursue them, have pertinence as they ensure bureaucratic proliferation of administrators and self-maintenance, at the expense of growth if necessary.

The New Authority

Life in the crystal palaces of corporate headquarters is considered normal and satisfactory when it is *quiet*. The placid and secure pace of people without anxiety pervades the ranks of the middle-management body politic. Since risks are widely shared, it is the *system* that bears the brunt of bringing on innovation. Errors are fewer, since the possibilities of large gains, involving as they must the risk of larger losses, are eschewed. The hierarchy exerts its group authority from above to minimize the individual authority of those below. Committees occupy three-quarters of the typical executive's time according to one study. Touching bases on a field with ten bases keeps functionaries padding quietly over headquarters rugs the whole of their working lives.

In fact, the new leader makes no decisions but operates a decision-making apparatus reports Professor Mason Haire of the University of California at Berkeley. And Professor Douglas McGregor, of the Massachusetts Institute of Technology, says that leadership is a relationship, rather than a function performed by one person, and that it pulls together a symbolic chief and participating followers.[5] Three forces work to shape the actions of leaders in the new corporate society: (1) *Selection* for the qualities that make for effective membership in the bureaucratic framework; (2) *training* in scientific management and rational systems of leadership and executive functioning; and (3) *alteration of the environment* to isolate and possibly expel traditional entrepreneurs, risk takers, and innovators from any sensitive location where their impact might be disruptive.

Even small business managers model themselves on this new style of corporate leadership. Having inherited the business, the Harvard graduate buys the "right" wardrobe, the "right" furniture for the office, and joins with other members of the Young President's Organization in taking sensitivity training. Regular checks from the Small Business Administration ease hard times in the market.

Schumpeter's prediction, made some fifteen years ago, would then appear to have some pertinence today. Does the decline of capitalism and the new style of business leadership point inevitably to socialism? Not necessarily. Things happen because people want them to happen. The restoration of innovation and vision in leadership is not impossible,

even in the noncapitalistic, yet still nonsocialist, corporate system we
live in. That restoration will not come automatically, however. It can
only happen if managers make it happen.

Though we may agree that Schumpeter was right in predicting the
demise of old-style capitalism, this does not necessarily point to the conclusion that socialism is the only remedy for a society in rebellion
against the oppressive effects of the old system. The belief that a society
must be either "right" or "left" was actually the product of a world
accustomed to thinking in ideological terms.

The modern world, however, is in no mood to think in this way.
Gladstone might have blushed to be caught unaware of the latest political theory, but since 1918, statesmen of all political hues have tended to
dislike the academic and ideological theorist. As a result, says Professor
Isaiah Berlin, no "commanding work of political philosophy has appeared in the twentieth century." Though his critics have refuted this
conclusion by pointing to the works of Lenin and Mao Tse-tung, they
agree that there is no philosophy of freedom uniting the Western world.
Schumpeter belonged to an earlier generation and thus thought in
ideological terms. People today adhere more to the position that ideology is the "opiate of the intellectuals" and they deal with their problems as they come.

In fact, to describe our coming condition as socialism is now mere
gong striking. The sound reverberates, but there is no longer any substance to it. It is more to the point to recognize that our environment
now dictates the adoption of a more compelling kind of business
leadership—the kind of leadership that will restore to individual managers their personal risk for loss or gain.

In the following chapters we shall show how the system of management by objectives incorporates most of the requirements for this
kind of leadership.

PART 2

Management by Objectives: A Systems Approach to Management

The systems approach is a modern way of looking at things in order to predict, direct, and control what goes on. In Part 2 we shall become talented amateurs in the systems approach and in the process show how MBO functions as a system.

A word of caution: You won't find the systems way of thinking easy at the beginning—not because it is complicated, but because it is different from our customary ways of thinking. Our education has taught us, by its structure into compartments (a bookbag of separate objects), that knowledge comes in little blocks called disciplines. The systems approach forces us to see things in related wholes. That's not easy. What does this have to do with MBO? Well, MBO is basic, for the first step in the systems approach is to *define the system's objectives*. Thus, if you use the systems approach, your first step is objectives. Or, to put it another way, when you manage by objectives, you are stepping off briskly into a systems approach.

Let us consider how that looks in a managerial environment.

CHAPTER 4

Looking at Your Organization as a System

The specialist concentrates on detail and disregards the wider structure which gives it context. The new scientist, however, concentrates on structure on all levels of magnitude and complexity and fits detail into its general framework.
— Ervin Laszlo[1]

MBO qualifies as a general theory of management because it looks at organizations, people, resources, and work differently. It considers the whole and how those segments that make up the whole relate to one another. In this chapter, you will get the world's shortest course in the systems approach. You'll see how you can look at your job, your organization, and your life as a system and the numerous advantages of doing so.

The Systems Approach and Goals Displacement

The major impetus for making MBO as widespread as it is today—and a recent survey shows it to be very widespread in major firms—has been the rise, even the ascendency, of the systems approach.

1. The systems approach, with its simple and completely plausible explanation of everything, joins Hegel's dialectic and other ultimate explanations as having numerous applications.
2. It deals with disparate parts and their relationships in an integrated whole.

42

3. It requires that you keep three elements in mind—inputs, activity, and outputs—with some feedback to tie the first and third.
4. It is organic rather than mechanistic in its logic, which is suitable for clarifying that which had not been clarified before.

Of the numerous kinds of systems that could fall within a general systems theory, the *cybernetic or feedback system* is usually considered the most typical, and it can be applied to the economics of the organization. Three elements make up such a system (see Figure 4.1):

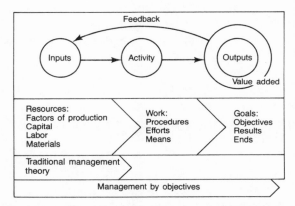

Figure 4.1 Schematic of a cybernetic system, the most commonly used of the systems approaches.

1. *Inputs* are the resources committed to an idea to make it a tangible, going concern. They include capital (fixed, working, cash, receivables, inventories), labor, and materials.
2. *Activities* are the behaviors of people—designing, making, selling, keeping books, engineering, bargaining, and the like—which *add value* (presumably) to the inputs.
3. *Outputs* are the goods and services, hardware and software, that *come out* of the system. These outputs are more valuable than all of the inputs used up in their making, and a *value added* can be computed.

This *value added* is the profit, the need being filled, the *purpose for the input being committed, and the activity carried out.* Two ways of disposing of this surplus value are customary: (1) They are *fed back* into the systems. (2) They are *distributed* to the beneficiaries of the system as dividends, learning, satisfactions, benefits, needs met, and the like.

While this minicourse in the systems approach is somewhat instruc-tive as a map, it is also a diagram of the traps for managers and other people who are *part* of the system.

The easy trap is for one involved in a system to become emotion-ally overattached to one element of what must be a three-element sys-tem:

1. Some people become *input*-obsessed and spend their time pre-venting expenditure. (Think of the person who will disapprove your expense account.)
2. Others become *output* fanatics and heartily resist considering whether the inputs and resources are adequate or the activities possible. (Think of the desk pounder and "I demand results not alibis" type.)
3. Far more prevalent, however, is the *activity*-obsessed person who is competent, professional, often dedicated, but has lost sight of inputs used up or even *results* sought.

Thus, in system terms, management by objectives is a system that begins by defining outputs and then applies these output statements as criteria to judge the quality of activity (behavior) and to govern the release and effectiveness of the inputs.

In more ordinary language, MBO is a system under which the manager and subordinate sit down at the beginning of each period and talk until agreement upon job goals is achieved. During the period, the subordinate is given wide latitude in choice of method. At the end of the period the results are jointly reviewed against agreed-upon goals, and an assessment of the degree of success is made. The process is then begun again.

The Activity Trap

Some of the largest and most affluent corporations are caught in the activity trap, but it afflicts small corporations, too, and extends beyond the business world to governments, schools, hospitals, churches, even families. Unless victims are aware of it, the activity trap will ensnare the wisest, most experienced old hands.

What is the activity trap? It is the abysmal situation people find themselves in when they start out for what once was an important and clear objective, then become so enmeshed in the activity of getting there that they forget where they were going.[2]

Every business started out to achieve some objective, usually to make and increase profit. Resources were assembled from stockholders, loans, or savings and poured into the enterprise. Everyone got busy, engaging in *activity* designed to carry the organization toward its objectives. But once-clear goals may evolve into something else, while the activity remains the same and becomes an end in itself. The goal moves, but the activity persists and becomes a false goal. This false goal becomes the criterion for making decisions, and the decisions get progressively worse.

Here are some examples of the activity trap:

- Quality-control directors act as if the enterprise were created so they could shut it down and hold up everything produced yesterday.
- Accountants act as if the business were created so they could keep books on it. No longer do they keep books so the boss can run it better.
- The sales manager acts as if there were no problems that could not be solved by more volume. Sales go up, but profits fall.
- Production managers get tonnage out the back gate by shipping junk, or using wrong labels and faulty addresses, then ride the backs of the help to get more production out tomorrow.
- Personnel managers behave as if the entire purpose of hiring all those people, providing them with tools and equipment, and building a plant was so the personnel department could make them happy.
- Labor relations directors act as if the company were formed so that they could fight with union officers.

Meanwhile, the stockholders and the president sit atop the mess wondering where the profit went.

The activity trap is a self-feeding mechanism if you don't turn it around. Everybody becomes emotionally attached to some irrelevancy and does his or her job *too well*. The ultimate stage is reached when company presidents themselves lose sight of why they are in business and demand more and more activity rather than results. They add layers of professionals to help them control the activity, perhaps acres of lawyers, each outstripping the other in preventing everybody from producing anything, and then, as profits decline, batteries of accountants who produce considerable accounting and also considerable costs. Engineers fight engineering problems by hiring more engineers, each with a technical opinion designed to prevent something from happening some place else in the firm. Many professionals spend their entire working lives taking in each other's administrative laundry, creating jobs and administrative hierarchies to generate more activity that is increasingly unrelated to the purpose of the company's existence.

Service clubs spend more and more time exhorting the members to "support our activity" with no hint of a worthwhile payoff. Churches, too, become enmeshed with covered dish suppers and basketball leagues—activities generating little other than indigestion and flat feet. Families get so entangled in the mechanical process of living that they forget what families were started for. There's a story about the perfect housewife whose kid got up at night to go to the bathroom. When he came back, his bed had been made.

Meanwhile, all this activity eats up resources, money, space, budgets, savings, and human energy like a mammoth tapeworm.

While it is apparent that the activity trap cuts profits, loses ball games, and fails to achieve missions, it has an equally dangerous side effect on people: they *shrink* personally and professionally. Take any boss and subordinate. Ask the employee to write down what specific results the boss wants in the next quarter. Now ask the boss, "What *results* would you like to see that employee produce next quarter?" The average manager and subordinate won't agree, though they may be reasonably close on the activities to be conducted. Answers will differ, and the differences will cause the subordinate to shrink, essentially, in potential.

Research shows that:

1. On regular, ongoing responsibilities, the average boss and subordinate caught in the activity trap will fail to agree on expected outputs at a level of 25 percent.
2. At the same time, because of this failure to agree on regular responsibilities, they will disagree on what the subordinate's major problems are at a level of 50 percent.
3. The worst gap of all is the failure of boss and subordinate to agree on how the subordinate's job should be improved. On this latter count, they fail to agree at a level of 90 percent.

As a result, nothing really changes in the way things are done. The environment changes, the customers' tastes change, the values of employees change. But the methods remain static, and the organization is crippled by the outdated acts of its own employees.

The human consequence is that the organization drains its people of their zap and finds itself employing pygmies. They look like real people, wear neckties, drive cars, and pay taxes, but they are performance midgets. They nod their heads when the boss chastises them but know that they have been cheated. They are stabbed daily in duels they didn't know were under way. Trees fall upon them, and *then* somebody yells, "Timber!" Their defensive recourse? Keep *active*.

Employees redouble their energies when they have lost sight of their goals. They may be chastised or even fired for doing something wrong when they didn't know what *right* was to begin with. They run a race without knowing how long the track is. They wonder if it's time to sprint for the wire, but they can't guess when, because it might be a 100-yard dash or the Boston Marathon.

The effect is cumulative. Because employees don't know the ordinary objectives of their jobs, they are hit for failures growing out of not knowing what spells success. This produces a reluctance to discover shortcomings. Suggesting something new in such an environment is risky. Better to stick with the old activity. Looking busy becomes safer than being productive.

This tendency toward activity is not inevitable if top people try to correct it. The law of gravity is always with us, but some people fly airplanes.

In America's best-managed organizations, the management has leadership systems that concentrate on outputs and results. In such organizations, every manager and subordinate manager periodically sit down and talk about "What are you going to produce for me next quarter or next year?" The two talk about objectives, outputs, results, and indicators until they agree on what the future shall hold. One of the parties then confirms the agreement with a memo.

Now when the curtain goes up, both actors have the same script, and this improves the quality of the acting considerably:

- The emphasis is on outputs, not activities.
- All employees know what is expected of them and can tell immediately how well they are doing.
- They know they are responsible for results and have committed themselves to trying to achieve them.

- They feel free to make necessary decisions and take necessary actions to achieve the objectives.
- At the end of the period, the manager and subordinate sit down once more and talk again. "Here is what you said you were going to produce. How well did you do, and what are you going to do next quarter?"

The key person in this type of productive organization is the top person. The chief determines that the organization will be managed by objectives, not activity, and decides what the corporate objectives and strategic goals will be. The subordinate managers define their operational objectives to fit those top-level goals and strategies. The top person should not be involved in day-to-day operations but should manage them by the objectives that have been accepted.

Nonbusiness organizations need explicit objectives, too. Families with defined objectives can get off the backs of their offspring, permitting a wider latitude of activity and behavior if the end result is good. Service clubs find that definite objectives attract resources and talent.

Virtually any organization can get caught in the activity trap because the bait is so alluring, but the security of the trap is inherently false and the rewards diminish at an accelerated rate. Organization, after all, is not an end in itself—it is a means of achieving specific objectives. To attain these objectives the participants, if they, themselves, are to survive, must eventually get down to business rather than the "busyness" of the activity trap.

MBO is an antidote to the activity trap. It requires that objectives start at the top of the organization and that people understand what is expected of them, where their help and resources will come from, how much freedom they have and what reporting relationships are necessary. It requires that they know how well they are doing in their work while they are doing it and how rewards and punishments will be handed out by their organizational employer.

What MBO Should Accomplish

As a result of the MBO procedure, several benefits to the organization and the individual should become more likely.

1. *A natural tendency toward "goals displacement" (a famous term originated by Robert Merton in 1940) will be alleviated.* Some research seems to show that in human organizations a normal (or at least explainable) tendency exists for people to *start out* toward goals but to become so enmeshed in activity that the goal is lost.[3] In its most aggravated form, *activity management* becomes a matter of deep-rooted procedures (as with salary administration, job descriptions, and the like), and attempts to revert to basic purposes meet with strong resistance. ("Do it my way.") *From the top management perspective, MBO is a direct attempt to build into management systems an unremitting attention to purpose.*

2. *Conflict and ambiguity between individual managers and subordinates will decrease as objectives become clear.* There is evidence that, left to their own devices, the average manager and subordinate manager are not apt to be in agreement about the subordinate manager's responsibilities in terms of outputs for any given period of time ahead.[4] Under such a lack of agreement it becomes impossible for the subordinate to *succeed,* with corresponding ill effects to him in pay, bonus, promotion, and recorded performance reports. Even further ill effects ensue when attempts to *improve* the subordinate delve into matters such as personality, attitude, motives, background, or similarly vague explanations of failure. *MBO attacks directly the gap of expectations and defines "success" in specific output terms.*

3. *MBO should be causally associated with overall success of the organization.* Drucker has noted that in leading corporations, General Motors, Ford, IBM, GE, where size has required divisionalized forms of organization, "Management *is* management by objectives."[5] My own prolonged observations in leading firms is that in the more successful firms (they achieve goals) more people are aware of their goals than in less successful organizations. The Sears manager knows his or her goal better than does the failing small merchant. Participative management is not uniformly present but is perhaps more possible under MBO than under intuitive or autocratic centralized management. This style is discretionary, but in many kinds of organi-

zation (where the people have been taught to expect it) it is mandatory to avoidance of disruption. Clarity of objectives between all links of individual managers is more likely to produce cumulative clarity of objectives. *Thus, MBO should improve overall organization performance and increase the level of participation.*

4. *Performance will improve when individuals are clear about their job objectives.* It is to be expected that individual performance will improve when people's goals are clarified, without seeking to achieve other side effects even though they might well be predicted also. Questions of motivation, attitude, enthusiasm, and the alleviation of barriers to such activating forces are left to the individuals themselves for resolution. *MBO should achieve such individual improvement and growth.* The assumption here is an important one. MBO should be both *functional* (gets the job done) and *developmental* (helps the individual grow). This congruence is vital to the survival of our economic system and the social and political system so intimately associated with it. If individual growth and corporate success were necessarily antithetical, the system could be self-destroying. In adopting MBO as a system, we recognize that organizations create products and produce people who are workers. *MBO thus appeals to higher-ranking, profit-oriented chief executives. It also meets the requirements of the personnel and developmental staff.*

Summary

Merton's *goals displacement* can be explained in systems language as a system defect in which objectives (hoped-for-outputs) have been defined but forgotten as we engage in the activity initiated to get there. What starts as a momentary lapse becomes a habit, then a procedure, and finally a religion. Meanwhile, the activity is consuming inputs which are increasingly related only to activity and not to outputs.

The consequences, however, are not limited to material input losses, which are real, but also to human development. The organization that locks fanatically into the input-activity loop produces a bureaucrat of new dimensions. The superior is often hostile, exacting, judgmental, and primitive. The subordinates become *professionally irresponsible,* so enamored of their professions that they resist the very idea of making commitments to outputs of either tangible or intangible character. "Give me resources continually, but don't ask me to commit in return to try for a specific output." The only recourse of the providers of inputs is to reduce or eliminate inputs and observe what losses might occur. This is certainly a painful way of learning, yet it is prevalent in part because of an unwillingness of persons to behave in a responsible and committed fashion and of bosses to define goals, to provide help in getting them, to leave employees alone while they are working, to let them know how well they are doing by self-control systems, or to reward them according to accomplishments.

CHAPTER 5

The System of Management by Objectives

The systems concept is primarily a way of thinking about the job of managing.
—R. Johnson, F. A. Kast, and J. E. Rosensweig

At the outset, let me make it plain that the system of management by objectives goes beyond being a set of rules, a series of procedures, or even a set method of managing. As the above quotation points out, it is a particular way of thinking about management. Let us begin, then, by placing our system in its conceptual framework:

1. The basic structure of the corporation is the organizational form often called a *hierarchy*. This is the familiar arrangement of boxes showing the boss in the top box and two, three, or more subordinates in the boxes one level down. Management by objectives is a system for making that structure work and for bringing about more vitality and personal involvement of the people in the hierarchy.

2. Management by objectives provides for the maintenance and orderly growth of the organization by means of stating what is expected for everyone involved and measuring what is actually achieved. It assigns risks to all responsible leaders and makes their progress—even their tenure—dependent upon their producing results. It stresses the ability and achievements of leaders rather than their personality.

3. As a system, management by objectives is especially applicable to professional and managerial employees. It can extend as far down as first-line supervisors and also cover many staff and technical positions. Though the same basic system (measuring

results against standards) is used in managing hourly rated personnel or clerical workers, the methods of setting standards and measuring results are significantly different.

4. Management by objectives helps overcome many of the chronic problems of managing managers and professionals. For example:

   a. It provides a means of measuring the true contribution of managerial and professional personnel.

   b. By defining the common goals of people and organizations and measuring individual contributions to them, it enhances the possibility of obtaining coordinated effort and teamwork without eliminating personal risk taking.

   c. It provides solutions to the key problem of defining the major areas of responsibility for each person in the organization, including joint or shared responsibilities.

   d. Its processes are geared to achieving the results desired, both for the organization as a whole and for the individual contributors.

   e. It eliminates the need for people to change their personalities, as well as for appraising people on the basis of their personality traits.

   f. It provides a means of determining each manager's span of control.

   g. It offers an answer to the key question of salary administration—"How should we allocate pay increase from available funds if we want to pay for results?"

   h. It aids in identifying potential for advancement and in finding promotable people.

A Brief Definition

In brief, the system of management by objectives can be described as a process whereby the superior and subordinate managers of an organization jointly identify its common goals, define each individual's major areas of responsibility in terms of the results expected, and use these measures as guides for operating the unit and assessing the contribution of each of its members.

The words we shall use in describing this system will be those every manager knows: authority, responsibility, delegation, and so on. We will refer to such familiar procedures as the performance review, the salary review, cost accounting, and other everyday management terms. You will not be called upon to master a new glossary or to grapple with the jargon of social science. Why? Because management by objectives is essentially a system of incorporating into a more logical and effective pattern the things many people are already doing, albeit in a somewhat chaotic fashion or in a way that obscures personal risk and responsibility.

The primary effects of operating by management by objectives are to be seen in such tangible results as improved profit, more growth, lower costs, and increased revenues. On a more intangible plane, it also makes bureaucracy less tenable by affecting such secondary variables as production, quality, housekeeping, sales volume, staff work, and research effectiveness. The tertiary effects of management by objectives are visible in such areas as better morale, more promotable people, improved quality of service, and improved delegation of decision making.

Sources of Management Knowledge

One of the most obvious facts about management is that there are effective bosses and ineffective ones. An organization may have an impressive array of experts in engineering, investment, purchasing, accounting, finance, sales, and heaven knows what else, and yet still fall dismally short of its objectives. Yet later, the same organization headed by a different manager (or the same manager using different management methods) will succeed brilliantly. How to achieve this turning around of an organization is thus the subject of much discussion.

One conclusion that has been reached on this question is that *managing* is a function or activity that affects total organizational performance far more than any other. In fact, it makes the functions and activities effective or ineffective.

Another conclusion is that this managerial function is a set of actions and a kind of behavior that is *distinct from the activities it manages*.

How does one learn how to manage? By and large, there are three basic sources of management knowledge: imitation, situational thinking, and behavioral science.

Imitation

Probably the greatest single source of management knowledge is the boss's behavior. Thus, young men and women find they are learning how to manage at the same time as they take direction from a superior. This would suggest that it is sound career planning to choose good bosses to work for. It also implies that the superior has a responsibility to behave in a way that is worthy of imitation.

The biographies as well as the personal examples of successful managers are another often-followed guide. This is sound practice, provided the aspiring manager imitates the things that really made these people successful—not their idiosyncrasies or irrelevant acts.

More dubious are the organized studies of the "career patterns" of successful managers. Slavish or unsophisticated imitation of such things can lead to an obsession with certain kinds of educational backgrounds or experience and the fruitless search for the "executive personality." It also obscures the fact that successful management behavior is usually *situational,* related to the environment and the followers as well as to the leader and the leader's action or personality. Actually—and mere imitation offers no clues here—*objectives* often explain behavior better than any other contributing factor in a managerial situation, since it is objectives that provide the main energizing and directive force for managerial action.

Situational Thinking

The second way of finding out what makes managers successful is through situational analysis and situational thinking. Instead of studying the actions of individual managers, we study the entire situation in which they work. Managers work in a variety of environments, and the particular environment in which they are called upon to function can account for their success or failure as often as their personal actions.

Thus, the values and goals of the organization in which managers work invariably shape their behavior and are often the underlying reason for their success or failure. Managers relate to the organization and get their work done in, through, and occasionally around it. A knowledge of the organization's values, the way it operates, its people, and its policies is essential in understanding managerial achievement (or its absence).

Every manager also works in an economic environment. The availability of funds, the procedures for accounting, the level of competition, and hundreds of other economic factors must be considered in explaining managerial success.

Also to be taken into account is the manager's technical environment. To a considerable extent, the success of managers in such fields as banking, insurance, manufacturing, education, hospital administration, or accounting is shaped by the demands of the profession they manage and practice. Some managers can readily shift from one field to another. A few seem to be able to manage any kind of business. Some can only succeed in a single line.

For the most part, the higher you go in the organization, the more time and energy you spend on the managerial portion of your job. For this reason, top military people can move into top industrial or business posts, because at the top, wherever they are, they are exclusively managers. It is more difficult for lower-level managers to switch fields since the technical part of the job will differ from one spot to another. How the managerial content of a job increases and the technical or professional emphasis decreases as a manager rises in the organization is shown in Figure 5.1.

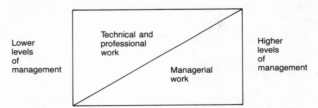

Figure 5.1 How managerial content increases and technical or professional content decreases as manager rises in organization.

There are many other situational forces that influence managerial action. Values, customs, mores—all sorts of social and political factors may place special demands on the manager and must be weighed in explaining managerial behavior.

Behavioral Science

Over the past thirty or forty years, the work of the manager has been the subject of intensive study by behavioral and social scientists. Though these researchers have undoubtedly enlarged our insights into the nature of the manager's job, they do not provide a complete explanation of managerial behavior and effective management action, nor does a knowledge of these findings serve as a substitute for managing.

This may perhaps be most graphically seen in Figure 5.2. The large circle represents the whole range of behavior with which practicing managers are concerned. The surrounding circles are the social and behavioral science disciplines adding to and explaining a part of the manager's functions. *Yet, as the diagram clearly shows, the central core of management know-how lies in managing, not in the social sciences.*

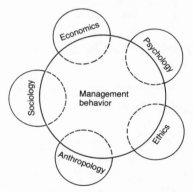

Figure 5.2 The core of management know-how lies in managing.

Managers use the findings of psychological research to understand, predict, and control such aspects of individual human behavior as learning, motivation, frustration, adjustment, and communication. They use sociological knowledge to understand how to deal with small groups, cliques, informal organization behaviors, crowds, mobs, and communities. From the anthropologist, especially the cultural anthropologist, they can gain an insight into the problems of cultural patterns in plants and offices. Yet so far as the average manager is concerned, all these sources of information must be put to work within the relatively simple framework in which most administrative work is done—a formal structure where authority rests near the top and in which goals must be set and results measured.

Most good work in management aims at accomplishing some specific end—achieving a particular goal, solving a particular problem, or reaching some fixed terminal point. The definition of these objectives for the whole organization, for all its subordinate organizations, and for the individuals in them is the logical starting place for management improvement because:

- If you don't have a goal, you have no idea whether you are on the right road or not.
- You can't assess results without some prior expectations against which to measure them.
- You don't know when things are drifting if you aren't clear what goal would comprise "nondrifting" or purposive action.
- People can't perform with maximum effectiveness if they don't know what goals the organization is seeking (and why) or how well they are doing in relation to those goals.

The Basic Organization Format

Professor Rensis Likert has described the organization of most firms, universities, and institutions as a series of "linking pins" in which the leader of a lower group is also a member of the next highest group. This is illustrated in Figure 5.3.

Here, we are mainly concerned about those higher-level linking positions, where in fact we are dealing with the *management of managers*. At this level, some of the goals will be received from the link above. Others will be developed within the unit.

Let us study that lower link more closely. The major elements in the system are illustrated in Figure 5.4.

1. Managers assume responsibility for identifying the common

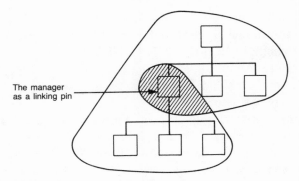

Figure 5.3 Likert's "linking pin" concept.

goals that all their subordinates share with them and toward the achievement of which they must converge their combined talents.

2. Each person is able to state, in advance of the attempt, *areas of responsibility* and *measures of acceptable results* for his or her position.

3. Each person has knowledge of the goals to be achieved, has worked out a plan for achieving them, and is measured by the *results,* insofar as these can be attributed to conditions that are controllable.

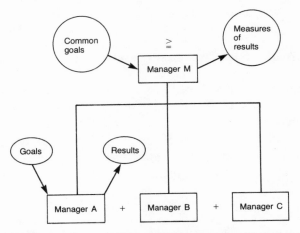

Figure 5.4 The basic system within which management functions.

While this system may seem obvious enough, the plain fact is that present systems of managing fall far short of this logical procedure. Michigan psychologist Norman R. F. Maier, in a study that explored the extent to which superiors and subordinates agreed on the major elements of the latter's job, found a divergence of opinion between the two groups on 25 percent of the items.[1]

When managers are employees in a large organization, their definition of *success* is inextricably tied to helping their boss succeed. Yet research evidence, in the Maier study and elsewhere, strongly indicates that most subordinate managers are not really clear about what their boss expects of them. In the absence of such understanding, it is little more than an accident or a special form of clairvoyance when a manager is considered very successful by the boss. The retreat into the security of bureaucratic life naturally ensues.

Let us take a typical organization in which Manager M works with three supervisors or subordinate managers (Figure 5.5). Manager M is concerned about getting maximum effort, creativity, and results from each subordinate. Looking at Manager A, M constructs a review of A's performance, as illustrated in Figure 5.6

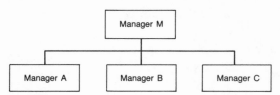

Figure 5.5 Three subordinates report to Manager M.

Though in many respects A's performance was satisfactory, M wonders why A bothered doing some things. There are also a few things A failed to do which the boss wishes had been done.

Faced with such a chart of results, M turns to the problem of *improving* them for next time. Here M has a choice of the three tools: selection, control, and development.

Selection

If Manager M considers A's performance grossly unsatisfactory, he or she may select A *out* and thus leave the way open for selecting *in*

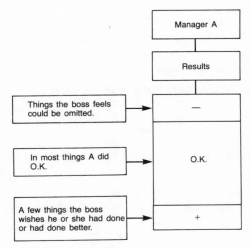

Figure 5.6 Manager M constructs review of A's performance.

another person whose results will be better. If, however, A's good results outweigh those things M is somewhat dissatisfied with, M will probably not use this tool but move on to one of the other two available.

Control

The boss may decide that the reason for A's failure to perform to expectations is somehow related to indifference, sloth, laxity, natural distaste for work, or inattention. The boss feels these failings can be overcome by closer supervision, tighter control, promise of benefit or threat of punishment, pressure, coercion, or some other form of control and direction. This places the burden upon M to supervise the person more closely.

Development

Here M concludes that lack of knowledge, skill, or ability may account for the unsatisfactory results. M must look more closely to discover what A is actually doing or not doing, then impart the missing knowledge, skill, or ability at the same time as the close watch is gradually relinquished. When M has eased the controls, if the development efforts have been successful, A will continue to progress satisfactorily under self-control.

Using General Motivation Methods as Indirect Controls

If M assumes that the causes of A's failures are sloth, indifference, laxity, or inattention, M may turn to certain popularized kinds of motivational formulas that have been widely disseminated in management and supervisory training courses. As M looks at A's performance for the recent past, he or she constructs a mental image, which resembles that shown in Figure 5.7.

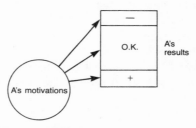

Figure 5.7   Manager M's mental image of A.

M has learned that people *in toto* are motivated by certain basic needs. These include *physical* needs, *ego* needs, and *social* needs. Thus, M's reasoning goes, if A can be supplied with one or more of these in the right combination then A will do the things that M wants done and eliminate the slothful, lackadaisical, or indifferent behavior.

M applies these formulas in a variety of specific ways, including bonuses, praise, chewing out, awards, and the like. M works at giving all his subordinates recognition, belonging, security, feelings of adequacy, and challenge. This approach suits bureaucrats just as well as it does risk seekers. It compels no acceptance of individual risks on the part of subordinates. They may, in fact, show startling improvement. But they may also show no improvement at all. At the end of the next period A's results may be better than before. This most often happens when M has failed to use the development tool.

Combining Motivation and Risk Acceptance

What is added to the manager's behavior when individual responsibility measurement occurs? Studies by Norman Maier and others have shown that when the expectations of bosses are not met, the simple fact is that subordinates did not know what was expected of *them* before they started the period in question.[2]

The basic step is for the subordinate and the boss to have an understanding in advance about the subordinate's major areas of activity and responsibility, what will constitute a good job (or a bad one), and what conditions should exist at the end of the period if results are to be considered satisfactory on all counts.

In the absence of such standards, no amount of generalized motivation can produce satisfactory results. Where the standards have been made clear, they have strong motivating effects in themselves.

Most research on motivation has been group research; that is, research into the morale and so on of a cluster of employees. Its usefulness lies mainly in inventing policies and procedures that affect the whole group. In dealing with individual A, the same policies may or may not be effective. A doctor doesn't consult an actuarial table to decide if patient Smith will die tomorrow. He studies Smith and his symptoms individually and in detail.

A management system should provide a framework for picturing the major factors in the situation as an integrated whole. It should be realistic. The system should simplify the complex rather than complicate the simple. It should also allow for some subsystems. At its best, a management system should incorporate both inputs and outputs, make individual managers responsible for the risks of business, and be considered as an almost self-contained whole. This does not exclude it from being part of a larger system, however, including the value system.

Management by objectives meets many of these criteria for a systematic approach to the manager's job. It deals with the organizational framework common to industry. It also relates to the larger problem of increasing the vitality and personal effectiveness of managers, as well as increasing their taking of risks.

MBO provides an answer to the problem of determining the manager's *span of control;* that is, how many people one can manage. The answer is that one can manage as many people as one (1) can set goals for with reasonable accuracy, and (2) can measure results for—and secure acceptance for both functions.

MBO defines what *kinds of people* a manager can handle in terms of the manager's knowledge contrasted with that of the subordinates. This is a system in which a manager can manage persons of any level of competence and education, provided the manager knows enough about their work to be able to work with them to accurately define the goals they will aim for and later to measure how well their results stand up to these goals.

MBO determines who shall get the *pay increases* from among the limitless demands for the limited funds available in the enterprise. The increases are allocated on the basis of the results achieved against agreed-upon goals at the beginning of the period.

MBO distills the complex problem of *communications* by giving first priority to the communication of job-related, risk-taking information, and treating the communications of goals and results as the primary problem.

MBO also solves much of the problem of *delegation* by treating it as a learning curve. The rate of control can be diminished at the rate at which superiors can teach subordinates to act on their own, and the rate of subordinate independence is a function of how fast they accept objectives and learn to move toward them.

The above list by no means exhausts the problems that can be handled by the manager who adopts MBO. Let it be understood, however, that MBO is far from being simple. In fact, nothing is more fatal than to conceive of a management system as a cut-and-dried procedure. Experience has repeatedly shown that when the architects of a management system regard it simply as one more mechanism, it is never accepted by the people who are called upon to put it into effect.

CHAPTER 6

Installing the System

How can technical change be introduced with such regard to the cultural pattern that human values are preserved? It is necessary to think about these patterns. . . .
—Margaret Mead

Having concluded the previous chapter by warning against being too mechanical in setting up and applying a system of management by objectives, I will now somewhat contrarily proceed to illustrate how such systems can be installed. The steps that I describe here have been distilled from the experience of many companies. Needless to say, they must be adapted to fit your particular circumstances.

The Necessary Conditions

The primary condition that must be met in installing a system of management by objectives is the support, endorsement, or permission of the principal manager in the organizational unit where the system is to be used. The premise that success for every subordinate means "helping the boss to succeed" indicates that the boss must be in accord with the goals of the subordinates and must not oppose the methods they use to achieve them.

Hence, the place to begin is with the top person in the organization. If the system is to be used at the corporate officer level, the top person will probably be the company president. At the divisional level, the system must include the general manager if the key functional heads are to use it as a way of managing. In manufacturing, sales, and en-

65

gineering departments, it must include the plant manager, sales manager, or chief engineer of each of these functional units.

This does not preclude any managers whose boss is not opposed to their using the system from going ahead and installing it in their own departments or units, so long as the managers have discretionary power over methods of managing.

The adoption of management by objectives in the national sales organization of Honeywell's Micro-Switch division, for example, was successfully carried out because the division's national sales manager decided that the system had strong possibilities for the sales organization, and his general manager enthusiastically backed this decision. In numerous other companies, personnel, research and development, and accounting departments, legal staffs, and other units have successfully installed management by objectives where the top person in the unit was free to do so and wanted it to be done. Usually the process includes the following phases:

1. The top person and those key executives reporting directly to that person study the system and how it operates.
2. The top person and subordinates set up measures of organization performance.
3. Goal-setting methods are then extended down through the organization to the first-line supervisory level through a series of meetings between the various organizational units and their superiors.
4. The necessary changes are made in such areas as the appraisal system, the salary and bonus procedures, and the delegation of responsibility. Ambiguous policies are clarified, and procedures that may be blocking effective operation of the system are amended. Other changes, such as the installation of a system of "responsibility accounting" by the cost department, are also made.

The Stages of Installation for the Individual Manager

If you are starting out to install this system in your own activity, you may ask, "How and where do I start? What steps are involved?" Following is a workable procedure for the individual manager at any level.

Two distinct but related activities are involved:

1. At the beginning of each budget year, you and each of your subordinates agree on the subordinate's targets of performance for that year.
2. At the end of the year you meet again to compare targets with results.

Let us look a little more closely at each of these activities and see what the manager does to accomplish them.

Setting Goals with Subordinates

The following steps are undertaken at the beginning of each budget period for which goals are to be established:

Step 1. Identify the common goals of the whole organizational unit for the coming period, based on your desired goals for the whole organization. State the goals in terms of the measures of organization performance you intend to apply at the end of the period. Some typical areas in which a statement of common goals may be needed are profitability, competitive position, productivity, technological leadership, employee development, public responsibility, and employee relations.

Usually the economic goals are stated in terms of the controllable areas of responsibility for the head of the unit concerned.

UNIT	ECONOMIC GOAL
General management	Profit
Sales	Revenues, margins, or contribution
Service	Cost of unit of service delivered
Manufacturing	Cost of product made
Staff or research	Budget and program promised

Step 2. Clarify your working organization chart. Sketch the actual organization of your group showing titles, duties, relationships, and impending changes.

As a manager you are responsible for achieving organizational results and personal responsibilities. You work out performance budgets only for subordinates reporting directly to you. Those below this level should work out their budgets with their own immediate supervisor.

Your objectives are your own goals plus the major goals of those reporting directly to you. Don't pyramid into one set of goals with all the many responsibilities of all the people below you in the organization. Carry the goal-setting process to your immediate subordinates. Take individual stock of the people with whom you'll be setting performance budgets. (Review all of your subordinates' past work assignments, appraisals, salary progress. Note any special factors about each of them and their work: their major responsibilities, what's going to be expected of them, and so on.)

Step 3. Set objectives for the next budget year with each person individually. Here's how you go about this:

    a. Ask the subordinate to make notes on what objectives he or she has in mind for next year, and set a date when you'd like to discuss these. Normally, these goals will fall into four categories: (1) routine duties, (2) problem-solving goals, (3) creative goals, and (4) personal goals.

    b. Before the meeting, list some objectives you'd like to see your subordinate include for the next year and have them ready. Note especially any innovations and improvements required of his or her function.

    c. In your personal conference, review the subordinate's own objectives in detail, then offer your own suggestions or changes.

    d. Have two copies of the final draft of the subordinate's objectives typed, one for each of you.

    e. Working from the final agreement, ask your subordinate what *you* can do to help reach the targets. Note any suggestions, keep them with your copy, and include them in your objectives, if pertinent.

Step 4. During the year check each subordinate's goals as promised milestones are reached:

    a. Are they meeting their targets? Time, cost, quantity, quality, and service should be measured here.

    b. Should their targets be amended? Don't hesitate to eliminate inappropriate goals or add new ones if a special opportunity arises.

c. Are you delivering the help you promised?

d. Use the jointly agreed-upon goals as a tool for coaching, developing, and improving each person's performance on a continuous basis. Reinforce good results by feedback of *success* when you see it. Allow people to make some mistakes (don't hound them) but use their failures as a platform for coaching.

Measuring Results Against Goals

These steps are undertaken as the end of the budget year draws near:

Step 1. Near the end of the budget year, ask each of your subordinates to prepare a brief *statement of performance against targets,* using the copy of his or her performance objectives as a guide. Tell the person not to rewrite the entire statement but to submit a written estimate (giving relevant figures where possible) of the accomplishments compared with the targets. In this statement the subordinate should also give reasons for any variances and list additional untargeted accomplishments.

Step 2. Set a date to go over each report in detail. Search for causes of variances. Ask yourself:

a. Was it your fault?

b. Was it some failure on the subordinate's part?

c. Was it beyond anyone's control?

Then get the subordinate's agreement on just how good the performance was and where it fell down.

Step 3. At this meeting, also, you can cover other things that may be on the subordinate's mind. You might discuss such matters as relationships on the job, opportunity, job-related personal problems, and so on. But don't rush this. If the employee prefers, set another date for talking about these things.

Step 4. Set the stage for establishing the subordinate's performance budget for the coming year.

Reviewing Organization Performance and Defining Goals for the Coming Year

Here, of course, you find yourself back at step 1 of the goal-setting stage, but better equipped by reason of your experience to set more realistic goals for the next budget period.

Unfortunately, simply setting forth a stark outline of this type may give rise to the misleading impression that the system calls for no more than slavish adherence to the prescribed pattern. Actually, any mere statement of procedure overlooks the factors of time and judgment and willingness to move with the deliberate speed required to overcome the cultural patterns that oppose the introduction of change.

Technical-assistance teams in underdeveloped nations, industrial engineers in inefficient factories, and community-development experts in rural America have all had to learn the hard way that people everywhere cling to expectations that offer them fulfillment of the values they hold dear. In the executive suites of the nation, as in the villages of India, the natives are under the sway of gods, graves, ghosts, sacred books, and high priests. One cannot sweep these aside with a weapon forged from the feeble material of logic alone. The procedure must allow for local customs and cultural idiosyncrasies and go forward at a pace determined by the elimination of these barriers rather than by the dictates of pure logic.

Still, technical and logical progress must be made.

Some Indispensable Preliminaries

In installing the system, managers would do well to look to the experience of others if they wish to avoid the costs of trial and error. When in the hope of reaping quick gains, managers ignore what others have learned, a certain amount of "backing up" and redoing will almost certainly become necessary, as many companies have found in trying to shortcut some of the following essential steps.

Secure Top Management Backing

If the often-delicate negotiations that are necessary to obtain the endorsement of the top manager are omitted, the subsequent steps are likely to fail pretty badly. Unless the top person and the key executives in each department know and accept what is being done, you might as well *defer your hopes until such endorsement is forthcoming*. It is no secret that there are many successful managers who enjoy personalized control and don't mind at all if things appear chaotic as long as control is effectively centered in their hands. Such leaders resist systemization for a variety of personal reasons. When they also possess abundant energy and long experience and run the business with vigor and zest, the results will probably be good. The question, though, is whether they will be succeeded by leaders who are their equals in ability, experience, and energy. It may also be questioned whether such people are, in fact, using their talents to best advantage.

When a company is in effect run by one person, several conditions usually exist that can hardly be considered favorable to the organization or the leader. The leader is probably tied closely to the present and is doing too little innovation. This is not always true, however. Many charismatic leaders are great innovators, continually pushing the organization into new (and not always appropriate) fields. At the same time, the innovative powers of others may be stultified by this domination.

Most leaders who practice personalized control are prisoners of their subordinates and the job. The prisoner and the guard are both in jail. The puppet-master and the puppets are at opposite ends of the same string.

Usually the personalized style of leadership results in the leaders' working at projects below their best abilities. As a rule, these are "vocational hobbies"—things the leaders particularly enjoy doing because they excel at them. Perhaps they once held the job now being done by subordinates and oversupervise them. Perhaps they gain personal satisfaction from a particular line of work and dally with it, though they are paying someone else to do it. The process of weaning managers away from such vocational hobbies is in part accelerated by a systematic approach to management.

Trying to obtain the endorsement, support, or permission of the leading figure in the organization to install management by objectives will be of little avail if he or she resists giving up personal control. If a leader is intractable in accepting systemization, is successful, has strong successors coming along, and is innovative, it may as well be accepted that a new system is likely to add little to the company's immediate profit and growth and had better be deferred.

In any event, if management by objectives does not promise to achieve some beneficial effects that can be measured, it should not be pressed into use at that time.

Clarify Common Goals Before Individual Goals

One of the more important reasons for involving the top leaders of the organization in the process is to engage them in setting common goals for the whole organization. This is more than a simple accumulation of the individual goals of subordinates. Such common goals may come from past history, from competitive records, from industry standards, or from higher levels of management, such as the board of directors.

Much of the literature of the social scientists who have studied and written about management by objectives has stressed "productivity" as a single measure of success. Experienced managers recognize this as but one of a dozen or so possible goals for an organization. These common goals might be in any one of the following areas:

- Amount of profit
- Rate of profit
- Profit as a percentage of sales
- Profit as a return on investment
- Profit as a return on equity
- Growth in assets, sales, or profit
- Market position or product-mix pattern
- Share of market
- Quantity and quality of service provided
- Productivity of people, machines, or capital
- Revenue levels
- Contributions to profit
- Employee relations, attitudes, turnover, and so on
- Public relations

The necessity of setting organization measures of performance before setting individual management measures of performance lies in this simple fact: *Not all organization goals will be divisible into the personal goals of managers at lower levels.*

Decisions taken at the highest level—for example, to buy rather than to manufacture (or vice versa); to accelerate growth through merger and acquisition; to increase productivity through automation or instrumentation—may affect the objectives of individuals in subordinate positions in a variety of ways. Individual managers at lower levels must know what these decisions are, and what limitations such decisions place on their discretionary powers before they can be asked to propose their own goals. Otherwise, superiors may find themselves seeking opinions or suggestions that, in fact, cannot be used because they conflict with decisions previously made higher up. It is far better never to ask subordinates to participate in decisions that affect them than to ask them and then ignore what they have to say.

For example, a grocery company found that its marketing methods needed a drastic overhaul in the face of rapid changes in food stores and the rise of the chains. The buyers had become more like purchasing agents of quantity lots while marketing methods were still geared to mom-and-pop stores. It became evident to top management that a complete revamping of the marketing plan was needed. Among the envisaged changes were early retirements for a substantial number of salespeople, the release of others, and the demotion of many sales managers. The pure use of participative management ("How do you think we should organize to fit the new marketing situation facing us?") produced a vast array of resistance to the drastic upheaval that was obviously called for. As a result, a great deal of bitterness ensued when the necessary change was enforced from the top. But what really irked the managers was that they had been asked their views and had given them freely, had been ignored, and then had the inevitable ill effects upon the sales group forced on them anyway.

The establishment of measures of organization performance before individual measures are set *defines the boundaries* within which subordinates can legitimately propose goals. Once these boundaries are known, individual goals and budgets should be solicited, and to the extent possible should be used in *adapting organization goals.*

In brief, *the establishment of measures of organization performance should precede goal-setting meetings between managers and subordinates.* These measures of organization performance delineate the areas of decision of both parties in the joint goal-setting process.

While many of the measures of organizational performance will be summations of the individual goals of managers, those which are not should be clearly identified.

Change the Organization Structure in Accordance with Goals

The sketching out of the actual organization structure follows goal-setting, since if goals are changed then changes in organization may well be needed. In the case cited above, it was the goal that shaped the organization and not the reverse. Changes in organization will lead to changes in individual areas of responsibility and authority and should be clarified before subordinate managers are asked to work out their performance goals and measures for the coming period.

The MBO Cycle

As Figure 6.1 shows, the system of management by objectives is a cycle. In this cycle, the newest feature is the *joint establishment* of the goals of subordinates. This is also the phase of the process that requires the most time from the most people.

This use of time on the manager's part is an important aspect of management by objectives and depends heavily upon three points:

1. *Management by objectives is a system of managing, not an addition to the manager's job.* To return to our example of Manager M, identifying common goals, restructuring the work unit, jointly setting goals with major subordinates (A, B, and C), and using these goals as measures of results, both for the entire period and for periodic review, means M will be too busy doing all this to do much else. In other words, M will be too busy managing to do much else.

2. *The manager who adopts management by objectives as a system of managing must plan to drop some of the more time-consuming vocational hobbies.* This is another way of saying that, as a manager, you must delegate or relinquish personal control of certain activities that you have hitherto personally manipulated or overseen in too much detail. The difference here

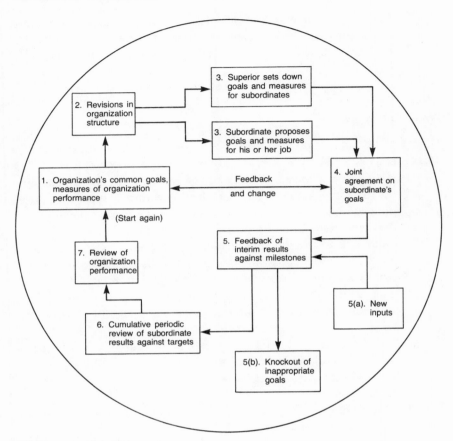

Figure 6.1 The MBO cycle.

is that you add the teaching of the subordinate to your duties, and your rate of relinquishing personal control is identical with the rate at which you teach the subordinate to perform as an independent operator. Thus, the *learning curve* for the subordinate is the *delegation curve* for the superior. Your former hobbies become responsibilities of the subordinate.

3. *The system of management by objectives entails a behavior change on the part of both superior and subordinate.* Your subordinates move in a more results-oriented fashion because they know what their goals are. You provide the instruction,

help, and behavior that will lead them to success. You must constantly ask, "What can I do, or do differently, or stop doing, to help you achieve the goals we're agreed on for your position?"

What Not to Do

There are certain key points in the foregoing procedure that can make or break the system. Here is a brief rundown of the major don'ts:

1. Don't get involved in personality discussions. It is becoming increasingly recognized that the chart-rating type of performance review is based on unsound premises and achieves no behavioral change of a predictable or productive nature. Confine your talk to the job, the results, and the reasons for variances.
2. Don't discuss salary and performance at the same meeting. I will treat salary administration and how it relates to performance in a separate chapter. Suffice it to say here that the two subjects involve many different facets and should be discussed at different times.
3. Don't discuss potential and promotability at the same time as you are working on the subordinate's responsibilities and results. Make that a separate discussion also. I will treat that topic later on, too.
4. Don't hold a person accountable for things that are totally beyond his or her control.
5. Don't dwell on isolated incidents at the expense of overall results.
6. Don't make up your mind about the results a person has achieved until the two of you have had your discussion.
7. Don't nag. By nagging we mean berating subordinates for their failure to do things they did not clearly know were expected of them.

CHAPTER 7

Organizationwide MBO

MBO isn't an additional program—it's a total way of managing an organization.

—George Odiorne

As we have stated, the system of MBO can be described as: *A process whereby the superior and subordinate managers of an organization jointly identify its common goals, define each individual's major areas of responsibility in terms of results expected, and use these measures as guides for operating the unit and assessing the contribution of each of its members.*

The logical beginning point for MBO in an organization is at the top. The sequence in which objectives will be set and reviewed comprises a rudimentary calendar of events that occur in the organization over a two-year cycle on a continuing basis.

How to Set Objectives: Management by Anticipation

The first step in goal setting is to define the *ordinary calendar of events* that must occur in the organization where MBO is to become the prevailing management system. This entails, as is shown in Table 7.1, some events that occur prior to the beginning of the target year and some events that will occur during that year.

The term *management by anticipation* is used to describe those goal-setting actions required of staff departments such as personnel, accounting, legal, traffic, finance, and controller.

77

Table 7.1 A Rudimentary MBO Strategic Planning Cycle for Business or Other Organization on a Calendar-Year Operation Basis

DATE	EVENT	COMMENTS
July 1	Annual edition of the five-year plan and review of prior year's five-year plan.	Responsibility of the top manager and all major functional (staff) heads, assembled by planning department.
October 1	Budgetary submission to budget decision group (for the following year).	Responsibility of all units upward, starting with sales forecast, cost estimates, and profit forecast to budgeteer.
	Review, revise, approve final budget figures.	Responsibility of executive committee.
January 1	Start the new budget year, release resources.	Issue detailed, approved, financial targets in final form.
January 15– February 1	Completion of individual operational objectives at all levels.	To set standards for managerial performance for the year.
	Annual goals conference by managers of departments.	To share goals and devise teamwork.
	Annual message of the president.	To give a challenge.
April–July 1, October 1	Quarterly reviews of individual results against goals, and adjustments as required.	Responsibility of all managers at all levels.
April 15	Audits, including program.	Responsibility of staff departments.
Monthly	*Meetings of the executive and finance committee to note exceptions and make corrective moves.*	
Passim	Position papers for circulation and discussion and policy committee actions as major issues are noted.	By staff experts or any responsible manager or professional or functional group.
July 1	Repeat the process.	

There are three major events during a year which comprise the planning cycle for the organization. As you'll note from inspecting Table 7.1, these three events come at the start of each quarter:

- April: Analyze all audits and program reviews to find strengths, weaknesses, problems, threats, risks, and opportunities.
- July: Prepare and submit the annual edition of the five-year plan.
- October: Submit the annual budget, profit plan, and fiscal plan.

1. Audit Information. This information, which includes program audits and overall reviews of the major strengths and weaknesses of each staff responsibility, should be reviewed to provide a basis for finding major opportunities and problems.

2. Five-Year Plan. The annual edition of the company five-year plan should be prepared for each of the major areas of responsibility. Thus, the annual edition of the five-year personnel plan, financial plan, technical plan, and the like should be prepared at a period some three months in advance of budget submission. For a company on a fiscal year starting January, the close-off date for the annual five-year plan would be about July 1 of the prior year. This permits opportunity to revise budgetary planning, move resources to new uses, find new funding requirements, and make decisions about the abandonment of programs or plans.

3. Annual Budgets. With audit information reviewed and the annual edition of the five-year plan written and circulated, the allocation of resources can occur. This permits more rational commitments of resources, including the use of zero-based budgeting for support services and of cost-effectiveness methods for facility and program decisions.

These three steps in management by anticipation are essential in the effective functioning of MBO in an organization. They provide for sound strategic objectives before efficient operational objectives are chosen. *Without strategic objectives stated in advance, measurable operational objectives may not be valid. You may simply be overseeing a well-run bankruptcy.*

In formulating strategic objectives, the following points should be considered:

1. Strategic objectives should be stated in advance of budgetary decisions.
2. Strategic objectives should define strengths, weaknesses, problems, threats, risks, and opportunities.
3. Strategic objectives should note trends and missions and define strategic options, including consequences of each option.
4. Good strategic objectives will answer the question "Are we doing the right things?" in contrast to the operational objectives which define "how to do things right."
5. Strategic-anticipation staff goals need not necessarily be measurable, but they should use both words and numbers with clarity to define long-run outcomes sought. For example, "Apex Corporation will become the leading seller of solid-state monitoring devices in the field by 1983." Such goals are often established by groups such as the board of directors, management committee, or personnel policy committee.

As shown in Figure 7.1 there are some specific considerations that will be included in the strategic-goals statement of every staff department and major business unit.

How to Set Objectives/Operational Goals:
Management by Commitment

At the beginning of the operational year, each manager and subordinate manager sit down and conduct a dialogue on specific operational objectives for the coming year for the subordinate position. Prior to the discussion each reviews the present situation, the results of the previous year, and some of the more likely requirements for change. Each person thus comes to the discussion prepared to arrive at commitments and to assume and delegate responsibilities.

The manager is armed with information on budget limitations, strategic goals agreed upon above, and actual results obtained in the previous period.

The subordinate comes with some expectations and knowledge of his or her own performance strengths, weaknesses, and problems as well as threats, risks, and opportunities.

1. Should be prepared three months in advance of budgeting decisions.

2. Should come up from below as proposed alternative strategies.

3. Should be prepared annually at half-year.

OUTLINE	COMMENTS
I. Present Conditions: Describe the present condition, statistically and verbally, on the following (add your professional opinion): A. Internally—strengths, weaknesses, problems. B. Externally—threats, risks, opportunities you see. II. Trends: If we didn't do anything differently in this area, where would we be in 1, 2, or 5 years? (Do you like this possible outcome?) III. Major Missions: What are we in business for? Who are our clients? What is our product? What should it be?	

IV. Optional Strategies (press for multiple options):	What would the consequences be?		
	Contribution	Costs	Feasibility
A. Do nothing differently. B. _____ C. _____ D. _____ E. _____			

V. Recommended Action Plan: To be turned into objectives.

Figure 7.1 Format for Annual Strategic Objectives Statements.

Operational management by objectives adds to the previous management by anticipation a new dimension, which is a face-to-face relationship with the superior and, through that superior, with the organization itself. This is *management by commitment.*

Commitment means that a subordinate makes some promises to somebody else whose opinion is important. This commitment is not general, but specific, explicit, measurable, and worthwhile.

Responsibility means that one accepts full accountability for the outcomes produced during the commitment period, without reference to excuses or explanations. This does not guarantee that the responsible person cannot fail for reasons beyond his or her control, but commitment still assumes a results responsibility. This implies adult behavior, professional effort, and mature self-control in one's work.

The superior is also committed. If the superior agrees in advance that the proposed operating goals are meritorious, then those objectives must be the criteria for judging performance at the end of the period. Such judgments could include salary adjustments and merit pay recommendations, bonus awards, appraisal, promotability notations and similar rewards for achievement. If the superior has accepted objectives in the beginning, the subordinate is protected against capricious or *ex post* judgments.

The key to management by commitment is that the hard bargaining about what comprises excellence of performance is done up front— before the period begins and not after a year or so of effort.

The process by which the operating goals (commitments) are established consists of a dialogue and a memorandum. The dialogue is one to which each participant brings something. It is neither solely top down nor solely bottom up, but a genuine discussion that is most satisfactory when it is conducted on an adult-adult level rather than a parent-child model.

How to Write Objectives for Commitment

The manager should write operating objectives in an order that suggests ascending levels of excellence. Properly arranged objectives will help to distinguish the good performance from the superior one. To do this, a manager must have a clear picture beforehand of his or her criteria for defining promotability and making assignments, for coaching and training subordinates, for delegating, administering discipline, and for making year-end decisions about compensation.

The subordinate should see the written objectives as arranged in rising levels of difficulty. During discussion these five questions should be answered to the subordinate's satisfaction:

1. What is expected of me? Let me know in advance.
2. What help and resources will be available to me in my work?
3. How much freedom may I expect, and what reporting times and forms should I assume?
4. How can I tell how well I am doing in my work while I am doing it?
5. Upon what performance bases will rewards be issued?

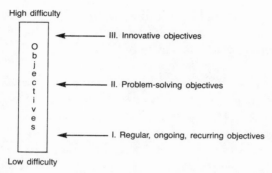

Figure 7.2 Writing objectives along a scale of difficulty and importance.

This last question is best answered by writing goals in three categories, as shown in Figure 7.2:

Category I. What are the *regular responsibilities* of the position? These are the ongoing, recurring, repetitive, and measurable objectives of the job, such as dollar volume of sales or units per shift.

Category II. What are the *major problems* that should be attacked and solved in this position during the coming period? A problem is a deviation from the standard that persists or that somebody important wants to have fixed.

Category III. What *innovations* will be attempted? These are active, not reactive goals. They are improvements, betterments, projects that will cause the area under the subordinate's control to operate better, cheaper, faster, safer, at higher quality, or with greater dignity for the personnel.

Some Typical Performance Measures

Starting with the regular objectives (Category I) of the general manager and his or her key subordinates, the goals should lock the organization together through some key indicators. Figure 7.3 shows some sample objectives of an ongoing, recurring character for a division general manager. The indicators of the regular category for this position include:

- Dollar volume of revenue per month
- Return on investment per quarter
- Cash on hand at quarter end
- Receivables, average age in days per quarter
- Inventory, average dollar level over the quarter
- Budget deviations as % on capital budgets
- Growth in dollar volume per quarter
- Labor stoppages per year

The indicators are never standard, but those listed were found to be common among a sample of fifty general managers. A study of Figure 7.3 highlights four features of indicator objectives:

1. They are stated as *outputs for a time period*. Statements of *activities* are not objectives but means.
2. The actual number chosen as an objective is stated in ranges. The superior starts by defining the middle figure, "Normal— realities," then lets the subordinate set the optimistic or stretch objectives, while the superior chooses the pessimistic figure. This latter figure comprises the *exception point,* at which the subordinate knows that he or she should *notify* the superior that things are not going according to plan. The middle point is based upon history, estimates, industrial engineering studies, or sales forecasts.
3. When deviations occur, the subordinate should know it before anyone else, should know why the deviation has occurred, have taken corrective action where it is possible, and notified and requested help from above early enough.
4. On the other hand, if the subordinate is attaining the middle level (normal–realistic goals), he or she should be left alone to operate without interference.

Figure 7.4 shows what a page of written problem-solving objectives (Category II) might look like. Usually these treat one or two major problems, defining:

- The present level or condition
- The desired level or condition
- The time when a problem is to be corrected (or brought to the desired level)

Category III objectives are also shown in Figure 7.4. These state the present condition, the desired condition, and some time-frame for the

Name _____   Period _____

GENERAL MANAGER

REGULAR-BASIC INDICATOR OBJECTIVES

Responsibility		Level of result sought		
Output indicator	Time period	Pessimistic	Normal–realistic	Optimistic
1. $ Volume of revenue per mo. .... Qtr.				
2. Profit: ROI .... Qtr. $ volume per mo. .... Qtr.				
3. Cash at mo. end $ .... Qtr.				
4. Receivables: $ mo. end .... Qtr. Days .... Qtr.				
5. Inventory: No. end $ .... Qtr. Turnover days .... Qtr.				
6. Capital budget % deviation .... Qtr.				
7. Labor problems—step 4 grievances .... Qtr.				
8. Share of market % .... Qtr.				
9. (Other) _____ .... ____				
_____ .... ____				
_____ .... ____				

RESULTS SCORE SHEET

Target No.	1st Qtr.	2nd Qtr.	3rd Qtr.	4th Qtr.	Total
1					
2					
3					
4					
5					
6					
7					
8					

Figure 7.3 Sample ongoing, recurring objectives for a division general manager (Category I).

innovative goals, perhaps including some stages of study or development.

The example given of the general manager's objectives, of course, must be supplemented by explicit objectives for each of the key subordinates reporting to the general manager. A manufacturing manager, for instance, might be committed to these regular (Category I) objectives:

```
II.   Statement of Major Problem-Solving Objective

      A.   Present condition or situation.

      B.   Desired condition or objective of the
           problem if solved satisfactorily.

      C.   Time commitments (always state as a
           range—pessimistic, realistic, optimistic).

III.  Statement of Innovative Project Commitment

      A.   Present condition or situation.

      B.   Innovation to be attempted.

      C.   Results sought (condition that would
           exist if the innovation were to work
           well).

      D.   Time commitment (state range—
           pessimistic, realistic, optimistic).
```

Figure 7.4 How to state a major problem-solving objective (Category II) and innovative project commitment (Category III).

- Average daily output per month
- Units per shift per month
- Indirect labor as a percentage of direct labor per month
- Factory overhead as a percent of total per month
- Average quality reject rate per month
- Warranty and policy costs per month
- Step 4 grievances per quarter
- Overtime hours per week per quarter
- Hours of supervisory training per quarter

A sales manager, on the other hand, does not have the same regular objectives as does the general manager, except for a few key result areas, but rather defines those indicators that will cover such major indicators of output as:

- Dollar volume per month per quarter
- Costs of producing the revenue per month per quarter
- New products introduced
- Dollar level of bad debts per quarter
- Days of sales training conducted per quarter
- New customers added per quarter
- Lost accounts per quarter

For each person reporting to the general manager, there would be indicators specific to that position but all would contain similar elements—namely, indicators of output for the time period stated in ranges, and problem-solving objectives and innovative goals.

How to Audit and Review Objectives

Three forms of review and audit are important in MBO—the periodic audit, the continuing review, and the annual review.

The Periodic Audit

This is a financial audit of a comprehensive nature usually based upon a sampling of the realities of the situation. It can be done by professional internal auditors or by an outside auditor such as a CPA. Program audits should be performed periodically not only for financial results and practices but for *program* operations as well.

Personnel audits and employee level audits for such matters as affirmative action, replacements of key persons, compliance with company or organizational personnel policy, and similar matters including labor relations should be included in periodic audits. Safety audits against OSHA standards done internally may prevent unfavorable audits by OSHA inspectors.

Other current practices of the best-run organizations include new forms of audit of programs. They might include technical audits, community relations audits, public responsibility audits, purchasing practices audits, and legal compliance audits for antitrust or patent protection.

The Continuing Review

Every manager having made commitments should be doing ongoing continuous reviews of his or her own performance. These reviews consist of observation and notation of actual results compared with the statements of objectives to which one is committed, and they cover the short time

periods (days, weeks, months, quarters) in which supervisory management gets reports of outputs.

*One of the major advantages of MBO is that it permits self-control
by the manager in relation to objectives agreed upon in advance.* Self-
control has some powerful motivational effects, for the tightest and most
perfect form of control is self-control. Commitment is a means of motivation and is considerably enhanced when self-correction is built into
the system.

As shown at the bottom of Figure 7.3, managers should be able to
post their own actual outcomes on the original objectives and send a
copy to their superiors. The function of the superior is to respond with
help and resources when requested or when notified that exceptions are
present.

The Annual Review

At the end of each year, the superior and subordinate pull out the objectives and review actual results in preparation for defining new objectives
for the coming year. With actual results against objectives in hand, the
superior can make such personnel decisions as are required.

This annual review discussion should be treated as an important
event and be held in a place free from distraction. It should deal with
objectives, results, problems, deviations, and improvements needed and
should avoid personality discussions. The superior should not adopt a
manner that is exacting, hostile, judgmental, or punitive.

CHAPTER 8

Measuring Organization Performance

Watch out when a man's work becomes more important than its objectives, when he disappears into his duties.
— Alan Harrington

It would seem strange to an old-style economist or anyone in business that I should have to begin by stating that business is first and foremost an economic institution. The reason for beginning thus is simply that the other effects of the corporation and the business community as a whole on the rest of society have been so emphasized in recent years that we may find ourselves overlooking this basic limit on our measurement of business performance.

There are hundreds of burdens that the business firm must bear, we are told, among the most frequent being:

- It must produce quality products.
- It must pay fair wages.
- It must pay its taxes.
- It must be a force for moral conduct.
- It must bargain collectively with unions.
- It should teach its workers to be free people.
- It should assist in the defense of its country.
- It should protect the property of its owners.
- It should provide for the old age of its workers.
- It should not demand conformity of its managers.
- It should not produce and sell useless products.
- It should not try to affect private lives.

- It should not conspire to set prices.
- It should not become too large.
- It should invent and innovate.
- It should not allow its employees to become immature.
- It should provide employment to workers.
- Its prices should respond to cost.
- Its management should be selected for ability.
- It should restrain its own power over others.

In fact, the roster of demands upon the firm and its managers, already large, grows daily. As professional managers have increased in numbers, the advice proferred to these nonowners on how to exercise their trusteeship has become more complex.[1] A kind of inchoate legalism now surrounds the corporation which, if ignored, leads quickly to statutory legal restraint. Is there a set of standards for managerial conduct? What priorities, if any, determine which set of values ranks ahead of all the rest?

It is the premise of this book that economic survival is still the primary demand placed upon management and that all other measures of corporate performance must follow and fit this goal.

If, in our zeal to impose new requirements upon professional managers, we bar them from achieving the primary purpose of the business enterprise, then we lose both the economic and the social objectives by which we measure it.

Of course, few modern managers would argue that profit is the sole measure of corporate management. It will be generally agreed that once the corporation has achieved this prime purpose it must quickly assume as many of the remaining obligations as are feasible without destroying its capacity to perform.

The key issue, then—the one that makes or breaks the business firm—is how to make profit, growth, and survival its primary goals, not only for the organization as a whole but also for each individual in its employ. Hence, the establishment of measurable, overall corporate goals must be accompanied by the establishment of measures of performance for each unit of the enterprise.

Out of the measures of total organization performance must grow the measures of organization performance for its smaller organizational units. Where do we look for such measures?

Primary Measures of Organization Performance

As a system, MBO requires objectives for every level of organization where some control over and improvement of performance is sought. While single organizations may have a single measure of performance (usually there are more, even for the single organization), it becomes obvious as we gain experience that the same measures will not apply to every unit.[2] Measures for a subsidiary unit should, however, be consistent with those of the larger unit of which they are a part. One schematic way of looking at measurements of organization performance is to simulate the organization chart.

This hierarchal structuring of organizational measures of performance against their own goals is accompanied by a corollary. *In management positions, the measure of the manager's performance is largely the measure of his or her organization's performance.*[3] That is, managers are measured by the performance of their followers rather than by their own personalities. In short, the manager is a skilled worker in organizations.

In establishing goals and responsibilities for higher-level managers, in fact, we find that the organization chart of their unit is (or should be) a fairly close proximation of their major areas of responsibility. This relationship is illustrated in Figure 8.1.

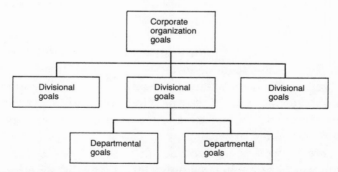

Figure 8.1 Organization chart can give close approximation of a manager's responsibility.

Take, for example, the personnel director of a company of 2,000 employees. She has a staff of fifteen in her department. She and her boss have agreed that her duties consist of: "Directing and administering the operation of the company's personnel and industrial relations policies, procedures, and programs." Her organization (showing immediate subordinates only) is diagrammed in Figure 8.2.

The list of responsibilities for her position would include all the major departments she directs and those things she does personally, such as advising the president on policy. If this personnel director were using management by objectives for her own position, her first step might be to define her major areas of responsibility, and the measures for each:

MAJOR AREAS	MEASURES OF SATISFACTORY PERFORMANCE
Labor relations	Continuous, productive operation.
Employment	Ample supply of qualified personnel
Benefits	Economic management of benefit programs and high employee satisfaction with their situation.
Salary administration	Equity and competitiveness in pay.
Training	Improvement in employee performance.

The actual measures of performance would, of course, include the goals imposed by the situation, including top management's perceived needs, as well as the suggestions of subordinates. Each subordinate, in turn, would define the specific responsibilities of his or her own position and discuss these with the personnel director until some agreement was reached and committed to writing.

Higher-level managers do not include in their goals all the detailed goals and measures of all their subordinates. If they did so, the pyramiding effect would soon make such a system unworkable. Each subordinate must define the common objectives for his or her unit and combine

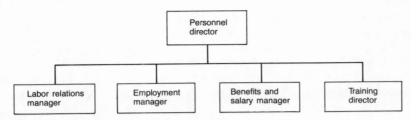

Figure 8.2 Personnel director's organization.

them into one total. This statement of the common organization goals of the lower unit thus becomes a measure for one area of the *boss's responsibility.* In short, subordinates have an agreement for total results and commit themselves to assist their boss to succeed.[4] What is success for the boss? If the subordinates achieve their common organizational goals, then these accomplishments combine to accomplish the total organizational goals of the higher unit.

Primary Goals and Intervening Variables

In the complex world of business, stating the results desired is not, of course, sufficient to achieve them. The time lag between research, production, and the eventual sale of a product or service is such that intermediate and early measurements of the steps toward results must be established. Such measurements of causes differ importantly from the measurement of results. Treatment of day-to-day affairs must be dynamic and short range. Nevertheless, working at a causal level is always more efficient when the manager is aware of the results sought in the total organization.

The first step in this process is to define the results sought, and define them in economic terms that are consistent with total company goals. The identification of intervening or basic causal variables must await this first step.

To measure results, it is helpful to adapt the categories that managerial accounting applies in measuring performance to the assessment of managerial behavior.

The Accounting Measures of Organization Performance

Cost accounting or the financial statement is a basic reflection of the economic consequences of the manager's behavior. Most cost accounting also attempts to identify where costs fall, in the sense of coming within the purview of a department head or unit leader. What are the basic accounting measurements by which we measure the financial performance of managers? The newer forms of *responsibility accounting* are most germane to our purpose here.

Figure 8.3 represents the different kinds of measures of organization performance that accounting provides. In setting objectives, the use of accounting methods should never conflict with personnel development goals, and so far as possible it should accelerate them. This often entails the shaping of the accounting system into one of responsibility accounting, which means that the financial objectives for each position shown in the diagram differ from those of other positions.[5]

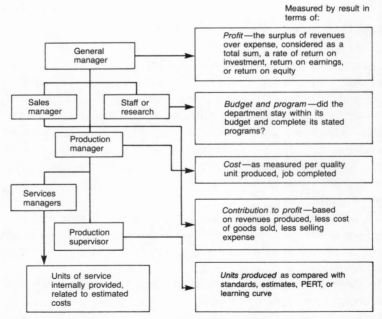

Figure 8.3 Financial measures of organization performance.

Profit as a Measure of Organization Performance. Essentially, profit means total revenues minus total costs. Very few people in an organization actually have profit responsibility in that they control or affect both revenues and costs. In a small or medium-sized firm, the president is the only manager who has profit responsibility. In the larger firm, the general manager of a decentralized division may have it, if he or she has control over both revenues and costs. In an even larger firm, a group vice president may have profit responsibility for a group of divisions—again provided his or her responsibilities are for *both revenues and costs.*

In any kind of appraisal system it is harmful to measure people by their profit responsibility if all they do is sell or manufacture. Profit as a result must be accompanied by control over both income and cost to be an effective measurement.

The naïve practice in some companies of plastering the premises with such exhortations as "Did my work make a profit for the company today?" is often harmful on two counts: (1) Very few of the people reading these signs make profits. (They contribute to them either by producing revenues, producing goods at a certain cost, or executing a program within a budget.) (2) Overattention to things for which individuals are not responsible and over which they have no control can divert employees' attention from doing creative work in areas such as cost, quality, safety, personnel management, accounting, and transportation. In any case, it is discouraging for the individual to be measured against achievements that are beyond his or her capacity to change, control, or affect.

Revenues or Income as a Measure of Organization Performance. A number of people in an organization can be measured by revenues or income attributable directly to their skill and effort. These include sales representatives and members of the marketing, advertising, and sales promotion departments. In some instances, the creation of *revenue centers,* with the manager in charge being measured by the revenue produced, represents an additional form of appraisal that is results oriented. A manager in such a revenue capacity may also spend money to obtain such revenues. Thus:

Income produced — Cost of goods sold = Gross margin

Gross margin − Selling expense = Contribution to profit

This measurement of managers in charge of revenue centers by contribution to profit is perfectly appropriate as an appraisal method. But it should be noted that such sales or marketing managers should not be charged with *profit* responsibility since they have no control over the cost of goods sold. Their contribution to profit could be controlled by these actions on their part:

- Pushing products with high mark-up.
- Pushing items with low selling expense.
- Avoiding the sale of unprofitable items.
- Adding to total volume without adding to expense.

Cost as a Measure of Organization Performance. In measuring the performance of the manufacturing organization, a different kind of end measurement is necessary. Here it is assumed that the manufacturing organization will produce a product of specified quality at a unit cost that permits it to be sold at a competitive price.[6]

In other words, cost-accounting data should be part of the final measurement of organization performance in manufacturing. These cost-accounting data should be incorporated into individual managers' goals, and the results achieved included in their personnel appraisal record as demonstrable evidence of their performance.

In order for such a move to have maximum effect on improving performance, the accounting system itself will need to be modified, as explained below. Ordinarily, such requirements are not part of accountants' concerns and must be explained to them or perhaps imposed upon them by personnel or general management as part of the latter's needs for measures of organizational and individual managers' performance.

Costs should be reported on a *responsibility* basis. That means that only those costs that are under managers' control and to which they have made a prior commitment should be reported as evidence of their achievement. All other financial information is incidental. If there are indications that noncontrollable expense has risen or something is otherwise unsatisfactory, these data should be separated from the costs the managers control.

Moreover, the feedback should be short range in scope. This may be accomplished by the use of accounting machines, which will speed up the rate at which reports are prepared. The best kind of cost reporting uses measures of performance which managers themselves can apply, thus enabling them to gauge their own levels of achievement while they are performing. This may require that organization performance measures be converted into units that managers can recognize as they work.

Thus, in certain manufacturing operations, cost objectives are translated into tons or dozens of products made in an operating hour. Manufacturing supervisors can take hourly counts of their units' outputs. These are often posted on charts or large blackboards where all employees can see how well they are doing. At a container-manufacturing plant, for example, the cost system was based on a certain standard number of workers on the line, with a standard number of containers expected to be produced by that much labor. The cost accountant and the manufacturing manager, on the basis of the previous year's experience, machine-speed ratings, and engineering studies, arrived at the unit costs shown in Table 8.1. The superintendent of the department then converted this goal into figures that were meaningful to supervisors and workers and placed a large blackboard at the end of the line where the containers were automatically counted before shipping (Table 8.2).

Now, each hour an employee checks the actual production shown on the counting meter, chalks it on the board beside the target for the time elapsed, and notes reasons for variances from the target ("No material," "Machine breakdown," and so on). Thus, the superintendent can quickly see every hour how his or her actual achievement compares with the target. Meanwhile the supervisor, who is on the floor all the time, keeps special watch on the progress of the line, identifying offending positions and then correcting them immediately.

Not every production system will permit measurement on such an immediate basis as this, but there are many mass-production operations where it could be applied and is not. The advantages are obvious. This

Table 8.1 Unit Costs in Container-Manufacturing Plant.

NUMBER OF WORKERS ON ONE LINE	TOTAL HOURLY LABOR COST	STANDARD HOURLY PRODUCTION	UNIT COSTS FOR LABOR
10	$50.00	10,000 containers	$.0050

		CREW SIZE	
		Standard:	10
Table 8.2. Production Board, Line No. 100.		Today's actual:	_____

OPERATING HOUR	TARGET	ACTUAL	REMARKS
1	10,000		
2	20,000		
3	30,000		
4	40,000		
5	50,000		
6	60,000		
7	70,000		
8	80,000		

type of measurement permits instant feedback of the results while there is still time to make changes before they become historical records and, indeed, before the employee's superior is required to exert any kind of pressure or direction for corrective action. Thus, self-control at the lowest level can be achieved.

In quality control, the use of visual-display charts of statistical quality control, which operators have before them and on which they themselves post sample results, has proved to have an incentive effect in instilling a sense of craftsmanship in the worker. It also instills a feeling of self-control and ability to measure one's own progress before pressures are exerted from higher up. Such a system requires that some kind of *unit cost* measurement be developed relating to the standard of output under the control of the lowest possible level of employee.

It should also be noted that this example applies to the container company's system of *flexible cost* measurement, since the removal of the crew from the line is a signal that only operating hours will be measured. Total volume is not as significant as the relative productivity of the crew while they are being paid for operating that line. It also permits the organization head to note whether or not the *manning table* is being adhered to or if some special condition has required that it be increased. Only information that is *controllable* goes back to the people who are being measured. For example, the reporting board does not throw in information about local tax rates, plant insurance, or overhead burden.

In other kinds of work, such as in the assembling of large items that may take several days, weeks, or months to complete, different kinds of control systems are required. The use of PERT or critical-path routing charts and networks may serve the same purpose. These show the relative stages of completion and their sequence—facts agreed upon in advance, against which the organization managers can measure their performances and, more importantly, *which provide them with feedback of their own progress* while they are engaged in doing their jobs.

The most undesirable forms of feedback are those where managers have not the slightest idea how well they are doing until some absent second party releases information about it.

Measuring Organization Performance by Cost

When the measures of organization performance to be used for performance improvement (rather than for pricing or other financial purposes) are being shaped, it may be necessary to modify the measurement system and reporting procedures to fix responsibility for individual supervisors and managers according to their area of responsibility and the type of work they direct. Some general guides here are as follows:

1. The cost system should relate to the plant layout, the flow of work, and most especially to the responsibilities of the individuals in charge. Continuous mass-production plants should have different reporting systems than should specialty job shops. Process-cost systems (such as the one mentioned) may differ in measurements of managers from those in job-cost systems (where PERT was suggested).
2. *Actual costs* need not be reported to the manager in charge unless all these costs are under his or her control.
3. *Estimated costs,* in which the cost of labor and materials and the controllable factory expense of producing the job have been predetermined, should be fixed in collaboration with the manager whose performance will be measured by them.
4. *Standard costs* should be determined for each element, but only those elements under the manager's control should become part of his or her objectives in running the department. Since the standard is determined for processes before the operation takes place, the responsible manager should know what these stan-

dards are and should have had an opportunity to take exception to them for reason. Such standard costs should be stated in units, and means of measurement should be established to permit immediate measurement and self-control.

5. *Marginal costs* or declining costs for the production of additional units are a special production condition that should be established with the manager before production starts. The application of the learning curve to measurement of relative levels of output for specific lots or jobs should be worked out in cooperation with the manager who will be measured by the standard. Airplane, electronics, and missile manufacturers make use of learning curves in cost estimating, scheduling, employee-level planning, budgeting, purchasing, and pricing. Learning curves may also be used to assess the relative performance of managers in areas where no prior standards of a historical or engineering nature can be constructed.

Program Budgets as Measures of Organization Performance

Many subunits of companies simply cannot be measured by revenues, contribution to profit, or costs related to output units. These would include such organizational units as the personnel, research, legal, and public relations departments. In such units, the measure of performance are subjective and judgmental, but they can be controlled in some respects once such judgments or policy decisions have been made. Employees in these units:

- Can be given a budget within which they must live. This is the input.
- Can propose programs they wish to complete. This is the output.

Performance Budgeting. Sometimes staff departments or other groups whose performance cannot be measured by revenues or units produced are assigned a fixed sum of money and required to develop a program that will make this money go as far as possible. This kind of budgeting usually results in what has been called the "equitable distribution of discontent." In a few instances, it might also result in the kind of management typified by such administrative horrors as these:

- Department heads ask for twice as much as they expect to get because they know their asking figure will always be trimmed by half, no matter how worthy it may be.
- As the end of the budget year nears, the managers of the departments operating under such budgets will make an extra effort to spend anything left over, lest the surplus be taken as an indication that the total sum was not really needed and will accordingly be cut next year.

The only corrective for this kind of action is one in which the *program* goes before the *budget*. Under performance budgets, the manager of each unit providing staff output will consult with his or her superior and with those who are the main users of the advice provided. Usually this output will fall into three major categories.

1. Advice. In providing advice the staff department is putting its expertise to use in suggesting ways of improving the effectiveness of operations in other departments. This advice may come in response to requests, it may be proffered without request, or it may be imposed. It may also be given to several levels or to one. It may be advice to top management on policy, to line managers on operations, or to other staff departments on procedures. Thus, the legal department may advise the sales department on antitrust, top management on mergers, and the personnel department on employee benefits, all from the legal angle.

2. Control. Staff activities falling into this category may take the form of surveillance of operations, with a view to feeding back to top management, line management, or other staff departments evidence that they or others are deviating from policy. Control activities may also consist of reporting accounting information to sales or changing patterns of salary administration within the company to top management. Control may be exercised simply by the staff unit's providing information about itself to another unit upon which that unit can base its corrective actions. In some instances, this information may be accompanied by the power to direct that changes or corrections be made without stating specifically how to make them.

3. Service functions. Some staff departments sell services to other departments, either at the expense of the user or as part of a general administrative cost. The unit cost of a service can be calculated just as the unit cost of a manufactured product can be calculated and provides a measure of departmental performance. When cost of services can be obtained, overall performance measurement is more precise. Normally cost of services between departments will be estimated in advance for a given period, then charged to the user at standard rates. The department offering the service is responsible for assuring that each service unit delivered is produced within the estimated cost.

Under such a system, the budget becomes an extension (in accounting terms) of the cost of delivering the promised performance. The decisions are made at the performance level when the decision maker at the general management level who is responsible for profits (revenues-minus-costs) determines the likelihood of the program's contribution to the profitability of the firm.

Most performance-program decisions of this kind are judgmental and empirical. They are based on the premise that achievement of the program will either improve profits for the accounting period at hand or will enhance the likelihood of profits accruing sometime in the future. In such areas as personnel management, labor relations, public relations, or educational assistance, these decisions often become *investment* decisions and are accorded the same treatment in the mind of the general manager that conventional investment decisions receive. The following kinds of programs are among those that might be established as staff, service, advice, or control decisions:

TYPE OF PROGRAM	ADJUDGED EFFECT OVER TIME
Management development	Continued growth and stability
Public relations	Freedom to operate
House organ	Amelioration of employee discontent
Cost accounting	Loss prevention
Operations research	Revenue increase or cost reduction

The results of such programs can be determined only through the subjective judgment of experienced managers, who predict that the programs will have the desired effects and will not produce negative effects in return for the money spent on them.

For the manager of a staff department, then, the best and perhaps the only measure of performance is achievement of predetermined programs within budgets.

Measuring Key Variables

In this chapter the discussion centered on the *result* variables that characterize different kinds of organizations in business. It is not suggested that simply knowing these results will automatically bring about their achievement. Often, in complex organizations, the major effort must be concentrated on some causal variable. A causal variable is one which, if diligently pursued, will contribute to a result. *The measurement of intervening or causal variables must always follow the definition of desired results.*

One of the flaws in many recent attempts to spell out the kinds of intervening variables to which management should pay attention is that management is hazy about the results it hopes to achieve. A so-called intervening variable is neutral in its effect unless the result itself is spelled out.

Productivity as a measure of results may be useful or useless, depending upon an understanding of what productivity adds to profit and growth. Such haziness about ultimate results breeds numerous ill effects in business. Let us take some actual examples.

The sales department of the XYZ Company, for example, has always stressed *volume* of sales. All its management practices have been designed to motivate sales representatives to produce a high volume of orders and a rising dollar volume of sales. Yet in the year 1979 this sales force brought in $90 million more in sales with no increase in profit to the firm. What can we say about the motivation of this sales force? Obviously, its members were responsive to the motivation of their managers. They were consulted on how to enlarge volume. They set high-volume goals and achieved them. Nevertheless, these efforts ultimately had a bad effect on the company's prosperity and economic performance. No differences were made between selling products with a high cost of goods sold and selling those with a low cost of goods sold. Selling costs were not considered as part of the sales objectives. As a result, the contribution of the sales force to profit was extremely poor, even though the sales representatives' response to the motivational actions of their managers was superb. Motivation of itself is neutral. Without some economically sound common goals and a clear statement of results including a good measure of organization performance, those neutral intervening variables nearly ruined the organization.

Productivity is often used as a measure, whereas in fact it may or may not be suitable as a method of gauging the economic performance of the organization. Take the ABC Company, a producer of animal feed. Management found that its unit cost per ton of feed would be lower if the plant could run at over 80 percent of its fixed capacity during the year. Accordingly, it exerted pressure on the sales organization to bring about a high volume of orders in order to utilize the plant and thereby increase productivity. The sales department lowered credit requirements and sold tons of fertilizer to farmers and grain stores whose credit was shaky. While this achieved the desired result of raising productivity immensely (the plant ran three shifts to fill all orders), the ill effects were not long in coming. The following winter when collections began to fall drastically, accounts receivable were at unheard-of levels, and the many defaults wiped out all the profits that the better productivity was expected to achieve.

In fact, the concept of productivity as a measure of the effects of motivational or intervening variables is naïve in many respects. It presumes that productivity is a single measure that uniformly produces profits and growth, whereas it may have some damaging effects if the other conditions of sound economic performance are not met. The home gardener who buys an expensive power mower to cut a minuscule grass plot may well find that productivity has been vastly increased but that, unfortunately, the total cost of grass cutting has become exorbitantly high at the same time. This kind of an intervening variable merely indicates a lack of understanding of the nature of the business process and how it operates as a system.

Table 8.3 indicates schematically how the respective levels of a modern corporation might be measured in terms of results sought, the intervening variables, and the key causal variables. In terms of the common goals sought by any unit, this chart illustrates how such goals

Table 8.3 How Levels of a Corporation Might Be Measured.

USE THESE STANDARDS TO MEASURE PERFORMANCE OF	RESULTS SOUGHT	INTERMEDIATE VARIABLES	SOME KEY CAUSAL VARIABLES
Board of directors	The firm will survive, grow, and be profitable.	The firm has objectives, plans, policies, controls and is well managed in depth, has ample facilities.	Board members are experienced, proven people, show strong interest in the firm, and attention to their role.
President, group vice-president, or general manager of a division	*Profits*, growth, market share as measured by return on investment, earnings as percentage, or return on equity.	Strong officers, capable employees, sound policies, clean-cut goals for entire organization.	President has strong proprietary interest, creates a desire to excel, provides supportive environment to key officers, opportunities open to able, financial incentives.
Manufacturing and manufacturing staff	*Cost per unit* produced, at specified quality, as needed (in time) as measured by standards, estimated, PERT, or learning curve.	Productivity, quality standards and performance, yield, scrap, downtime, machine loading, safety, technical organization.	Skilled people, technical excellence, necessary controls, ample training, employee motivation, organization culture conducive to productivity, favorable attitudes, opportunity and incentive.
Sales and marketing staff	*Contribution to profit* (revenue less selling expense) as measured by estimates, historical standard, program, or competition.	Volume, gross margin, market share, penetration, cost of selling, advertising effectiveness, product mix.	Same as above.
Corporate staff department (or research)	*Program budget* achieves predetermined program within budgeted limits as subjectively agreed upon.	Programs, policy manuals, procedures, patents, papers, produced, installed or reviewed.	Same as above, plus acceptance of role and function by line department and top management.

differ in the three measurement areas. It also points up the limitations of regarding any intervening variables as having universal application, and the need for shaping measures of organization performance to fit each organizational unit to be measured.

PART 3

Goal-Setting Techniques

While it is true that MBO is a philosophy and a concept that applies the systems approach, it also requires some very specific skills in writing and defining goals and in getting agreement upon them with somebody else. This is not easy, for millions of people have tried to set goals and failed. In the following six chapters I have tried to deal with many of the problems of defining goals.

You won't know how useful this material is until you try it. Then you'll discover what every good goal setter learns: goal setting is more than a cookbook matter. You need to understand the philosophy, concept, and system, then the details can be worked out to fit your own special situation, if you really want to try.

CHAPTER 9

What Successful Goal Setters Do

Radical rationalism could lead to a preoccupation so strenuous that it would expose man to the dilemma of that centipede which found itself completely immobilized because it had been asked to watch carefully which of its feet it was going to put forward next.

—Erik H. Erikson

In the twenty-five years that make up the history of MBO as a management system, a considerable amount of attention has been paid to the errors that can be made in goal setting. Thomas Kleber's forty common errors,[1] Dale McConkey's twenty most common errors,[2] and my own list of twenty common errors (written in 1965) have worked this valuable critical approach to an extensive degree.[3] Young doctoral candidates often seek out the views of managers in MBO-centered firms on why their company has not done well in applying the system.

Yet MBO persists and works in many firms, and my purpose in reporting the research here is to show what competent and satisfied managers using MBO report as the reasons for the health of their programs.

The Sophisticated Manager's Guide to Goal Setting

Common errors in MBO usually committed by amateurs or inexperienced practitioners have been documented by at least a dozen research studies. The following list, on the other hand, is based upon what managers who made MBO work said they have done *right*.

The twenty-seven rules that follow were provided by a dozen directors of management development, MBO administrators, and executives from twelve organizations who have found their MBO programs successful. Their firms have used MBO techniques for five years to twenty-one. The managers were asked to state a few things they have learned from their successes that they would like to share with other managers, and this summary of their cumulative advice contains several hundred tips.

The twelve organizations include one large government agency, seven divisionalized companies with a total of ninety-six divisions managed by objectives, two medium-sized companies that are not divisionalized, and one small firm that does highly technical work. Total dollar expenditures of these organizations are about $61 billion.

The conclusions here are not founded upon a statistical survey but on interviews and written narratives. Thus, the method is mainly subjective, empirical, and experience-based. The responses are what survey research calls "free response." That is, the persons interviewed responded to questions about the number of years of organization use of MBO and their satisfaction with it. All felt that MBO had made substantial contributions to the success of the business or purpose of the organization, and their answers were selected for that reason. The responses, which were obtained in 1977, are classified under major categories according to the question asked.

What Makes the Best Kind of Goal?

1. *Don't Stress the Obvious*

Good goal setters, the MBO managers report, don't merely write down obvious things but set exceptional improvement and innovative goals. This requires that people study the obvious with fresh eyes and find ways of improving on it, rather than simply projecting some incremental kind of minor change or, worse, repeating the past.

2. Every Goal You Accept Means You Have Rejected Some Other Goals

Because resources are scarce, if you commit your organization to one goal, you must have rejected some alternative goals. This means that you should have looked at many alternatives before choosing the best one. It also means that the chosen goal was fixed after it was agreed to sacrifice those not chosen. The good goal setter knows what those rejected options were and why they were rejected.

3. Many of the Goals Statements Are Hard to Set

Every list of goals, even those set by the most experienced goal setter, includes some goals that will not be achieved either because of circumstances or because people weren't tough enough during the process of choosing goals. This does not mean the process was worthless, but it does mean that goal setting is hard to do.

4. A Mistake in Goals Will Produce a Mistake in Activity

Choosing the wrong goal or stating it improperly will produce a chain of behaviors and activity. If the company is seriously concerned about making MBO work for the benefit of the organization, goal setting cannot be treated as a mere bureaucratic exercise, for activity will follow goals at the same level of excellence. Bad goals produce worthless activity. Good goals produce rewarding activity.

5. Some Goals Are Deliberately Designed to Deceive

Divisional managers, professionals, and key staff people will often deliberately state goals that will get them larger budgets or better organizational positions or that will baffle the people who use the goals as standards of performance. A state legislature, for instance, might not fund real goals, but will fund deceptive goals statements. The budget committee might not fund the divisional plan if the political character of the goals is stated candidly. In a company, a division that is competing with another division (Buick versus Chevrolet, for example) may not state its goals in truthful terms but will use noble and glowing statements such as "increasing market share over foreign competitors."

6. Goals Are Most Useful When Stated as Indicators

The most exciting goal and lofty purpose must be converted into some kind of indicator which can be used to measure performance. A church's goal to "make man more Godlike" must be converted into statements of baptisms, confessions, or membership figures. While this may generate activity for its own sake, it is nonetheless invaluable. Counting the number of managers trained, for example, does not ensure quality training, but it makes such quality possible, for if nobody was trained, the quality would be zero.

7. Goals Can Reflect Real Effectiveness or Apparent Effectiveness

It is not always possible to tell by outside examination whether a goal reflects some important contribution or not. This calls for experience, and the knowledge of both boss and subordinate is what an organization really needs. A designated hitter with an average of .200 who wins games may be more valuable than a superstar who bats .400 over the season but never hits in a clutch. Real effectiveness means making a real contribution to corporate strategy, not just being a statistically great performer or organizational hotshot in operations.

8. Some Goals Are an Ego Trip

Experience with good goal setting shows that managers must be alert to people who lay out goals to glorify themselves or to build a good appraisal record and résumé rather than to be good team players and do a job for the company.

9. You Can Induce Good Goals from Overall Organizational Performance

An overall high level of organizational results is sometimes produced by people who merely do their own thing very well, without there being a single superstar on the roster. Superstars who achieve goals at the expense of other people achieving theirs are sometimes found in low-performance organizations. Thus, achievement of goals should include the number of assists and the number of managers promoted out of the unit. Goals should encompass the building of overall strength and long-run effectiveness, not merely one year or periodic bursts of excellence.

10. There Can Be Both Verbal and Written Goals

While most goals should be confirmed in writing, people should be willing to make commitments that they would not want to have on record. For instance, a president may want to dress up a division in order to sell it to somebody. However, such a goal should not be stated in writing. That would only produce undesirable countereffects in the division's ranks. Record only the measures that would add up to that goal.

11. Measurement of Goals Is Easier If There Is No Reason to Conceal Them

Most evasions of goal setting are for political reasons, not because something could not be measured. The anti-nuclear energy society that states that its goal is "to delay construction of nuclear power plants by two years, thus saving lives from nuclear accidents" may, in fact, have as its real goal, "to heighten the political consciousness of participants." Of course, the latter won't appear in the announced goals. In corporate life, the pursuit of higher divisional budgets is not often stated as such, but if it were, then it could be measured.

12. Force a Measurement, and If It Does Not Work Out, Drop It

The introduction of a new product may start with a goal in specific dollars picked out of the air and foisted on everyone by arbitrary judgment. A better way might be a market study or a trend estimate of a scientific nature. Still, even an arbitrarily chosen goal will produce better results than no goal at all. Of course if it proves to have been grossly inaccurate, it should be amended.

13. Other Things Being Equal, Try Participative Goal Setting First

These days some managers and professionals seem to expect to be invited to participate in goal setting. If you have no reason to think subordinates will withhold effort or try to deceive the organization, then let them participate. In those rare cases where you suspect some serious foot-dragging, don't let any false lust for participative management deter you from *imposing* goals. Breaking a general rule about allowing participation can be done if there is good reason.

14. If Your Goals Will Make Your Boss Uneasy, Back Off

If stating your most optimistic goals makes your boss and everyone else skeptical or hostile, back off and state lower goals, then turn on the energy and deliver the high ones. Next time they will believe you, and in any case it seldom hurts to exceed your goal by a substantial amount.

15. If Goals Are Conditional, State the Conditions

You might be able to state goals as conditional upon another set of circumstances being true. For instance, a sales manager might say, "If United Technology gets that helicopter contract, I would set a goal of half a million in added sales for us. If they don't, we will do half that or less." You can also state possible side effects you will try to prevent, but build in a hedge for good measure. This is called making our goals *realistic*. For instance, "If we get the large contract we bid on, this will require a lot of overtime in the plant, and higher inspection budgets."

16. Side Effects Cannot Always Be Predicted in Detail

Goals that state organizationally controlled factors are easier to set than goals that predict specific side effects. You can manage by anticipation more than you thought possible, but there will always be the surprise outcomes, some good, some bad—bad enough to kill a project.

17. Imagined Side Effects Should Not Be Allowed to Stop Goal Setting

If a subordinate says, "Maybe some strikes or material shortages will occur during the year, and therefore I can't make a commitment," this should not be allowed. It is better to assume that the ordinary things will occur and not let one's imagination run wild anticipating obstacles that may or may not happen. You should expect ordinary conditions to continue unless you have some hard evidence to the contrary.

18. Experience Is a Pretty Good Teacher, and Experienced Goal Setters Set Better Goals

Old hands (or Old Turks, as Herzberg calls them) set better goals than people relying on sheer brains or instincts. Like estimating, goal setting gets better the more often it is done. Thus, you can rely upon the estimates of experienced personnel more than you can upon those of people who have 440 volts between their ears but are working from pure scientific or rational prediction. This does not mean you should not rely upon science and rational forecasts, and in the best of all worlds you should rely on a scientific and rational forecast from an *experienced* scientific forecaster. But when the chips are down and you must choose, it is best to rely upon experienced goal setters. Their method may be intuitive, but beneath the apparent fuzziness of system is a hard discipline called experience. Science plus high motivation is better than science alone.

19. The Business Environment Is Always Part of Reality-based Goal Setting

Goal setting is always done within a context, and the context should be included as part of the rationale for a goal. If OSHA did not exist, production goals and costs might be lower, but OSHA *does* exist and must be included in calculations. This means that goals are reality-based, and the context must be acknowledged, related to, and if possible acted upon in goal setting. The manager of the American division of a large Japanese firm put it this way: "Every problem, no matter what its origin, is a business problem when you are setting business goals. This includes government, energy crises, inflation, or simply the weather. If it won't have any effect, then it's not a business problem, it's an interesting irrelevancy."

20. Goals Are a Means of Power Attainment

People set goals to assist them in their drive for power. When goals produce a diminution of power, they won't be set or won't be vigorously pursued. Managers whose goals are to put their divisions into bankruptcy or reduce their status, function, and power in the organization probably will not set such goals very well, and if forced to do so will not execute them very well. People resist power flowing away from them, and seek power coming toward them through goal setting.

21. Goals that Are Routine Won't Excite Anybody

One large company limits its goals to statistical indicators reflecting the past year, and all goals are stated as a percentage of the past year's results. But goals that are merely a compulsory repeat of the past won't do much for the manager setting them nor for his or her organization.

22. Low Confidence Means Low Goals, High Confidence High Goals

Many respondents stated that they observed that the more timid managers set timid goals and more self-reliant, assertive, and confident managers set higher goals—sometimes unrealistically so.

23. Any Legitimate Client Demand Must Become Somebody's Goal

The demand for some product or service by a client, either inside the firm or outside of it, should be firmly fixed in somebody's goals. If such a demand is left hanging and nobody is committed to it, then the organizational goal-setting system needs tightening up. The reverse of this is that every goal should relate to the production of something that somebody important wants, not just the person stating it.

24. Good Goals Create the Resources to Produce Them

A good idea is always funded, and a worthy project will be done if it is needed and contributes heavily. Funds can be shifted from less worthy goals. People should be informed that no important contribution should be withheld for lack of funds and that a good goal should bump another less worthy goal and employ that lesser goal's funds.

25. It Is a Good Idea to Pick a Goal to Command Resources

The best goal is one that promises to add value to the resources that will be consumed in producing it. Setting goals to command resources will often turn attention to that value added. The resistance to adding value to resources is fairly widespread, and goals that show promise of being profitable will supplant goals that do not promise such added value or that are unclear on what the value might be.

26. The Goal Setter Is an Important Part of the Quality of the Goal

A good goal is often a good goal because it is set by a proven performer, and a bad goal—no matter how lofty in wording or ambitious in numbers and intent—is often a bad goal because it is set by an irresponsible performer or one not committed to the organization's purposes.

27. Let People Fool You a Little Bit in Their Goals Statements

If the overall effect of the goals people set looks good, don't be so finicky that you pick them apart for minor details. If sales representatives want to set their goals too high, let them have a year of running to attain them. If you are dealing with the timorous who like to hedge every bet, don't fight over pennies. Just urge them to succeed in the goals and even exceed them. This does not mean you should allow totally unrealistic goals, but don't pick at minor variations from what your judgment tells you would be more precise. The fallacy of misplaced precision can stifle initiative.

Conclusion

Goal setting is a forward-looking process that is done by imperfect people in an imperfect world. The major emphasis should be on doing better. As Andrew Carnegie once said of his steel company, "All's perfect, we're getting better."

CHAPTER 10

Management's Vital Signs: The Indicators We Live By

Any good doctor knows . . . that the patient's complaint is more extensive than his symptom.

—Erik H. Erikson

When pilots are flying with 300 people on board, they always trust their instruments—their indicators—not their instincts. Perhaps there is a lesson here for managers—namely, they should operate for next year's objectives as well as for the long-term, strategic objectives.

Indicators are needed for the regular, routine, ongoing aspects of a job. They tell us how well we are doing in reaching our regular objectives. Indicators are also necessary for the objectives of problem solving and innovation.

As organizations become more complex, the requirement for stabilization and control becomes imperative. The principle here, and an important one, is this: Anything to which we can apply indicators can be managed. Anything that does not have indicators applied to it is not being managed, it is drifting.

According to Dun & Bradstreet, the master scorekeeper of business failures, one of the greatest causes of failure is that frequently the owner of the business does not have it under control. Relating this to indicators, it means that the manager must not only be able to read the indicators but also must be able to make indicators when problems occur.

118

A manager reads statements from the accounting department, cost reports, source and application of funds statements, credit reports, and other indicators. However, in order to control the organization and to obtain a stable base from which to innovate and to measure problems, the manager must also create indicators.[1] We shall look at some of these indicators, for they are similar to the skills of management.

Regular Objectives

What do the regular objectives look like? For a sales manager, one such objective might be the dollar volume of sales per month. Another objective might be controlling the selling expense that was required to generate that dollar volume. Administrative reports must also be completed. Service indicators, such as new accounts, old accounts lost, customer complaints, and a ratio of complaints to compliments, might also be used.

A manager taking over a new position with greater responsibility will likely find certain kinds of reports in the "new" basket. These reports come from the controller, the sales department, the production department, the timekeepers, and from clerical people at all levels. The reports flow into the manager, who naturally falls into the habit of reading them and, if puzzled about a certain report, will circumspectly ask about its origin, meaning, and purpose. A secretary is likely to explain that this particular report was always received by the manager's predecessor, and so, very shortly, the manager will assume that this is part of the atmosphere to which he or she has been elevated, that these facets of the new position are unique to the company or job, and will miss the fact that there is an important principle here. If the principle were understood, it would help the manager develop skills and perhaps teach them to other people.

What is the principle? It is that one executive skill is effective use of information. And one of the vital ingredients in using information is developing indicators and reading those indicators accurately.

How do you go about developing indicators for next year's job or for the long term? You start with strategic indicators.

Strategic Indicators

Strategic indicators are long term in nature and are often the basic indicators covering the entire organization and its direction. Return on investment is one such indicator. Return on gross assets is another. Earnings per share is yet another. It is not always apparent that the indicators themselves have great strategic importance to the organization. In the 1960s, for example, a large land development company operated against a strategic indicator of increased earnings per share. This indicator was widely promulgated and all agreed it was an important one. However, it served the company badly. Rather than go to equity financing in their western land development, they went to debt financing through banks. Halfway through a major project of $100 million, the banks ran out of money, owing to a liquidity crisis; the company was left with a series of half-completed developments that were neither convertible to cash nor salable. This company took a tremendous financial bath and required years to recover.

Often organizations pursue return on investment as their strategic indicator. However, a strategic indicator must meet the requirements listed in Figure 10.1.

```
1. The organization must first select one.

2. The strategic indicator must be related to the
   economics of the business.

3. The strategic indicator should be communicated
   to every responsible functional and general
   manager.

4. Systems should be built to show accomplishment
   against the strategic indicator.
```

Figure 10.1   Requirements of strategic indicators.

Converting from Strategic to Operational

There are seven steps to converting strategic indicators or objectives to operational indicators or objectives (Figure 10.2). First, we must find a responsible person. Next we must get that person committed for a specific period of time and to a very specific output.

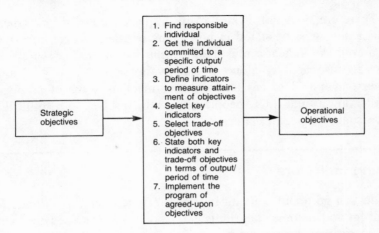

Figure 10.2 The process of converting strategic objectives to operational objectives.

Thus, in reaching regular objectives, the skill of the manager involves finding outputs for a period of time which will act as indicators to that individual and his or her superior, subordinates, and peers. These indicators will show whether or not the person is on course.

Why do we talk about outputs? Because the alternative is to talk about activities.

Take the case of the manager of college recruiting for a large corporation. His or her goal is stated as "visiting the colleges." This is really an activity statement. A goals statement should be specified in terms of outputs, results, or consequences for a specified period of time. A goals statement for the recruiter should include such items as number of students hired, total cost of the recruiting program for the year, ratio of students hired to students interviewed, and perhaps cost per student hired. These would be tangible indicators stated in terms of outputs.

Statements of goal areas, in order to be suitable as indicators, should be stated in terms of time. Without time there is no commitment. Have you ever had the experience of promising something, and then discovering that you did not want to do it? It becomes embarrassing to you only when the person to whom you made the promise pins you down to a time commitment by asking "When?" From a very early age this reaction is built into our culture and our value systems: a commitment is "real" when it involves a time commitment.

Therefore, it is not enough to pin a person down to an indicator. The indicator must be stated in how many per day, week, shift, month, or whatever. An indicator must be an *output per period of time*. It is an output because activity alone is usually not a useful way of telling whether the individual has met a commitment in terms of production. When stating a time limit, people commit themselves to a result that is of a reasonably specific nature.

Defining Indicators

How do you go about defining indicators? When defining outputs for a specific period of time, key indicators should be discussed first with a subordinate, who knows the base points around which other objectives revolve. For the employment manager, one base point is the number of persons hired by job category. For the accounting manager or the controller, it may be time reports, report accuracy, or report reruns.

In discussing indicators with subordinates, you will find that they will be able to identify the key indicators, and that the key indicators are going to be identified as outputs for a period of time (see Figure 10.3).[2]

How many objectives are needed? Single objectives are insufficient; objectives beyond the key objectives must also be established. There must also be indicators other than the key indicators. The key indicators are those around which the others revolve. The other objectives are *trade-off objectives,* additional objectives that must be achieved as well as the key objectives. They are called trade-off objectives because they compete with the other objectives. We are continually juggling quantity, quality, service, and time. For example, an employee might excel in production if quality control did not exist. Profit may compete with service; gross margin may compete with dollar volume. Recruiting managers might obtain a greater number of recruits if they did not have to worry about cost per hire. Objectives that address such secondary aspects are trade-off objectives.

How should objectives be set—too high, too low, or just right? This is a chronic problem. What will be too high to discourage an individual or just high enough to stretch him? Is the objective too low so there is no challenge? What time periods should be set? How does one determine where reality lies?

Range of levels or indicators of output

Objectives statements (output/time)	Pessimistic	Realistic	Optimistic
Key indicators: 1. 2. 3. 4. 5.			
Trade-off goals * * * *			

Figure 10.3 An objectives statement.

A manager needs two skills in setting objectives with subordinates: first, the ability to live by symbols; second, the ability to create those symbols. How should the goals be set? Too high, too low, or just right? Should the boss set them or should the subordinate?

Perhaps the most difficult question of all is how to set goals and define areas in the future to measure the unmeasurable. People asked about estimates for the future feel quite uncomfortable, and rightly so, for you are asking them to commit themselves to something not wholly under their control. They are obviously going to have a great many suspicions about your motives. Also, they will want to know what will happen if they fail—as they well might if the conditions are beyond their control.

Yet, if we look at the human condition we see that people really are able to see future trends and that they will state them freely. We must recognize that reality in the future does not lie at a single point or at a single instant in time. It lies within a range.

If you drive home from work, for instance, you may project that the drive will take from 30 to 40 minutes. If you were asked to state *exactly* how long it takes you to drive home, you would balk, but if you were asked to give a "ball-park figure," things would be different. This is an example of one person in communication with another and asking not for control over the acts of God, but for an estimate of the future.

Starting with Reality

Indicators are set after the output has been stated for a period of time. You should start with a bracket of objectives, a range, so that you know you are starting with reality and have greater maneuvering room. Of course, acts of God *can* occur, and no one can predict the future with precision. We do know, however, that within a range, the amount of accuracy in knowing future events is quite high. If an engineer tells you a certain project will take between six and eight weeks, it would appear that six weeks would be the earliest time, and eight weeks an outside figure. Seven would perhaps be a "realistic" expectation. If the project required ten weeks, then this would imply that something exceptional occurred.[3]

The setting of objectives in a range is important, and it increases the acceptance of the objectives. It gives the subordinate more self-control than a single number does, and it permits a boss a planning guide. It also allows the boss to use management by exception. One of the worst aspects of setting a single numerical goal is that an individual will go to every extreme to do better. This may cost the company dearly.

A range lets us know where the outcome will lie within the restraints imposed by the environment. If the outcome lies below the pessimistic figure, an explanation is in order. The general planning guide can be the middle (or *realistic*) figure.

In setting objectives within a range, you must be realistic. Two points are important. The first is to identify an objective. The second is to identify a range and choose a realistic midpoint between a pessimistic figure and an optimistic figure. How do you do this? What would you expect to be a realistic indicator of the production of newspapers from a high-speed press? What would be success? We could start with the reality of what was the hourly average last year. This does not imply that we should live in the past, or live each year twice. But this is a beginning point. After all, last year *really* happened.

If you had a steady secular growth (rather than several incredible catastrophies), then you would extrapolate from last year to this year. This can be built into reality now. Odiorne's Law applies here: "Things that do not change remain the same."

One misapplication is "zero defects." Does this mean, I have asked, that a plant will produce absolutely defect-free work for an entire year?

"Absolutely! This is our objective, and we are going to insist upon it."

What was the defect rate last year?

"Five percent."

What was it during the first quarter of this year?

"Five percent."

Now, what is it going to be for the next quarter?

"Zero defects."

This is not facing reality. Looking at the five percent, what would be a very favorable estimate? If you have faced reality, what would be an optimistic objective (see Figure 10.4)? This becomes the upper part of the range. If the realistic objective is reached, and you go beyond it, then you are in a success range. If you go beyond the optimistic objective, you have qualified as a performer.

Pessimistic	Realistic	Optimistic
This point is the "exception point." It is the lowest acceptable level of attainment of the objective. This point often indicates that the goal will not be met unless action is taken.	This is the most likely figure to be reached when the goal is attained. It may be last year's figure if nothing has changed or is to be changed. This point in the range is the most apt to be reached.	This figure could be the best ever done. It is not just a theoretical figure; it has been reached before, even if only one time.

Figure 10.4 Range of possible outcomes.

What would be the pessimistic objective? This is the point at which you realize you are falling below the expectations level.

Sales managers, services managers, production managers, and accounting managers can all use the exception principle if they have stated objectives within a realistic range. If the objective has been built properly and if a pessimistic figure has been considered, you are able to manage by exception. The pessimistic figure implies trouble to be corrected. If you set a good range:

1. You will know the apparent problem before anyone else.
2. You will know why the realistic objective is not being met.
3. You will initiate every corrective action under your control to solve the problem.
4. If you still need help, you can ask for it in time.

The Necessity for an Indicator System

In 1971 the president of ITT, Harold Geneen, in an interview for *Dun's Review* when ITT was named as one of the ten best-managed companies, indicated he had two articles of faith. First, all key objectives should be set face to face. Second, problems at a lower level should be brought up to the next higher level in order to obtain sufficient help in solving them.

This process requires an indicator system. It requires the equivalent of an instrument panel in front of the manager. A manager who can devise indicators for his or her organization is managing that organization.

How does one measure the unmeasurable? If you cannot measure something, work up verbal descriptions of it. If you cannot develop verbal descriptions for it, it might be a good idea to ask yourself if this is truly a necessary function.

The great challenge of the future will be to read indicators and to develop new ones.

11

Setting Routine and Emergency Goals

If we are concerned with the shortage of talent in our society, we must inevitably give attention to those who have never really explored their talents fully.

—John W. Gardner

With the entire framework of the system in mind, the key premise of MBO is that the goals established between the subordinate and boss will achieve better results than chaotic or random methods could produce. In this chapter, I will deal with some of the characteristics of good goals and some of the kinds of goals that might be set by a manager and subordinate. The next chapter will describe the vital question of the *process* of goal and individual standards setting, and how much participation subordinates should have in establishing their objectives.

The guiding principle of goal setting is: *High performance goals are needed in every area of responsibility and every position where performance and results directly and vitally affect the contribution of the employee to the organization.*

The goals system should provide all managers with a means of planning and measuring their performances and those of their subordinates. It should give managers some means of knowing when they are deviating from their target in sufficient time to do something about their errors. Goals should be established in areas over which the managers have control through their personal efforts. There should be ample opportunity for feedback and the chance to obtain genuine satisfaction from achieving predicted targets. The system should eliminate anxiety about possible failures, when such anxiety is rooted in ignorance of what is expected.[1]

Can Managers Be Measured Like Other Workers?

For half a century, industrial engineers and motion-study experts have had fairly specific ideas about how to measure the performance of hourly workers in factories. Time study, and the sophisticated techniques evolved from the basic methods of measuring physical work, are quite well established. In brief, such performance measurement consists of three phases:

1. Break a job down into its component elements arranged in cycles. Each job in the factory consists of a definite series of actions which follow one another in an established pattern. Inevitably workers go through this cyclical pattern in their work, and each step in this cycle can be identified.
2. Establish a standard time for the performance of each of the stages in this cycle of work. Add in certain delay times as an element of the cycle. These may be for personal rest periods, delays for various predictable causes such as machine breakdown, and for fatigue as the day goes along.
3. Add all these standard times together and arrive at an average time for the cycle, then convert into hours. Since each cycle produces a finite number of pieces of work, the standard quantities of work can be counted for each hour a worker is being paid. If you know the worker's hourly pay rate, you can arrive at a standard cost of production for each piece of work. This is useful in rating worker efficiency, in establishing the price of the product, and in other manufacturing management considerations.[2]

Such methods, vastly more complex in their development but basically rooted in this three-phase program, have also been applied to office clerical workers, to service workers such as maintenance people, and to workers in other areas.

The major requirement for using industrial engineering techniques to set standards of performance is that there be a beginning and an ending to the work cycle or task, and output related to measurable effort. However, *this is not true of technical managerial and professional work, since we are measuring responsibility and results, not effort.*

Almost without exception, the application of time-study techniques to managerial work has failed. If the job being studied lends itself to measurement of repetitive cycles of work performed, it probably is not supervisory work to begin with. *Increased effort* does not necessarily produce better results; *selective choices of effort* are more important.

The attempts to measure the work of professionals such as scientists and engineers along time-study or industrial-engineering lines have been equally unsuccessful. For one thing, the cycle of work seldom repeats itself. Often the cycle is technical, professional, managerial, and staff work is such that it *never* repeats itself, or it may be a year or two in length, as, for example, in the work of the accountant or auditor.

In view of the repeated failures to measure the performance of managers on conventional time-study or engineered-work lines, it is evident that some new methods of measuring individual managerial and professional performance are called for. The new methods must be adapted to the kind of effort managers put forth. More importantly, they must concentrate less upon the methods the managers use than upon assessment of the results they achieve.

This emphasis upon results or goals as the measurement of managerial performance does not mean that the methods used in getting there are considered unimportant. It is simply a recognition that the method itself may or may not produce the desired results. Both research and practical experience show that the successful manager in different situations may use different methods. Sometimes two different methods will each achieve excellent results.

At the same time, it does not make sense to measure results or performance when either of the following conditions exist:

- Managers have windfalls or pure good luck, which cannot be attributed to their methods or skill.
- They have poor results owing to conditions beyond their control. ("I want results not excuses.")

Moreover, results must often be measured against a standard for which any number of persons share responsibility. Where there is joint responsibility, measurement should be against a shared standard and the division explained. Unless the individual's contribution can be singled out from the contributions of all the others, he or she should be charged or credited with only a pro rata share of the group's achievement.

We know that managers in profit-making firms should be making
some kind of contribution to profit. The manager who does a good job,
however, may not always be measured directly, immediately, or personally by the profits the firm makes that year. It may well be that while
one does an excellent job, others do badly, or the market, the competition, the weather, or a host of other causes run in such a way that the
company loses money. Many managers declare that they work harder
and smarter when the going is rough than when everything is going well
for them. ("When the going gets tough, the tough get going.") But
suppose the going gets tough, the manager works hard, and, though he
or she is able to stave off disaster, the results are still poor compared
with last year's expectations of stockholders. Should the manager be
considered a failure?

The Assumption of Personal Risk

The initial attempt at goal setting between a superior and a subordinate
often results in generalized statements of goals which do little more than
restate some of the kinds of bureaucratic safeguards to which middle
managers have become accustomed in their work. Typical of these evasions are such proposed goals as:

- To perform all my duties in a superior manner.
- During the coming year I will show more diligence in executing
  the duties assigned to me.
- It is my hope that I will personally channel my energies more
  effectively toward company prosperity.

Such sentiments are highly laudable but hopelessly vague. Implicit
in them also is the patent attempt to evade specific statements of results
sought and the acceptance of personal risk through being measured by
individual performance.

This reluctance should be considered not so much a shortcoming of
the subordinate as tangible evidence of the need for tighter establishment of results-centered leadership. Compare the above statements of
objectives with these:

- During 1980, I will install and have operating a machine accounting system for this division.

- By June 1981, I will have negotiated out of the labor agreement the clause for arbitration of standards.
- By November, I will have completed the feasibility study for the application of computers to payroll preparation.
- During this year I will have our campus recruiting brochure rewritten and ready for distribution.

Such commitments, though admittedly more risky than others for a manager or staff person to become committed to, are more tangible. They are attached to the risk that the individual may fail—a consequence that may have adverse effects upon chances for promotion, raise in pay, or even tenure in the job.

In the goals-setting process, the superior will find that there are four categories that can be used to characterize the goals sought. These are:

1. Statements of *routine* matters.
2. Provision for *emergency* actions.
3. *Innovative* and creative projects.
4. *Personal growth* and development goals.

Setting Routine Goals

In this chapter I shall discuss goal setting in the first two categories mentioned above leaving innovative and personal development goals for succeeding chapters.

Every managerial or staff position includes some routine duties that must be carried out. Though repetitive and commonplace, these activities need to be spelled out specifically for a variety of reasons:

1. The boss should be cognizant of many of the small things that preoccupy the subordinate. Though the superior often is not even aware of these routine operations, they may be important in that failure to do them well could have serious consequences, whereas when they are well done their effect is apparently invisible.
2. Routine matters are often loss-prevention actions that divert the larger attention that will be needed later if they are poorly executed.

3. In estimating the distribution of duties among various staff members, the superior needs to be cognizant of this routine work in order to estimate the coverage of all of the facets of the operation and the management of the time of each subordinate.

4. In deciding on the distribution of the work, the boss must spell out these routine duties first. Such statements then form the basis for a more orderly clustering of duties to allow for their most effective performance.

Here, for example, are some typical routine responsibilities of a plant supervisor in a metal-working plant:

- To prepare the work assignment sheet daily.
- To investigate all cases of absenteeism upon the worker's return to the job.
- To maintain the supervisor's notebook, filing policies, memos and changes in procedure.
- To read and initial all time reports, inspection reports, and production reports.
- To maintain the inventory records for piece parts, and reorder from the warehouse when stocks reach reorder levels.

Such routine responsibilities may be included as part of the *job description* for the position, as prepared by the job-evaluation staff. In a sense, the job description is a statement of the purpose and duties of the position and is a charter to perform certain duties attached to it. The system of management by objectives enlarges the job description in two significant aspects:

1. All such duties are reviewed annually, and changes are noted in writing. Mutual agreement on these duties is a result.

2. Measures are established specifying when these routine duties are well done.

The measurement of performance in routine duties is a two-phase process. The first phase is the prior agreement between the superior and the subordinate upon what these routine duties are. This ensures more complete performance of duties than would be the case if no such agreement existed.

The second phase consists of statements of *exceptions* as measures of performance in routine duties. Subordinates agree that they are responsible for the performance of certain routine duties. They state in advance what exceptions to these routines they consider reasonable for the boss to expect.

A paymaster, for example, may report that routine duties cluster around getting the weekly payroll out every Friday. It is agreed that the measure of exception here will be zero—in other words, the boss should expect no exceptions to the diligent performance of this routine duty. Thus, the failure any week to produce a payroll on Friday will be considered an exception that calls for explanation by the subordinate. If the cause were reasonably under his or her control or could have been averted by extra care or effort, the absence of the payroll will be considered a failure on the part of the subordinate.

Another example. A production manager may agree that all incoming orders from the sales department will be acknowledged within four hours, with an upper limit of one percent exception. Thus, if all acknowledgments are issued within this limit of exception, the manager has performed satisfactorily. If failure to acknowledge rises to four or five percent, and the causes were attributable to conditions under the manager's control, he or she must assume personal responsibility for the failure, and explain.

Some typical responsibilities of a routine nature which can be measured by the exception principle might include the following:

- To meet all promised dates for delivery without exception.
- To issue insurance checks within 48 hours of claim filing.
- To average one pair of gloves per worker per day.
- To report all major violation reports from governing agencies.
- To operate at a spoilage level of three percent, with no more than one percent excess variance.

The common characteristic of these statements is a specification of an ideal condition that would exist if the routine duty were performed according to a *standard*. The measure of compliance covers what variances from the standard are permissible, and the point at which they become exceptions. If some variation is permitted, then it is not an exception. The exception begins when the agreed-upon variance is exceeded. For such a system to work in routine managerial or staff responsibilities, two guides must be observed:

1. *Reduce everything quantifiable to numbers.* Such responsibilities as production, quality, safety rates, spoilage, costs, and yield rates may be easily reduced to numbers, with the variances likewise stated in numerical terms. Other jobs in management do not permit such precision.

2. *Where numerical measurement is impossible, prepare verbal descriptions of the ideal conditions and of permissible variations.* In certain areas such as community relations, employee relations, and so on, it may seem impossible to reduce the standard to numbers. Actually, this can be done more often than is believed possible. Specific key indicators may be adopted for use as measurements. For total effect, however, if quantification has been tried without success, a verbal statement of the conditions that will exist when the duty is well performed should be used.

Let us assume that Manager M has received statements of routine responsibilities from subordinate managers A, B, and C (Figure 11.1). The opportunity for a redistribution of responsibilities is worth taking at that time. Making a *responsibility redistribution* has two major facets:
1. Getting statements of responsibility areas for routine duties from each of the managers or subordinates.
2. Laying out on a spread sheet the distribution of responsibilities for the whole department or group reporting to Manager M (see Figure 11.2).

Manager A is responsible for sales, B for the office, and C for the plant. As the responsibility distribution chart indicates, both Sales and Office state that they check credit of possible customers. A checks their standing through records, and B conducts field investigations. Manager M may choose to leave things as they are; or, if there have been some failures in the past, Manager M may assign full responsibility for credit checking to Office. Noting that all three do purchasing of certain items, Manager M may decide to continue with this practice or come to the

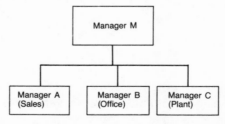

Figure 11.1 Analyzing routine duty standards for responsibility distribution.

Name	Manager A	Manager B	Manager C
Responsibility	Sales	Office	Plant
Check credit	Yes	Yes	No
Purchasing material	Some	Some	Some
Estimating	Yes	No	Yes
Bidding	Yes	No	No

Figure 11.2 Responsibility distribution chart of managers reporting to Manager M.

conclusion that economies could be made by centralized purchasing in the hands of one manager. Noting also that estimating is done by both Plant and Sales, he or she may ask for a clearer definition of who does what, leaving the present system in effect, or may shift total responsibility to one or the other as a means of ensuring more effective estimating performance.

Where joint responsibility exists, as it must in many cases, specific statements as to what measures of exception should be attributed to which subordinate should be obtained in order to obtain unity of effort and to measure results of the responsible person.

So, if both Sales and Office state that they are responsible for credit ratings, some definition such as the following must be obtained from each:

Sales is to report new customers in advance of solicitation in order that their credit rating may be checked by the office manager. Manager A must also report any information obtained in sales visits, including statements by other suppliers and by the potential customers.

Office is responsible for credit, and performance here is measured if Manager B maintains company membership in appropriate credit associations, checks all potential customers' ratings with such agencies, and reports these findings back to sales before any orders are taken from new customers. Manager B responsibility may also include sending to Sales regular credit rating reports on all present and past customers.

Sales in turn is responsible for receiving such reports and refraining from accepting orders from potential customers who fall below safe standards of credit. It becomes Manager A's responsibility to communicate this information to the sales organization and to be measured by credit losses, providing credit information is accurate and on time from the office manager.

Such a systematic analysis means that responsibility distributions must be settled in advance of the year's program, and that special attention must be paid to places where unclear definition of joint responsibility has resulted in losses or other performance failures. Typical areas where joint responsibility exists are where staff departments share advice and timely reporting functions with line departments, which need to act promptly and correctly upon information received—for example, industrial engineering and production, personnel and line manufacturing management, personnel and public relations, traffic and purchasing, accounting and manufacturing on cost control, sales and credit, sales and research, sales and manufacturing scheduling, production planning and assembly.

The definition of major areas of responsibility and the conditions that will exist when these responsibilities of a routine nature are performed comprise the minimum standards for holding a job.

Usually such standards mean that the person hired to occupy such a position has the required knowledge and skills to do these routine things. One hired for the position who must learn such skills will perform less than fully expected and should be measured as a trainee, apprentice, understudy, or learner. When a trainee is performing the routine duties according to the measures the boss can accept, then he or she is acceptable. It should be noted, however:

- Such a performance level might not include the ability to solve emergencies that could occur in the performance of routine.
- Routine performance may not entail much creativity or innovation in the job.
- The risk to the incumbent who levels off at the maintenance of routine levels of performance is that failure can result in removal from the job, if this failure is continually repeated or there is repeated evidence that he or she is incompetent to discharge these minimum routine expectations.

- This routine level of performance is the basis for nominal pay level—no higher than average—and should never be considered as meriting a bonus, incentive payment, or merit increase. Such additional compensation should be payment for performance beyond the routine.

Setting Goals for Emergency Actions

Emergencies and unpredictable eventualities may be considered as ordinary in every job, in the sense that we may expect that they will happen at some time or other. Unexpected problems arise because of changes in the environment, changed demands of users of the service, the errors of others, past errors not caught in time, acts of God, or other unforeseeable forces. The principal measure of the emergency is the demands it makes on a manager's time and the extent to which it diverts that manager from discharging routine duties or innovation.

The difficulty is predicting just which emergency will appear and when. How, then, can a superior allow in advance for the time and effort the subordinate will have to divert in solving the unforeseen? Still, in the goal-setting process, *some* estimate of emergency time required and the needed autonomy to act must be explicitly stated and time allotted for coping.

Most managers will tell you that the things that interfere most with the effective use of their time are:
- Attendance at meetings
- Incoming telephone calls
- Running meetings
- Visitors
- Social callers
- Travel
- Customers
- Employees with problems

Moreover, they will add, "I can get more work done alone in the office after hours or on Saturday than I can all week with the phone and other people interfering." The well-stuffed briefcase is a search for isolation to work in.

Yet, it is through the telephone, the meeting, and the personal contacts that the most effective work of managers must be done. Furthermore, close analysis of these unpredictable interruptions shows that after some analysis of the time consumed in each, many of them could be programmed.

One large firm, for example, made a study of its top staff and found that its managers averaged six hours a day in conferences, committees, and other meetings. Yet the same managers reported that the greatest interference with the use of their time was "meetings." Something is obviously askew here. If a study can show such close approximation to reality in the time spent on a specific activity then such use of time is predictable. Knowing how much time is spent on the phone, in conferences, in meetings, and the like permits them to be planned. The exact time that an incoming phone call may occur is almost impossible to predict. But the prediction of *how many* phone calls the manager will receive and the total time he or she will consume in such "distractions" is easy. With such facts in hand two alternatives are open. Managers can begin to take steps to cut down the time they spend on these activities by doing them more effectively or they can plan the rest of their time around such schedules. In either event, if they can predict and partly control such use of their time, it need no longer be called emergency work.

The management of time requires you to log the time you spend in specific kinds of behavior and establish other plans to accommodate these activities. If you closely analyze your time by categories of behavior, you can usually reduce the number and duration of goals thought of as "emergencies" since they can be planned.

It should be noted, though, that only the subordinate, not the boss, is in a good position to make estimates of the way he or she distributes time among different kinds of activity. Setting goals to cope with emergencies should force some action on the subordinate's part along this line. If a performance review during the budget period or a periodic review of results attained at the end of the period shows that there has been a failure to attain either routine or innovative goals because of unforeseen demands upon the subordinate's time, a time-utilization study should become an objective for the coming period.

Many activities presently seen as emergencies or not foreseen at all by the manager—a premise that, if valid, would constitute an escape from accountability for failure to achieve his or her goals—could be planned with considerable precision if a deliberate effort were made to do so. For instance, some typical goals that subordinate and boss might establish to cover the general category of emergency or unpredictable duties are:

1. Personally investigating all customer complaints and taking corrective action.
2. Entertaining visiting executives from company headquarters.
3. Interviewing candidates for positions.
4. Investigating accidents.
5. Talking to acquaintances who call or drop in.
6. Coping with illnesses and deaths of employees.

However, a careful study may reveal that such matters are often predictable in terms of the average time consumed and should be categorized as routine rather than emergency. When setting goals with the subordinate, the boss should try to obtain more systematic estimates of emergency activities and reduce them to routine matters. Over time, only those things that could not under any circumstances be predicted or estimated in advance should be permitted to be identified as emergency or unpredictable goals.

Managing Bad Luck by Objectives

Of course, the burning of a filament or an unprecedented act of God can send all of our lovely forecasts down the drain, but in certain kinds of organizations it seems that an inordinate amount of executive time is consumed in responding to panic events rather than on the more orderly processes of planning and executing. For many managers, the existence of such accidental events appears to be a basic flaw in the entire concept of management by objectives and therefore permits them to avoid setting *any* kinds of goals. "We can't tell what's next, so how can we set goals?" they ask. Is it, indeed, a weakness or theoretical flaw in the MBO idea or is it a matter of competent application?

Now certainly some events are determined solely by chance. Machiavelli once said that half of our destinies are determined by chance and the rest by ourselves. Recent statistics on business failures might indicate that this percentage distribution is inaccurate. The figures show that, of every 100 businesses that fail, 92 will be caused by bad management and 8 by acts of God. These statistics suggest the value of managing by objectives in order to gain some mastery of one's own future.[3]

There are the risks of nature and there are the risks of misman-agement. MBO cannot pretend to control acts of God but only to reduce exposure to the risks of mismanagement.

Modern systems theory can be of considerable help in managing those risks of mismanagement that seem to be products of pure luck. This application of systems requires that there be a *will to manage.* The mentality of the antiplanner toward such events should be supplanted with a determination to surmount all that is surmountable in the face of what on the surface seems to be nothing more than a swirling and chaotic mess. Systems thinking does not admit to chaos.

There are no messes in nature or in data. The mess is in the mind of the beholder. With clarification of perceptions, order often emerges from chaos.

It is often noted that when you are hip deep in alligators, it's hard to recall your objective was to drain the swamp. Yet alligators have existed for 150 million years, have always lived in swamps, and if you were a systematic person, you might have foreseen that you would meet a few. The failure to drain the swamp isn't in the swamp or alligators but in our own planning ability.

CHAPTER 12
Problem Solving by Objectives

The biggest problem in the world could have been solved when it was small. . . .

— Witteu Bynner

There are dozens of reasons why problems don't get solved. Perhaps they are impossible to solve. Perhaps they are being blocked by the carelessness or inattention of somebody in a high position. Perhaps people don't have the technical skill to overcome some technical glitch in the system. Or perhaps some obstinate person wants the problem to remain unsolved just to embarrass somebody.

The chances are quite high, however, that most problems don't get solved and some of them get worse because *nobody responsible has made a commitment to solve them to somebody else whose opinion is important.* Indeed, research studies show that often the bosses and the subordinates of this world are not in agreement as to what problems exist in the subordinate's job, what the priorities are among those problems that do exist, and what would be an acceptable time and cost for solution.

That's where management by objectives can be of considerable value:

1. It requires that the boss and subordinate sit down and get an agreement on what the major problems are.
2. It defines the problem in more specific terms, which in effect *turns the problem into an objective.* This has numerous advantages over a more leisurely and disorganized approach to problem solving and enhances the likelihood of the problem's being solved.
3. It defines the conditions that will exist if the problem is solved.

141

4. Problem solving by objectives ties closely to the indicators, such as accounting figures and regular objectives, defined in the first stage of MBO. Any indicator that goes beyond acceptable limits is by definition a problem.[1]

What Is a Problem?

The definition of a problem in problem solving by objectives thus becomes "achieving the objectives agreed upon." As Figure 12.1 shows, the dimension of the problem is defined by first defining two other elements—the present condition and the desired condition (objective). In other words, to define the problem requires that you know where you are now (if you don't know the facts, you don't know the problem or whether you have one) and know where you wish you were (if you like it where you are, you don't have a problem). *If you know where you are, but wish you were somewhere else, then you have a definition of your problem—getting there.*

Thus, the problem-solving objective is a three-part quiz that the boss makes with the subordinate:

1. "What are you trying to accomplish?" (Dig in until you get a reply.)

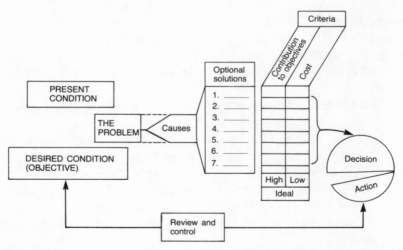

Figure 12.1 A model for problem solving and decision making by objectives.

2. "Where are you right now?" (Go get more facts, if necessary.)
3. "Let me summarize: Your problem is getting from A to B, isn't it? When will you be there? What will that cost in time and money? Please make a commitment for arrival time and cost."

Remember that the objective isn't perfection but improvement. You may be trying to get things back on the track. Or you may simply want to get back to last year's level. You would, of course, like to see things perfect but restoring normality is a more realistic goal. This is what Professor Herbert Simon of Carnegie Mellon has called "satisficing" the problem (a composite of satisfactory and sufficient). While it might be nice to see perfection, it isn't a sound managerial practice, for the last couple of inches needed to get there could be the most expensive part of the trip and not worth the incremental last effort.

- Improvement means that people are responsible for changing things for the better and correcting them when they go astray.
- Responsible doesn't mean "Who did it?" but rather "Who is going to fix it?"
- An objective calls for a commitment to restore normality.

Once this commitment is in hand, the superior should be available to help but does not necessarily interfere unless requested to help.

Suppose the subordinate doesn't know how to tackle a problem? If the subordinate knows the situation, knows the goal, and agrees on the dimension of the problem, that should be sufficient to clarify the problem-solving objectives. If, however, the subordinate does not have a clear plan for solution, then the entire process pictured in Figure 12.1 should be applied in the goal-setting process. In any event, the use of systematic problem solving will increase the likelihood of solution.

How Problem Solving by Objectives Works

Here is how the process works in problem solving:
- Have an *objective* in mind before you start.
- Collect and organize all of the pertinent facts.
- Identify the problem (the difference between what actually exists now and your objectives) and its causes.
- Work out your solution and some options to it.
- Screen the optional solutions through some decision criteria.

• Set up some insurance actions to prevent failure in the form of controls.

Since this book isn't intended to be a technical treatise, we'll stick with the bare essentials. Our point here is that the best decision makers in management, it is agreed, are precise thinkers and certainly know how to make up their minds. If you would like to acquire some of that skill, understanding this problem-solving method might help.

Have an Objective in Mind

You cannot really solve a problem or make a decision unless you have some idea *why* you want to solve it or what an ideal outcome would be—cost-effectiveness, increased profit, or whatever. You need some objective to judge whether or not your decision is O.K. once you have made it. You should clearly identify your goals. What are they?

1. To raise sales volume by $1 million?
2. To cut costs by $100,000?
3. To make up your mind about whether or not you approve of your daughter's suitor?

Your decision-making processes will be affected by your objectives. Once you have these goals clearly spelled out, you are then ready to move on to the rest of the plan—namely, to get more information (facts) upon which to make up your mind.

Collect and Organize All Pertinent Facts

Immersing yourself in the situation at hand seems to be a good guide. Get all of the data, the relationships between people, the numbers, the examples. One good way of getting at the facts is to list them chronologically, as if you were keeping a diary on the situation. Sometimes by seeing how events occurred one after another you can find a better way of getting out of a bad situation.

Another way of pulling the facts together is to draw some kind of sketch showing graphically how the facts lie in relation to one another.

Still another way is to make a chart or graph of the facts. By arranging them in this visual or chart form, you see them in relationships that point up the true nature of the problem you are trying to solve.

One pitfall to be avoided in fact gathering is treating things as facts when there is no evidence that they are true. If you conclude that opinion is fact, you start out with no common ground of arriving at a decision that can be implemented. *Facts should be verifiable and agreed-upon data. They should be backed up by some evidence to which all can agree. It's a fact if you can measure it, see it, smell it, hear it, taste it, or otherwise check it with your senses.*

Much decision making goes wrong because people don't treat facts objectively. They try to treat opinions, biases, hunches, or conclusions as if they were facts. Having jumped ahead thus, they may then overlook something important because it means that they have barred other possible solutions.

Here's a small test of your grasp of this idea:

> John Jones, 21, was arrested last night while driving on Jackson Road by Officer Harrison of the local sheriff's department. He was held for driving without a license and for possession of liquor.

Which of the following statements represent fact in this case?
1. Jones's parents should be blamed as well as John.
2. John was probably drunk.
3. John was arrested and put in jail.
4. Officer Harrison is of the local sheriff's office.
5. John had forgotten his license.
6. Driver education in the schools doesn't do any good.

The only fact in this list is no. 4. The rest is speculation, opinion, and gossip. If you fell into the trap of assuming that one of the others was fact, you went beyond your evidence.

Identify the Problem and Causes

The mere existence of a fact does not of itself make a problem. Let us say, for example, that John Jones, who was arrested by Officer Harrison, was a stranger. The news item becomes a piece of idle information. There may be a serious problem for young Jones or his family, but not for you.

Add this factual bit of information about the arrest to another fact that the same John Jones has been seeing quite a bit of your daughter lately. It may not be a problem, then, until you tie these facts to your objective regarding your daughter's marriage choice. Now you may indeed think you have a problem. Let us suppose the following two items were the case:

1. Your objective: You wish to have your daughter marry a young man of good character who will make her happy.
2. Your fact: John Jones, whom she has been seeing often, was arrested last night, as reported in the paper.

Your problem? It's basically the difference between what you want to achieve and the fact that indicates a possible difference exists. Can you meet your objective for your daughter's marriage if she continues to see John Jones? If Jones drives without a license and has liquor in his car, is he a suitable mate? The problem in this case is potential (it lies ahead) rather than existing at present. She isn't married yet. You induce the probability that the objective won't be achieved by her marriage to Jones as he presently appears to you.

The point of all this isn't that Dear Abby should be more scientific, nor is it intended to teach you how to run your daughter's life. Even if you make what to you seems like a logical decision, your daughter may not accept it. The point is that *a problem is the difference between what you see factually to be the present situation and what you would like to see to meet your objective.*

For example, if you had read or heard instead that John had won a National Merit Scholarship, or had been elected to his class presidency, you wouldn't see a problem. What you want (your objective) would be consistent with what you were getting. Result? No problem.

To define a problem takes two ingredients; an objective and some facts about present conditions that would show differences.[2] Before you condemn young Jones and upset your daughter more than she was by the news item, it might be better to get *all* the facts on Jones. Why was he arrested in the first place? Was he drunk? Were there extenuating circumstances? Does the news story refer to the same John Jones your daughter has been seeing?

It is also wise to really spell out your objective. Do you really want her to marry a young man of good character if he's a terrible bore?

What if he's bright and successful? Suppose he's a ne'er-do-well? What do you really want her to marry for? How important are *your* wishes to your daughter? What would you settle for? (You may have minimum and maximum objectives.)

With these guidelines you can pinpoint your problem.

Once you've clarified your problem, you can start thinking about some possible solutions.

Let us look at a few more examples, not tied to a domestic problem.

- You would like to manage your sales force in a way that would produce a million-dollar volume, but you reach only $600,000. You note that your sales representatives don't make more than one call a day and are indifferent to customers' expressions of interest. Your *problem* is low sales by $400,000, and the facts point to some possible causes of the problem.

- You would like to be promoted to a corporate officer rank in your firm and stand three levels below that position now. You also note the facts that all of those above you in rank are younger than you, are doing a good job, and like their jobs. Your *problem* is that your aspirations to high rank are blocked and the circumstances won't be eased in the foreseeable future.

Try defining a few of your own actual problems in these terms of (1) your objectives, and (2) the facts which point up (3) the difference. Now you are ready to turn to a more creative and imaginative kind of activity.

Developing a Solution and Some Options

Note that we're pressing at this point for alternative solutions, one of which may prove to be best. Your ultimate solution may be better if you have a wide range of options from which to make your final choice. You might prepare this set of options as a simple listing of alternatives. For example, take some possible optional solutions to your concern about Jones.

1. You might suggest your daughter take a parent-paid trip to Europe.
2. You might discuss your concern with Jones.

3. You might discuss your concern with your daughter.
4. You might ignore the whole thing.
5. You might introduce her to several young men and hope she will have second thoughts about Jones.
6. You might give her direct orders to avoid Jones.

And so on.

Screen the Optional Solutions

Once you have listed all the options you can think of (and perhaps you have had others help you think), you now need a filter of some kind to eliminate the worst ones and clearly label the best option. You make a simple decision-screening grid, as shown in Figure 12.2.

Then you use the decision-screening grid in Figure 12.3 to help solve your problem. The actual estimates of the correct wording to use in filling in the boxes must be based on your judgment in each frame. Presuming that you know your daughter's temperament, your mutual relationship, and the degree of influence you have with her, you now have structured the information in a way to make the decision easier.

1. It seems that only two feasible options exist. Either push for the trip to Europe (which she would like very much) or ignore the whole thing.
2. If cost is a major consideration (you aren't wealthy and have heavy expenses already), you ignore your concern. If, on the other hand, your finances are O.K., buying her a ticket for Europe will put your mind at rest. Or, will it?

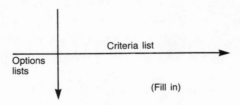

Figure 12.2 Simple decision-screening grid of optional solutions.

List the various options here	List your objectives and criteria for choosing one option across here. For example: "You wish to have your daughter marry a young man of good character who will make her happy."		
	Contribution to objective	Cost	Feasibility (will it work)
1. Send her to Europe.	Medium	High	High
2. Talk it over with Jones.	High	Low	Low
3. Talk it over with her.	Uncertain	Low	Low
4. Ignore the whole thing.	Low	Low	High
5. Introduce her to other men.	Uncertain	Low	Medium
6. Order her to avoid Jones.	Uncertain	Low	Low
Desired outcome	High	Low	High

Figure 12.3 Decision-screening grid of optional solutions to your concern about your daughter's suitor.

Set Up Some Insurance Actions

The array of solutions does not really solve your problem nor make up more than a first (logical) pass at devising a real solution. A sound search for options should also entail some follow-up, *if-then* calculations as a guide to making the action effective.

If the solution is the European trip option:
1. *Then* she might forget Jones.
2. *Or* she might find that absence makes the heart grow fonder.
3. *Or* she might meet another man whom you will like.
4. *Or* she might meet another man whom you will distrust more than Jones.

Such calculations for each of the various solution options can be tested by the use of probability guides or decision criteria. For example, if the chances of her forgetting him rather than growing fonder by being

away are 50-50 (one chance in two), you must then press on and study
the chances of her meeting somebody else who is likely to mean something special to her only if the memory of Jones is dimming. Say the
chances of finding someone you like better are also 50-50 (one chance
in two), then we must multiply the odds so that the probability of the
event (she'll go to Europe, forget Jones, and find someone else) are one
in four. Now you must face the chances of her meeting a ne'er-do-well
abroad. You calculate them at 50-50 (one in two). This ratio must be
applied to the one-in-four possibility previously arrived at. This means
that the chances are only *one in eight* that she will find a suitor you like
in Europe. The chances are also *one in eight* that she'll meet another
man that concerns you. This puts a new perspective on paying out all
that money. On the other hand, the chances are one out of two that she
will forget Jones and will not find a new suitor on her European trip.
You still won't have achieved your objective; you'll merely have given
your daughter the opportunity to re-think her plans for marriage with
Jones.

If you decide to try the European trip as a solution, then it's time
to move to the next step in your decision-making process—namely, set
up some controls to make the decision work better.

Since the chances are one out of two that the trip will lead to her
forgetting Jones, your controls should do these things:

1. You should help her plan a trip so interesting that her mind
   won't keep wandering back home. Boredom, and reminders of
   Jones should be prevented.
2. Since the chances of her finding a low-concern man are the
   same as finding a high-concern one, and both are meager, she
   shouldn't be overly exposed to men.

Your final decision, then, is shaped to fit these criteria:

• She is to take a well-planned trip to Europe accompanied by her
  favorite young married aunt who is anything but a typical
  chaperone, but can be firm when necessary, and has your daughter's respect.
• She is to tour constantly, perhaps in a rented car and will not
  stay in any one place too long where she might spend time with
  young men.
• The whole idea must be acceptable to her.

Summary

The point of all this example, of course, hasn't a thing to do with you or your daughter. It's merely been an illustration of a model for decision making. You've gone through a process that in review follows this pattern:

- Have an objective in mind before making up your mind.
- Get all of the relevant facts.
- Identify the problem (and its causes).
- Develop some solution, with options.
- Predict the effects and screen your option through criteria.
- Set up some controls to assure that your decision will work.
- Get acceptance of your decision.

If you've been impatient with this simplified example, we'd suggest that right here you should practice the method of making up your mind on a real problem of your own. It may be a business problem, a professional decision, a domestic problem, or a career choice. Put the book down and try it. Then come back for more details on each of these major steps in making up your mind. Figure 12.4 is a widely used form employed by operating managers to state their problem-solving objectives.[3]

How to Establish Problem-Solving Objectives with Subordinates

The process of establishing problem-solving objectives with subordinates should be done using a questioning or an interrogatory style rather than a lecturing or "tell 'em" style. You ask:

- What are the facts?
- What are some good objectives?
- What, then, would be your summary of the problem?

The boss, then, is not the major source of information about facts, objectives, problem definition, and so on. This is somewhat different from some of the regular, ongoing kinds of goals, for there the evidence of past performance may be overriding. The boss, in fact, may have both the choice or option of asking people what would be a suitable objective, for the situation demands certain standards of performance. In short, *where the standards are predetermined, you should tell people what those standards are. When you are hoping to obtain creative problem solving, using an interrogatory style will be much more productive.*

1. Identify problem area: _____

2. Definition of present level or condition: _____

3. Definition of reasonable desired level or condition: _____

4. Reevaluation (restate or edit to final form of problem): _____

5. Examination of cause of problem: _____

6. Selection of most likely causes (if possible): _____

7. Proposed solutions: _____

8. Evaluation of proposed solutions—criteria:

	Contribution to objectives	Cost	Feasibility	Side effects— desirable and undesirable
1.				
2.				
3.				
4.				
5.				
6.				
7.				

9. Time control: *Date*   *Action*   *Expected results*

_____

Figure 12.4 Form used by managers to state problem-solving objectives.

CHAPTER **13**

Setting Creative Goals

There is no hard and fast line at the point where the common sense synthesis of experience becomes a scientific ordering in a scientific system.

—R. B. Braithwaite

Perhaps the greatest single area where MBO can improve organizational results is in establishing commitments to goals in innovating—in creating new methods and introducing changes for the better into the organization.

No manager should be permitted to set goals for his or her position on the presumption that the status quo is good enough. The solution of perennial problems, or the introduction of new ideas to achieve better results than are presently being attained should be insisted upon during the goal-setting process.[1]

The right to demand such innovative or creative work has a number of related corollaries:

1. Managers who persistently fail to innovate in their own jobs are merely filling the maintenance requirements of their positions and, in so abstaining, bar themselves from consideration for promotion on merit, bonuses, pay increases other than general increases, or similar advantages.

2. Failure to perform routine duties, coupled with the lack of any attempt to improve their job performance, should be the basis for such managers' demotion or separation.

3. Of course, the rate of failure may be expected to be higher where imaginative or ambitious projects have been undertaken. The penalties for failure here should be less than for failure to perform the routine requirements of the position.

153

4. Opportunities for making breakthroughs or generous strides exist more in some positions than in others. While this obvious difference may allow for an element of windfall or bad luck in terms of opportunity, it does not account for the differences in achievement against possible gains to be found in any position. The manager who consistently takes maximum advantage of opportunities for improvement should be handed even greater opportunity, whereas the person who sees nothing but routine work in every situation should be shunted into positions where only such demands are made.

Creative goal setting in a technical, managerial, or staff position usually can be divided into two major categories:

1. *Extrinsic creativity*—the introduction of new ideas from outside.
2. *Intrinsic creativity*—the discovery of new ways, combinations, methods, or systems of doing the present job.

I will describe each in turn.

Setting Goals for Extrinsic Creativity

Not every job will lend itself to the application of new developments in science and technology. Such innovations as the conversion of recordkeeping to computers (teleprocessing, word processing, and high-speed copying), the application of motivational research to market analysis, and the use of linear programming in warehouse layout are based upon two factors:

1. Some new invention or system has been developed by others, perhaps research, engineering, or management experts outside the organization. This might be a development in the physical, social, or biological sciences, or of a new management method.
2. The new technique is mastered and applied to the specific problem or problems that exist within the organization through the special efforts of an individual manager or group of managers.

Ultrasonic cleaning of tools, application of zero-based budgets for staff functions, numerically controlled machines, new energy-conserving materials, and similar creative breakthroughs are usually introduced

into an organization through the curiosity of some individual in a responsible position who tests its feasibility and installs it.

It isn't necessary that the individual be the inventor of the extrinsic
idea to be credited with its innovation into the organization for which he
or she works. Here are some typical extrinsic ideas that have been converted by one plant manager into useful and effective innovations in his
organization:

- The use of radioisotopes for quality control.
- The introduction of statistical quality control.
- The use of linear programming in warehouse layout.
- The use of queuing theory in production scheduling.
- An electronic order picking system in the warehouse.
- Conversion of cost records to computer accounting.
- Use of programmed instruction to train machinist apprentices in
  math.

Other ideas could be listed, but for this actual list it should be
noted that the method, device, or scientific principle in question was not
invented by the plant manager at all. He simply maintained a healthy
curiosity about new developments in manufacturing and elsewhere.
Whenever he ran across a new invention or technique he asked himself,
"Could I use this in my plant?"

Usually the introduction of new techniques or methods follows a
three-step process:

1. The responsible party learns of the new idea and *obtains a lay
   knowledge* of the technology entailed. He or she may read about
   the idea, attend a seminar on it, consult with experts about it,
   or visit a location where it has been applied.
2. Armed with this much knowledge, the manager conducts a
   feasibility study to determine whether or not the new technique
   or device will fit into the operation of his or her organization.
   At this stage the manager is matching the idea with the problems and making cost and performance estimates that show
   whether or not the idea is economical, will solve problems, or
   will create more problems than it solves. There must also be
   some calculation of what the impact on the culture of the organization will be if the proposed change is introduced. What
   may be the adverse effects on what groups and what can be
   done to avert these effects. Usually, the innovator will map out

methods of obtaining the support of those affected and probe into the communications problems to be faced in instituting change. These cultural problems are the greatest barriers to the introduction of technical change into an organization and the most often overlooked.

3. The manager makes the change and installs the new method, using the insights obtained in the feasibility study. Change is sometimes introduced through testing first in a single department whose leader will be an enthusiastic and active supporter. In some kinds of programs, though, it may be necessary to make the change throughout the organization simultaneously.

The more widespread the innovation in the organization, the greater the necessity for an exhaustive feasibility study and the greater the need for attention to the cultural patterns that might cause the introduction of the new technique to meet with resistance and ultimate failure. There are five considerations an innovator must keep in mind when introducing technical change:

1. *Individuals will adhere to the familiar pattern of beliefs, attitudes, and behavior* unless something in their situation demands immediate change.

2. Technical change will be viewed as less of a change if it is *incorporated into the familiar pattern* or into an unchanged pattern of larger relationships.

3. The changing of individual behavior is a function of the individual's receiving a *series of reinforcers for small stages of development* of the new behavior.

4. The person who would innovate has *a wide range of methods to use in applying the new method*—for example, change the people, change the situation so as to change individual perceptions of it, provide individuals with satisfactions from the new method similar to those provided by the old. The mechanism of change in behavior is not one-dimensional.

5. Whenever change can be *introduced on a small scale* first and evaluated carefully before enlarging it, the innovator should follow this course. This permits careful analysis of the effects of the small change and may avert errors that might be disastrous if the change were made in the larger dimension of the organization.[2]

Setting Goals for Intrinsic Innovation

The second kind of innovation that can profitably be built into goal setting is of the intrinsic kind. While the introduction of new technology is important, the greatest opportunity for the working manager or staff person in the large organization probably lies in seeing the possibilities of innovation that exist in using present results as a basis for improvement and for establishing creative goals, with commitment to such change being carried on systematically.

When a manager and superior sit down to prepare goals for the period ahead, the time is right for the analysis of past results and for reshaping goals for the coming period based on those results. The missed opportunities at this time may have an adverse effect on future results, however, if the discussion digresses into any of the following paths:

- The superior decides to practice some amateur psychotherapy and alter the personality of the subordinate.
- The superior uses this occasion to apply pure pressure on the presumption that "motivation" means stirring the subordinate into faster action.
- The superior confines the discussion to a mutual analysis of results, instead of leading the subordinate into making a more precise analysis of the situation and developing goals for better results in a systematic, insightful way.

It usually pays off if the goal-setting process is one that forces both subordinate and superior to think deeply about the results obtained in the past, with a view to improvement in the future. This usually means that an orderly series of stages of analysis is followed.

1. Collection of the Facts. Before the goal-setting meetings begin, each of the participants should have amassed all the facts that can be obtained about results in the past. Each probably has some data that the other does not (or might wish the other to know). This could include special "side conditions" and results either not available or not automatically presented in such formal statements of results as sales reports, budgets, production reports, or cost statements. Such collections of facts should be handled in a *classification system that groups into areas all responsibilities included in the subordinates' jobs.*

2. Analysis. Breaking data down into many kinds of detail can assist in the next stage. This entails a study of causes, effects, and analysis of relations. Data may be grouped qualitatively, quantitatively (by statistical description) into frequency distribution, chronologically, locationally, or by dramatic instance.

3. Interpretation. This is the addition of meaning to the data presented in the arranged format. What are the conclusions for next year growing out of last year's results? What do the facts or figures tell us that is new, that reinforces or casts doubt upon previously held conclusions? What are the lapses between ideal and actual, and what are the reasons for them? Problems are identified in the interpretation, and problem-solving programs are proposed.

Problems are often most useful in goal setting if they are stated as questions—for example, "How can accidents be reduced from five to one per million manhours worked in the foundry?" Out of such questions and the detailed breakdown of data, *proposed solutions* can be converted into *action plans* or specific objectives that the subordinate can be committed to.

4. Statement of Objectives. This is the culmination of the analysis process, signifying that the individual manager has now laid out the objectives and has become committed to working toward them and that the boss has accepted these objectives as suitable activity for the subordinate to follow.

In one company, a division manager received a rather terse note from the senior vice president which castigated him for one of two shortcomings in results. The statement of results was a mixture of results over which the division manager had no control, a collection of old facts that dated back several years, comparisons with noncomparable divisions, and a vague but hortatory urging to "hit the ball." In the process of installing MBO, the subordinate used the occasion to prepare detailed summaries of results in each of his major areas of responsibility. He dealt with cost, quantity, quality, service, and time as indicators of results. He laid this statement before his senior. As a result, the attitude and behavior of his chief altered substantially.

If superiors do not feel they have the available information to make such an assessment of results, they may ask their subordinates to prepare such statements prior to the goal-setting interviews. Staff services may also need to be drawn upon to present the results in a perspective the subordinates might not see. Fact gathering should be based upon results for which there is some *evidence*. Facts are not worth dealing with in the analysis of results without some kind of tangible reference to evidence.[3]

This emphasis upon evidence rather than hunch does not exclude key opinions of individuals, if such opinions affect that behavior. The self-image of engineers, for example, has proven to be an important factor in their supervision. A fact may be considered as being supported by figures, charts, tables, graphs, statements of key people, dramatic or representative incidents, or verbal descriptions.

The manner in which the facts are arrayed becomes very significant. Let's look at two ways of arranging the same set of facts in a situation where supervisor and boss have the problem of setting some creative goals for the improvement of the existing situation.

Figure 13.1 shows the distribution of lost-time accidents for ten manufacturing departments. A casual inspection shows that departments

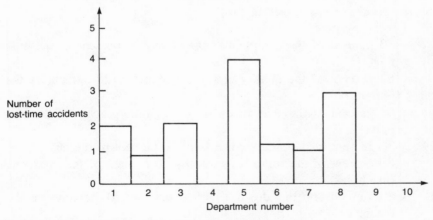

Figure 13.1 Lost-time accidents for ten departments.

5 and 8 have the largest number of accidents. If we let the factual analysis drop here instead of pushing it further, we may miss some excellent goal-setting opportunities. Suppose we press even further and rearrange the same facts by order of frequency of occurrence rather than by the department number sequence.

By rearranging the order in which we present the accident graph so that the highest magnitude is first and lowest magnitude is last, we set up a new insightful viewpoint. For one thing, we can compile a cumulative total as it goes up in major bites. As we study these facts, we note an interesting relationship between location or clustering of department and frequency—namely, the first four departments listed in order of magnitude account for 70 percent of the accidents. *In terms of the goals of the plant manager next year, this may mean that 70 percent of the safety effort should be expended in four of the departments.*

There is more room for pinpointing targets here, however. In using such definitions of differences between cause and effect in terms of effort and concentration of energy, there is a principle that is more important than the details of this particular plant's safety record—namely, *there is a normal and natural maldistribution among possible causes or focal points of trouble and the dispersion of effects.*

To be even more specific, for every problem or for every result achieved in the past, the Law of 20/80 can be assumed to be at work. This is the rule of the vital few and the trivial many among the causes of specific results. Let's illustrate this:

On the average:

- 80 percent of the complaints come from 20 percent of the customers.
- 80 percent of the quality errors are made by 20 percent of the operators.
- 80 percent of the grievances are filed by 20 percent of the employees.
- 80 percent of the orders come from 20 percent of the customers.
- 80 percent of the scrap is caused by 20 percent of the operators (machines).
- 80 percent of the down time occurs on 20 percent of the machines.

All of the above examples (of which there are countless more) illustrate this normal tendency for maldistribution between causes and effects.

In any situation where past results point to a management prob-
lem, the opportunity for improvement lies in concentrating effort on the
vital 20 percent of the factors concerned.

The Superior's Role in Creative Goal Setting

Where the principal method of trying to improve performance is unal-
loyed pressure from above, the likelihood of such analytical thinking is
reduced. Pressure, whatever else it may achieve, will also bring about
defensiveness in subordinates and an unwillingness to admit that they
could use some advice and help in problem solving. In the face of such
challenges as "Why don't you *plan* better?" subordinates will probably
admit that they do not know how and would welcome anything the boss
can teach them in this area. But after heartily assuring the boss of their
good intentions and giving false optimism its due, they will most likely
continue to perform at the same level as before.

In inducing creative goal setting, the superior's major role is to ask
specific questions that require reflective answers and to channel the subordinates' thinking toward constructive analysis of their own problems.
The boss might try to determine if subordinates have done any of the
following things in getting at possible solutions:

1. Have they examined the facts of their situation in sufficient
   depth and detail to provide insight into the vital areas where
   they should concentrate their attention?
2. Can they rearrange their facts in new combinations? (In the
   above example, the facts were first arrayed in terms of rank
   order and magnitude and then rearranged to show cumulative
   growth.) Facts may also be redisplayed chronologically, by frequency, or by geographic origin. Such simple rearrangements
   may reveal new facets of the problem that have previously been
   overlooked.
3. Have they considered the relations between possible causes and
   effects as possible solutions? Have they noted changes in
   ratios? Have they drawn upon past experience as standards for
   measuring current results? Have they measured, for internal
   consistency, ideas and facts that might indicate a difference between the actual and the ideal?

Here, too, superiors might ask themselves whether they have made it clear to subordinates what the major criteria for evaluating their possible programs or goals will be.

Thus, the sales manager who hopes to change the market mix of his or her sales effort might first explain the new pattern in terms of the total result sought for the department, and then go on to make it clear to subordinates how their personal goals must be converted to achieve this overall objective.

Creative Atmosphere and What Produces It

It is relatively safe to assume that people have more creativity than they demonstrate at work. In some cases, they aren't located in staff or research departments which tell them to be creative. In other instances, they are told by a hundred small messages, "Don't be innovative around here." In still other instances, they are told by verbal messages to be creative, but the rest of what they feel and hear punishes innovative behavior when it occurs. The manager can facilitate this creative and innovative atmosphere by means of a well-run MBO program. Here's how:

1. *If you want innovation, ask for it.* The assumption that innovation is bursting forth ready to spring into action and produce great things for the organization won't lead to productive change unless people are told explicitly that innovative thinking is expected of them.
2. *Just telling people to innovate isn't enough.* The process by which natural tendencies to seek variety and innovation in work convert into suggestions, ideas, and changes is sufficiently subtle that you cannot simply wait for it to come. You must work at it. This boss behavior means that, if you don't require innovation, you may be telling people that it is discouraged.
3. *You must get a commitment from individuals and teams.* The use of face-to-face discussion, the interrogation of people about opportunities that might be exploited, and the encouragement of commitment to innovative goals are specific steps toward creation of a general climate of innovation.
4. *Boss dissatisfaction with the status quo should be a part of the*

climate. Training people in work simplification and methods improvement, value engineering, and creative thinking are ways of telling people that change is desired and that the status quo is not good enough.

5. *Reward innovation when you see it.* Not only should the pay and merit system encourage and pay more for innovative behavior than routine behavior, but also the intangible rewards system should do favorable things to people who innovate. Too many organizations arrange the environment, systems, and feedback on the job in such a way that people are punished or placed in difficult working conditions for trying to improve things. When this condition exists, innovation declines. *There should be more favorable consequences than unfavorable consequences to people for innovation.*

6. *Personal support of the manager is crucial to produce employee innovation.* If the boss sits down with subordinates regularly, stresses the importance of innovation, asks for innovative commitments, attaches rewards to such innovation, follows up and endorses and supports innovation, then innovation will become an organizational way of life.

It might well be that the only way to obtain innovation is on a face-to-face basis between every boss and subordinate.

There are, however, many ways in which innovative behavior can be stifled or diverted into other activity.

Twenty Common Errors in Goal Setting for Innovation

The most common errors committed by managers in setting goals, according to one study that analyzed the stated goals of 1,100 managers, are the following:

1. Managers don't clarify common objectives for the whole unit.
2. They set goals too low to challenge the individual subordinate.
3. They don't use prior results as a basis for using intrinsic creativity to find new and unusual combinations.
4. They don't clearly shape their units' common objectives to fit those of the larger unit of which they are a part.

5. They overload individuals with patently inappropriate or impossible goals.
6. They fail to cluster responsibilities in the most appropriate positions.
7. They allow two or more individuals to believe themselves responsible for doing exactly the same things when having one responsible party is better.
8. They stress methods of working rather than clarifying individual areas of responsibility.
9. They emphasize tacitly that what counts is pleasing them rather than achieving the job objectives.
10. They make no policies as guides to action but wait for results, then issue ad hoc judgments in correction.
11. They don't probe to discover what program their subordinates propose to follow to achieve their goals. They accept every goal uncritically, without a plan for its successful achievement.
12. They are too reluctant to add their own (or higher management's) known needs to the program of their subordinates.
13. They ignore the very real obstacles that are likely to hinder subordinates in achieving their goals, including the numerous emergency or routine duties that consume time.
14. They ignore the new goals or ideas proposed by their subordinates and impose only those they deem suitable.
15. They don't think through and act upon what they must do to help their subordinates succeed.
16. They fail to set intermediate target dates (milestones) by which to measure progress.
17. They don't introduce new ideas from outside the organization, or permit or encourage subordinates to do so, thereby freezing the status quo.
18. They fail to permit their subordinates to seize targets of opportunity in lieu of stated objectives that are less important.
19. They are rigid about not scrapping previously agreed-upon goals that have subsequently proved unfeasible, irrelevant, or impossible.
20. They don't reinforce successful behavior when goals are achieved or correct unsuccessful behavior when they are missed.

CHAPTER **14**

Setting Personal Development Goals

The job environment of the individual is the most important variable affecting his development.

—Douglas McGregor

There are four major kinds of objectives that should be included in each manager's targets. Thus far, we have dealt with three of these:

1. Routine duties, measured by exceptions.
2. Emergency or problem-solving goals, measured by solutions and time.
3. Creative goals, measured by results against stated objectives.

We now turn to the *personal development* goals that might be included in the set of objectives to which a manager is committed.

The establishment of goals for personal development does not imply that a manager's strictly job-centered goals aren't a form of personal development also. In fact, these job-centered goals comprise the major development plan, since they relate to job performance. Even so, beyond this, there may be personal skills that, if acquired, will make it possible for managers to do their job better, and will stand them in good stead whether they are promoted or stay in their present position. This kind of development may take place as the result of guided experience on the job or through formal classes in management skills, technical and professional subjects, and so on.[1]

How much of these personal efforts should be left to the individual to initiate and pursue, and to what extent should the boss intervene to spur the subordinate on?

165

The Self-Made Manager Revisited

Since the turn of the century it has been increasingly possible for American men and women of varied backgrounds to acquire managerial positions of great responsibility. Most auto executives, we are told, come from humble beginnings, and the story of the young person without means who rises through the ranks to head a great corporation is a beguiling and commonplace one.

One result of these enticing prospects for the youth of modest origins is that many middle- and lower-level management people are today engaged in a frantic scramble to improve their status and rank through "self-development." Corporate management-development programs have encouraged this scramble to a large extent by piously proclaiming that "all management development is self-development." A further consequence of this movement has been a sort of crusade that has led thousands of frustrated young people to cultivate the skills of self-denial, leaving them self-absorbed and all too keenly aware of the sacrifices they are making in order to get to the top.

The trouble is that when self-development becomes too introspective, not only does it often fail in its immediate objective but, almost invariably, it also fails in its ultimate objective.

Can Behavior Be Changed?

William James is reported to have said that by the time one has reached the age of thirty, one's basic habits and personality pattern are fixed and will probably be retained in the same general configuration for life. Psychologist Robert McMurry has developed a most ingenious selection procedure on this thesis. It employs the *pattern interview* in which two basic patterns are used.[2]

The first pattern is derived from a group of questions about the individual's background. After putting these questions to a large number of people, the interviewer is able to detect a pattern among the answers. The second pattern emerges in the analysis of individual responses. The habits and attitudes thus revealed point to a particular configuration of personality which is quite useful in predicting the individual's future behavior. According to McMurry, "the pattern interview can be the equivalent of a long and personal acquaintanceship with a person." From the underlying logic of this approach, he has generalized that fundamentally "people don't change." A person's future is thus based on a sort of one-two combination that will govern his or her place in life—a combination of *good genes* and *good luck.*

Others hold that this line of thinking is not true at all. The essential nature of being human, they assert, is the capacity to improve. The American dream is based upon what de Tocqueville called "the perfectibility of man." The distinguishing quality of humankind, this school of thought maintains, is the educability and the capacity of the human mind to enlarge its knowledge. "Man," says anthropologist Ashley Montagu, "is the most plastic, the most malleable, the most educable creature in the world."

This latter viewpoint underlies many of the programs of self-development. Its optimism and idealism are naturally more attractive to the ambitious than the gloomy views of the people-don't-change school. Moreover, anyone who has had experience with the young knows how educable they are. On the other hand, many top managers can point to large numbers of workers, line supervisors, and middle managers who have become fairly rigid, except that, as these top executives will ruefully admit, "they sometimes get worse."

Perhaps the basis for self-development lies in retaining the human qualities that keep one educable. That this educability is widespread—more so than is sometimes conceded by the pessimists—is evidenced by the prevalence of adult education. Why do some people never lose their zest for living and learning, while others live careers of static repetition? It is probable that this is more a function of the environment than of the person. Continued success through self-change and self-development breeds more of the same, but if such effort is unrewarded, it dies. The suppressive effect of a male-dominated world upon women seeking non-traditional jobs illustrates this effect.[3]

Self-insight is not enough, then, to assure self-development. Certainly it should not lead us to conclude that self-inspection always leads to self-understanding. Such self-understanding is more apt to come through looking outward—to the study of others—than from prolonged scrutiny of one's own interior. Man is the best mirror of man, and in learning about others we understand better about ourselves. This is especially pertinent for leaders. In any event, in studying others we at least learn how to behave productively in society, even when we don't learn about ourselves.

From this set of premises we can now proceed to note some common fallacies in many of the self-development plans of aspiring executives.

Because so many management-development programs have failed to bring about any significant change in the behavior of the trainees, many experts have despairingly concluded, "After all, it's up to the individual." This conclusion has provided the rationale for a science of self-development in which successes can be attributed to the process, and failures laid at the door of the individual. The trap here is the assumption that by directing energy and passion *inward* one can master the *outward* environment. Success, as we all know, depends partly upon outside circumstances and partly upon oneself. In fact, the ability to move away from unfortunate circumstances may itself account for the majority of success stories. Where this option does not exist, people's upward progress in an organization may sometimes be accounted for by their capacity to change the limiting conditions to fit their capabilities.

Lastly, there is the elective of changing oneself to fit the environment through some self-imposed therapy upon one's own inner experience. This is a miserably weak strategy, however, for two reasons: first, because you are absorbed in observing yourself and lack the perspective of an observer outside the system you are trying to adapt to; and, second, because outward behavior does not always resemble the inner experiences that accompany it. No science of self-development based on this mirror gazing can possibly work. Where the organizational environment is at all favorable to your rising in it, you will succeed far more readily if your education, adjustments, and energies are directed *outward,* not dwelling perpetually on yourself.[4]

Successful people are those who have objective interests that absorb them, thus making them objects of interest to others.

The Myth of the Executive Personality

At the heart of many of the self-development plans of eager young people is the false notion that there is an ideal executive personality that is equally effective in any kind of organization. To date, however, despite the most intensive search, nobody has been able to find one. There is no single personality trait and no combination of traits always present in the successful executive and always missing in the one who doesn't make it. Let us test this hypothesis in a simple way with the most commonly held illusion in this area—namely, that one should have initiative.

Initiative is often thought of as a quality that every successful executive must have. Nothing proves it. Many executives rise and do a fine job as executives without initiative. Some inherit the business, reluctantly decide that their duty calls for them to devote their best efforts to it, and succeed. In other cases, executives themselves don't have any initiative, but their spouses do and prod them into moving upward. Sometimes, initiative plays no part in people's success at all. The fact is that they happened to be in the right place at the propitious moment and honor and responsibility were thrust upon them. A similar analysis can be made for any other trait.

The principal reason why a particular personality trait (or any combination of traits) cannot be used as a discriminatory measure is that executive performance is most often a combination of *actions* taking place within a *situation*. Self-development is the readiness and the ability to take action that suits the situation of the moment.

In fact, business leadership and responsibility can be regarded as both a container and the thing it contains—the container, the organization and its setting, and the contained, the manager.

To use another analogy, clearly the scene encompasses the actor. The motions and words of the actor—his or her managerial behavior—must be consistent with the scene or they become comic and awkward.

The kind of self-development in which the manager labors at cultivating a shut-in "executive" personality is not only useless, it also limits managers' ability to follow stage directions. It causes ignorance of the environment toward which their behavior and development must be attuned if they are to sustain their part and earn the right to be cast in even larger roles. This analogy does not mean, however, that the actor is without significance in the scene. If a manager did not have an impact on the environment, then managerial self-development would merely mean the acquisition of chameleonlike qualities, and a manager in a bad company would automatically become a bad manager, making no effort to bring personal qualities of superior action to a poor scene.

Yet, as professional actors soon learn, the faculty of selecting good plays (with good scenes) is just as important as the ability to faithfully enact the part prepared for them. So, in business, choosing an organization that matches one's skills and abilities is more important than cultivating a repertoire of personality traits to be applied regardless of the environment.

Since success is a combination of leader, followers, and situation, a sure-fire leadership personality is impossible to define. Being impossible to define, it's impossible to develop.

The Limits of Classroom Methods of Personal Development

The marvelous confidence of American educators in the power of the classroom teacher to remake the world is a refreshing phenomenon. Unfortunately, it is an assumption that is seriously open to question.[5] Much can be achieved in the classroom, of course. Verbal behavior, and perhaps written behavior also, can most certainly be changed. This is what happens in most college classes and in the formal school system. Graduates can now speak and write about things that they could not speak and write about before or, if they could, can now do so with greater facility. Laboratory courses teach them other kinds of behavior that they can repeat elsewhere. There is quite a respectable list of various kinds of managerial or professional behavior that can be wholly taught in the classroom (that is to say that when they are back on the job no special supporting conditions are needed for people to apply what they have learned). Thus, managers and professional employees can be taught in class:

- To make speeches.
- To lead conferences according to a method.
- To write better technical reports.
- To interview another person.
- To write better business letters.
- To perform mathematical calculations.
- To program a computer.

The reason we know that behavioral change can take place in such areas is that identification of the end behavior sought from training is almost entirely under the control of the instructor and success or failure can be measured inside the class itself. Consider, however, Figure 14.1. As a result of a class, the learner should move from A to B in definite steps. Further, B should be transferred out of the class into the job. Here, we are no longer concerned with the kinds of behavior that are susceptible to change within the control system of the classroom and the instructor. Now we are considering those kinds of behavioral changes that have significance only if they are carried over to the job. Among such behavioral changes are:

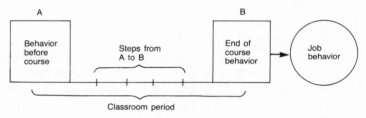

Figure 14.1 The elements of classroom instruction producing useful behavior.

- Managers delegate more.
- They make better decisions.
- They seek out subordinate viewpoints.
- They work through committees.
- They conduct cost-reduction programs.
- They solve grievances better.

Such activities can be taught up to the point where trainees *discuss* these topics in the classroom, but any actual change in their behavior is beyond the control of the classroom instructor or of the class method of teaching. The classroom training becomes merely one of the forces that reinforce or extinguish behavior on the job. Let us look at job behavior and see some of the other kinds of forces that may determine whether people change their job behavior or not as a result of what they have learned in class (see Figure 14.2).

1. If they have acquired *new knowledge,* as a rule they won't lose it back on the job. But if this knowledge is rather complex and technical, they may find it fading away if they don't use it. Whether or not they apply it, however, may be more a function

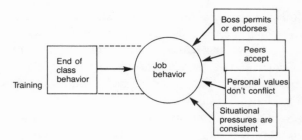

Figure 14.2 Forces that determine whether what people learn in class changes their job behavior.

of their responsibilities and duties than of the effectiveness of the class teaching.

2. If they have acquired *new attitudes* in the class, and measurement of their behavior at the end of the course shows that the class has affected their attitudes, these may persist or they may fade away or be extinguished on the job. The fading away or extinguishing of newly acquired attitudes can result from unfavorable reception by superiors or peers, second thoughts about the course in comparison with certain values found useful on the job, or steady situational pressures.

3. If they have acquired *new skills,* they may use them on the job, provided the use of these skills doesn't conflict with the boss's ideas of correct behavior. They may use the new skills so long as this doesn't mean flying in the face of their peers and flouting the cultural pattern of acceptable behavior. Using new skills must also be consistent with the situational pressures in their work. Any or all of these forces may work to overcome people's inclination to use their class-acquired skills on the job.[6]

Here's one example of the limitations of classroom instruction. Several manufacturing managers from a large firm went to an evening course at a local university. The course instructor, a professor of psychology, was an advocate of group decision making, and the supervisors readily learned how the procedure worked. In role-playing sessions in the class, they demonstrated their ability to follow it. However, the managers then went back to their jobs where all their people were closely tied to machines of the continuous-process type. When a problem came up, managers had to make snap judgments, with little margin for error. This they were able to do most of the time because they all had long experience on the job and few questions arose to which they could not quickly come up with an answer that worked perfectly well. As a result, they never used group decision making in their jobs.

One of the most common experiences of industrial trainers who conduct a supervisory course and then distribute evaluation cards for the trainees to fill out is to be greeted by the overwhelming response: "Why don't you give this course to my boss? The boss never does any of these things."

Such a response probably means that the skills imparted in class won't be used on the job. The trainer might have averted this by doing one of these things:

1. Teaching the subordinates their boss's favorite method of managing.
2. Holding the course, perhaps in briefer form, for top management and getting their acceptance for the subject to be taught to the lower-level managers. If permission for or endorsement of the proposed course is not forthcoming at the end of the top manager's course, the trainer should not offer the course to the subordinates, or two results may be expected: (a) the supervisors will behave in a way that their boss disapproves of and perhaps be rated low because of it, or (b) they will acquire one kind of skill and be forced to practice a different kind, which will lead only to frustration and disappointment.

Here are some guidelines for ensuring the success of a management training course:

1. Confer with the top manager of the unit in which the managers are to be trained or taught. Spell out the kind of behavior change aimed at, and make sure he or she is willing to accept it.
2. Give the top management of the organization a brief preview of summary of the course, if not the whole course, before giving it to the subordinates. Ask the top managers to endorse the new behavior or even to start practicing it.
3. At the same time as this top management endorsement and participation is obtained, the environment in which the supervisor

works should be studied to see whether or not the proposed new behavior is consistent with it. This can be done by visiting the proposed trainees and noting the conditions of pressure, time, cost, quantity, service, and discipline under which they function. If these conditions appear to be unsuited to the kind of training proposed, it is better not to offer the course.

4. Give the course to the lower-level managers and obtain the cooperation of higher management in reinforcing application of the training back on the job. This can be done by superiors' checking on their subordinates and telling them they approve of the new behavior.

5. Action types of training that involve learners in simulations of situations they will encounter back on the job make the carryover to the job easier. Role playing, case studies, management games, and the like can all help to bring about behavioral change. They need to be accompanied, though, by discussion and critique.

The Goals of Personal Development

Personal development goals will usually comprise only a small segment of a manager's total objectives for the goal-setting period. Exceptions to this might be younger men or women trainees whose primary responsibility is to learn. Working managers, however, will probably limit themselves to two or three self-development goals. Here they have a somewhat bewildering selection to choose from:

- Completion of evening courses toward a college degree.
- Attendance at two seminars a year.
- Membership and active participation in a professional group.
- Subscription to two or more periodicals.
- Completion of adult education courses.
- Completion of company training courses.
- Attendance at an advanced management course.
- Visits to other plants or offices.
- Visits to customers or supplier plants and offices.
- Participation in one or two community service activities.
- Service on high-level committees inside the company.
- Special assignments in other areas of the business.

- Covering another department during vacation.
- Conducting special investigations.
- Participation on junior boards or functional committees.
- Personal health-building programs (with medical advice).
- Conducting training classes for subordinates.
- Teaching adult education or evening university courses.
- Being a guest speaker at university classes.
- Being a seminar leader for a trade association.
- Writing a paper for a professional publication.
- Reading a specific number of management books.
- Preparing special speeches or presentations for an executive.
- Serving as secretary of boards or management committees.

Looking at this list, which for some individuals could be extended still further, it is evident that some managers could spend most of their time on this kind of thing. In fact, a small number of managers *do* spend an inordinate amount of time on such activities. They are perennial attenders of courses and seminars and often concentrate on these self-development efforts at the expense of performing some function of direct value to the company.

People on the training staff may find themselves attending many meetings to determine their worth for other members of the organization, but the operating manager in a manufacturing, sales, or general management position should limit attendance to no more than three or four. In any event, if personal development activities are to serve any real purpose, the following rules should be observed:

1. There should be a specific reason in mind for undertaking the activity.
2. The effect of the desired change in behavior on the person's job performance, either present or potential, should be weighed.
3. A commitment in writing stating when these personal development goals will be completed should be obtained from the subordinate. This statement should be specific in terms of what is to be done, when it will be completed, and the general approach or method to be used. There should also be some indication of how the boss can measure the results.
4. A subordinate should be asked for some kind of follow-up. This can take the form of either a written or an oral report on the progress being made toward self-development, and how this progress relates to work performance.

4

MBO in Operation: The Subsystems Affected

Management by objectives entails far more than a couple of personal chats at the beginning and end of each year. It is not some additional program but a *way of managing*. In this part we will focus on some of the important kinds of changes required in related company systems:

You should pick people by objectives, pay them by objectives, budget by objectives, promote by objectives, and do performance appraisals by objectives. In other words, you should manage by objectives.

CHAPTER 15
Selection by Objectives

A society such as ours is dependent upon many kinds of achievement.

—John W. Gardner

The application and implementation of MBO often becomes fixated upon a mythical scene. A boss and subordinate sit in the boss's office, and the boss talks over goals or results with the subordinate. Actually, this use of the MBO concept is not the most significant utilization of the MBO idea, despite the amount of attention it attracts, for it leaves unanswered numerous questions about the interview.

- How did that subordinate get in that spot?
- Similarly, how did the superior attain his or her post?
- Aren't most of the troublesome moments in this discussion really attributable to the fact that the wrong person is in one chair or the other?
- If the goals and results are terribly bad, perhaps it is not a matter of counseling so much as replacing. How will you be assured that it won't all happen again?

The application of MBO to the managerial selection process—call it "selection by objectives"—will become its most promising application in the next decade.

The Evil Effects of Poor Selection

A number of serious ill effects occur in organizations when selection procedures go awry. To note a few of them:

1. *The top executive suffers and the organization suffers.* "I

178

picked the wrong person for sales manager. Sure, he looked
good, in fact, he swept us all off our feet. But when the chips
were down, he couldn't get the job done. Now we are faced
with the painful process of removing him, or changing his behavior, and both promise to be tough. Even if we fire him, how
can we be sure we won't simply repeat the process?" Thus said
a company president recently. Income was off. Morale of the
sales force was low. Programs were delayed. Financial problems were cropping up. All were caused by faulty selection.

2. *Bad choices perpetuate themselves.* A large university conducted an extensive search for the post of dean of one of its
largest colleges. After some extensive committee work, it settled upon a handsome, pleasant man who had considerable
qualifications as a scholar, but none as an administrator. Put in
charge of the college, he made every mistake that had ever been
made in administration at least once. This was not the worst
effect, however. In the subsequent years, he drove out, in rage
or frustration, every competent supervisor, manager, and department head who came under his direction. In their place, he
put people as incompetent as himself. By the time he had
learned his trade, he was approaching his retirement, but fought
to the end to solve problems created by the incompetents of his
own choosing.

3. *People lose confidence in the system.* When young people of
talent and brains work in an organization that is careless about
promotional policy, they become disillusioned. The young
lieutenant who sees the bumbling incompetent wearing two
stars starts to think seriously about finding a new career outside
the service. One of the worst effects of the Vietnam War to the
military as an organization was the large number of qualified
persons who were repelled by the military, thus opening the
paths for less competent but highly ambitious people to find
avenues to the top. Even when subordinates' contacts with top
people are second or third hand or even more remote, the presence of incompetence at the highest levels resounds throughout
the ranks, and younger men and women depart while they still
can.

4. *The corrective measure is always painful.* When it is realized
beyond doubt that an error in selection has been made, the costs

can be exorbitant. It is reported that Henry Ford II paid more than $1 million in accrued bonuses and benefits for firing Semon Knudsen, hired only a year before from General Motors. While such costs are not ordinary by any means, they are proportionately high at every level of executive hiring and firing. When a decision is made to patch up a mistake in selection of a manager by putting him or her on a shelf, it almost inevitably sets a bad example and the manager frequently becomes an executive mischief maker.

Criteria and the Candidate

Criteria comprise a yardstick against which specific alternatives can be tested. Selection is a decision process, and the decision is made best when the criteria are clear in the mind of the decision maker, the candidates (or alternative choices) are evaluated against these criteria, and the choice is the one that fits best.

Whether you are a manager faced with a vacant position to be filled, or an ambitious young person who aspires to a vacant position, knowing the criteria is invaluable. If you aspire to a post, two classes of information can help you in attaining the job:

1. You can take inventory of your own qualifications, experience, education, past successes and failures, personal likes and dislikes.
2. You can match them against the criteria set for the position.

Applicants who are clear on the criteria can arrange their stories, résumés, references, and interview behavior to make presentations that suit the criteria admirably. If they know their own qualifications but are unclear on the criteria, perhaps because the employer hasn't thought them out, applicants may be able to shape the criteria by selling their credentials as best for the position.

In one large manufacturing firm, waste and rising overhead were evident to one applicant. The personnel director of the firm was somewhat wishy-washy in his specifications. Sensing this, the man being interviewed told him, "Mr. Jones, what you need is a man who has a capability for cutting costs, in fact, being a hard-nosed cost reducer. If you don't get such a man soon, the whole division will go down the tube." His prognosis struck a responsive chord with several people who recognized the merit of his analysis and he was hired. His subsequent success in cutting costs and improving profits lasted for several years, at which time, he was compelled, by pressures from subordinates and peers, to ease up on his hard-nosed style.

Another applicant, a man of similar capabilities determined that such a hard-nosed course was required, but after a further look he realized that it would be impossible to implement such a course of action. Several of the president's relatives were in key positions and it would be difficult to get tough with them. Accordingly, he withdrew.

In another firm, a large retail chain, the president invited a strong candidate for vice-president to his home for further discussion of his joining the firm. While he was there, he was introduced to the president's family, which included six bright and interested young sons. At the end of the evening, the candidate announced, "With that crew of young fellows coming along, I don't think I'll ever make president of this firm, and therefore I withdraw my application." The father then returned to the dining room and called a family conference. "Boys, it is apparent that I'm not going to get the man I want for vice-president, and so you had all better start learning the business, and learn it well."

People who are underqualified or overqualified for a job are wise to voluntarily withdraw if their honest assessment of the criteria and their own qualifications tell them that in all probability they will not succeed. For instance, a young Mormon being considered for a high post noted that the job's heavy social schedule required that one be a two-fisted drinker, or at least a regular social drinker, and so he withdrew knowing that to accept would lead to difficulties for him in the future. In another instance, a man with strong social skills who enjoyed robust masculine activities interviewed for a job in a medium-sized company located in an isolated city where the dominant culture was austere and rather puritanical for his standards. Foreseeing the potential for friction and discontent in that environment, he wisely withdrew.

What Makes for Good and Bad Criteria

Good criteria should comprise a test of preferredness or fitness. For one thing, good criteria should be *multiple* in nature and not singular. They comprise a model of behavior for the manager after he or she is in the new position. This means that the manager has in mind not merely a list of adjectives (a static model) but a dynamic model that indicates the flow of events that must occur. For another thing, good criteria should summarize the *combinations* of consequences preferred from the less desirable ones. This means that the criteria must always be considered *situationally*, and the skills a person possesses may be invaluable in one situation or damaging or useless in another. A high tolerance for frustration may be absolutely essential in certain political environments, but useless in another where impatience and hard-driving, energetic attacks would pay off—such as launching a new model in the automobile business. Having a high regard for authority figures above and a keen dependency upon leadership from those in authority, could be either an asset or a liability, depending upon the organization culture in the new position.

A third requirement of good criteria is that they are best stated in *ranges or proximations,* rather than in explicit single numbers or terms. John Lee Pratt, once treasurer of General Motors, always required that division managers state their business forecasts in ranges of outcomes —pessimistic, realistic, and optimistic. This required a more complete business analysis and a general manager who could live within ranges and tolerances, rather than rigidly stating exact predictions of outcome.

Finally, good criteria should be stated in a form that comprises an *ascending scale of excellence.* The minimum or nominal requirements of the position, if it is to be done at normal levels, should be supplemented by definitions of higher and higher levels of excellence until the highest possible level of attainment is defined.

What's Wrong with Present Selection Methods

The major problems of present-day selection methods seem to fall into these major categories:

1. *Techniques are mainly for low-level workers.* Since Hugo Munsterberg and others about 70 years ago seriously undertook the study of employment testing, the major emphasis has been

upon the selection of workers.[1] The problems of early identification of high-talent personnel, and the techniques of hiring and promoting managers, engineers, and staff persons are different and at this stage very problematical.[2]

2. *Psychological testing has come under serious fire.* From within the profession and from outside, numerous attacks have been leveled at psychological tests. They comprise an invasion of privacy, some hold. They have logical improprieties, say others. They breed conformity, say still others. They violate equal employment laws, say still others.[3] Whatever the merits of these charges, the effect has been to cast a cloud over the use of these tests in selection. A small fringe of charlatans promising psychological miracles in a manner akin to the snake-oil peddlers of old have not done much to clarify the issues.

3. *The civil rights and equal opportunity laws have changed many long-accepted practices.* The civil rights laws of 1964 and 1969 have shaken traditional employment practices seriously.[4] Discrimination against women and minorities is barred but effective new guidelines have not come easily.

4. *The mad rush is back to college graduates.* Despite a rapidly rising curve of enrollments in the colleges, the rush at the exit door of the institutions of higher learning is greater.[5] Surely, one of the most bizarre and absurd fads ever to sweep industry, the clamor to collect degree holders for every white-collar position, shows no sign of abatement. There is apparently little attempt to determine which job requires a degree and which one does not. More than half of entry-level positions reported on one survey are reserved for degree holders.

While all of these problems could be expanded at length, and the list itself lengthened, they comprise typical evidence of the illness that presently besets the hiring and promoting processes.

Steps to Better Selection

The first step in management selection is to establish objectives and to obtain commitments in advance to meet them.[6] It presumes that the person who has achieved objectives consistently in the past is more likely to achieve them in new situations. It is further proposed that these selection criteria have primacy over testing, hunch, behavioral inventories, or background. Thus, the major purpose of selection procedures should be to uncover evidence of achievements against objectives in the past.

Personnel staffing decisions are gambles in much the same way that a decision to bet on a particular horse is a gamble. Both decisions are based on predictions of performance among alternative choices. Predictions of the future are estimates or expectations based upon observations of past and present achievements and the known or assumed relationship between these observations and future wants.[7] For the horseplayer, prediction of the outcome of a race might be based in part on such variables as ancestry of the horse, performance in previous outings, current times, and physical condition of the horse and the jockey. For the manager involved in personnel staffing decisions, the prediction of a candidate's performance will be based upon observations of variables believed to be associated with, or determinative of, the desired level of future performance. In either case, the horseplayer or the manager is seeking to identify the winner. Needless to say, there are many poor choices and many disappointed people.

The Four Criteria Now in Use

The systems of selection used to date fall into four major categories, described here in summary form. These selection techniques are based upon the major presumptions of the person applying them.

1. The Personal Preference Method. This is still the most commonly used method, even when disguised by the apparatus of science. The hunch of the manager, his or her biases, likes, and dislikes determine the selection of employees.

2. The Internal Characteristics Approach. Earliest of the scientifically based methods, this method applies aptitude measurements to applicants, and allows one to attempt to predict success on the job.

3. The Behavioral or Skills Approach. Another scientific approach to selection of employees is that of identifying behavior patterns in the past and predicting that such behavior (as demonstrated in tests or verified through résumé and reference checks) will continue into the future. With these results matched against job requirements, success can be predicted.

4. The Background Approach. The fourth method is evidenced most strongly in the career pattern studies of Warner and Abblegen and seen in the search for college graduates in campus recruiting. It presumes that successful managers and professionals can best be selected by studying the careers of the already successful and hiring those who best seem to duplicate them.

What I am suggesting here is that a new approach is now possible, synthesizing the useful features of the others and adding a new method of selection. Because it proposes to supplant the others, and in fact has proven more successful where applied, a brief review of each of the former four methods is in order.

1. The Personal Preference Method

The proprietary right of an owner to make the decisions about who shall be hired and who shall not be hired to work in his or her business grows out of the property rights of ownership. If small merchants or manufacturers decide to hire only members of their own lodge, church, or family, there are few constraints upon them. Title VII of the Civil Rights Act of 1964, if applicable to them, theoretically limits their exercise of this right in the public interest. Clearly, they cannot openly flout the law, but their preferences may lead them to the creation of standards that make the law ineffective while serving their preferential biases. The administration of the law in future years may corner them in these subterfuges, although at present the strong voluntary compliance aspects of the law can leave them relatively untouched. Since many of their biases are unconscious—and hotly denied if pointed out—they are difficult to eradicate from outside the firm. The 1964 studies by Robert Kahn of the University of Michigan of the employment of Jews,[8] and the open challenging of the use of psychological tests on the basis of their "culture-biased" aspects illustrate aspects of concealed bias.

These personal preferences originate in the emotions and sentiments of employers and extend from hiring alumni to Zulus, simply because employers feel the way they do about the people they want around.

2. The Internal Characteristics Approach

Since psychologists are usually the only professionals qualified to devise and validate tests of psychological characteristics, it is not surprising that testing of various kinds has all of the strengths and limitations of psychology itself as a science. In recent years, this approach has come under fire for a variety of reasons. Writers of a moralist type have written with great fervor about the invasion of privacy that attends testing. By selecting questions out of the body of extensive test batteries, congressional committees and critical writers have generated righteous wrath. For example, "Did you ever want to kill your father?" reads poorly when it becomes a headline in a Washington newspaper. Martin Gross, Vance Packard, and others have attacked the indignities that occur when psychologists pry.[9] Other criticisms have come from within the profession itself. Logical improprieties in testing are often discussed in professional journals. Still other critics include behavioral scientists who have queried the scientific propriety of some testing methods.[10] As a result, it is now forbidden in government agencies to use personality tests upon job applicants, and in 1975 this ban was extended to government contractors. Tests are not totally banned, but this list of limits placed upon their use has been sufficiently complicated that the actual effect will be a falling off of this kind of testing. Courts have been strongly favorable to petitioners charging bias-through-personality-testing.

The purpose here is not to outline the varieties of tests and their advantages and disadvantages; the aim is to outline only the objectives of tests that comprise the "inward characteristics" approach to selection. Achievement tests would not fall into this category since they measure demonstrable behavior, but two others do: aptitude and personality tests.

Aptitude Tests. Because of the magnitude of the wastes and losses in selection, there has arisen a more and more insistent demand to reduce errors in staffing decisions. It is this necessity that has given rise to aptitude prediction by means of testing. At present, various kinds of psychological tests are the chief means for making aptitude prognoses.

Testing in all applied sciences is performed on the basis of samples, and aptitude testing is not essentially different from the application of tests in other sciences. The thing sampled in aptitude tests is, in most cases, human behavior. Specifically, a psychological test is the measurement of some phase of a carefully chosen sample of an individual's behavior from which extrapolations and inferences are made. Measuring differences among people through the use of psychological tests has made a signal advance to understanding and predicting human behavior.

In its simplest terms, aptitude testing rests on a relationship between a normally distributed predictor variable (which may or may not be related to the skills and abilities required on the job) on the one hand, and another normally distributed measure of satisfactory performance on the other hand.[11] The simple matching task is to eliminate, on the basis of the relatively inexpensive predictor variable, those individuals with little likelihood of success on the job—obviously an easy task in theory but beset by complexities in practice.

The conception of specialized aptitudes and the desirability of having tests of behavior that will indicate in advance latent capacity has its roots in ancient history. More than 2,300 years ago, Plato proposed a series of tests for the guardians of his ideal republic. His proposal was instrumented in the United States Army mental tests of World War I.

The use of tests to measure aptitudes did not receive much interest until the late nineteenth century when a number of psychologists became interested in mental testing and the psychology of individual differences.[12] The early tests were largely individual. This approach changed with the advent of World War I. Based on the pioneering work of A. S. Otis, a set of tests that not only could be administered to a large number of subjects at the same time but could be scored by semimechanical means appeared on the scene.[13] Nearly two million army recruits were tested, and aptitude testing on a group basis was born.

Following rapidly upon the heels of the spectacular accomplishment of psychological testing in the army, industry picked up the cue that tests could be effectively used in employment and personnel work. The individual worker came to be considered a conglomerate of traits that could be measured by tests. It did not matter whether these traits were regarded as innate or acquired. What mattered from the employer's viewpoint was that tests could be utilized in the selection and job placement of workers. The result of this hasty and ill-advised exploitation of an approach that was useful in another field was temporary failure and disillusionment. Quite naturally, a distinct reaction against aptitude testing set in.

The road back from almost complete denial of aptitude testing in industry has been paved with both successes and failures. Today aptitude testing is finding ever-increasing use in American industry. Aptitude testing has proven to be helpful in staffing decisions involving clerical personnel, sales representatives, and certain other industrial occupations; however, in that area where effective prediction is most desperately needed—in managerial selection—aptitude testing has met with only limited success.[14]

One of the most telling criticisms of aptitude testing is that made by the late Clark Hull in 1928.[15] He suggested that something in the neighborhood of .50 might be a practical limit for validities of tests. Nothing in the history of selection testing has radically revised this figure after almost 50 years. Nevertheless, the quest goes on—to develop tests that can efficiently estimate or forecast aptitudes and success on the job from test scores.

Personality Tests. Success on the job is not solely determined by ability; it is also attributable in part to the personality and interest of the worker. Aptitude tests are not tests of motivation and interest; consequently, something else is needed to measure these dimensions of the worker. Not only are supervisors interested in finding out whether the worker *can* do the job, they are also interested in determining whether the worker *will* do the job. It is to this question that personality and interest inventories in the industrial setting are addressed.

The instruments used to assess the "will do" side in prediction come in all shapes and sizes. Some of these devices are simple inventories, others are based on specific personality or motivational theories. Some seek to measure those aspects of the personality called temperament traits. Still others are projective in design and are intended for "global assessments" of personality.[16]

These instruments are impressive in their diversity and approach. However, notwithstanding their multiplicity of technique and design, the success of personality and interest measurements in industrial selection has been something less than spectacular. Much of the variety in approaches to the measurement of personality stems from the desire to overcome the deficiencies in existing tests, and the fact that the relationship between the predictor variable and the criteria are infinitely complex and dynamic.

Many of the tests presently used in assessment, particularly in the selection of managers, are general personality tests that have not been validated for managerial performance but rather for the identification of particular personality traits. The relevance of these traits or characteristics to successful performance on the job frequently comes about because of some intuitive judgment as to the type of subordinate one would like to have. Relatively few attempts have been made to forecast accurately the demands placed on the applicant once he or she is in the organization. Thus, it seems that we may be playing Russian roulette with the future of the enterprise by attempting to select managers through screening devices that, in effect, merely assure us that all those admitted to managerial ranks are alike. Fortunately, this is not the problem for the organization today as it might be in the future. At present the validities of personality tests are low enough so that the consistent use of any of the personality tests will allow enough people to slip by to protect the organization against poor judgment about the qualities it thinks it is selecting.

What is needed by management with regard to its personnel staffing is apparently a heterogeneous supply of human resources from which individuals can be selected to fill a variety of specific but unpredictable needs. Thus, the problem with personality tests is much more than that of overcoming distortion due to faking, presenting an idealized concept of oneself rather than a realistic self-appraisal, and a lack of self-insight. The basic issue is ability to predict the future with an extremely high level of probability. This clairvoyance will be a long time in coming.[17]

3. The Behavioral or Skills Approach

A third approach to selection has been through tests that are less concerned with inner qualities or inferences about such qualities. Behavior—activity that can be seen or measured—has been the subject of measurement and observation in this cluster of selection devices. In its simplest form, it was the test applied to the itinerant craftsman who wandered from town to town in the early part of the century. The boss of the machine shop would simply give him a piece of metal and a drawing and tell him to "make this." If he made the piece to precise specifications, and did it quickly with few errors, he was hired. The test of typing skill was to place applicants in front of a typewriter and have them type. Their work was timed and checked for errors. If they performed well, they were hired.

The use of such tests—which aren't any more psychological than the height and weight of the applicant are psychological—are still used and are extremely useful screening devices. There has been an attempt to extend such testing to selection of managerial applicants, or candidates for sales, professional, or technical positions. Perhaps the most comprehensive plan for this approach is that of Robert N. McMurry, whose pattern interview program,[18] coupled with tests and full-dress exploration of behavior histories, is widely used by many firms.

McMurry's system is a combination of personality, aptitude, and behavior approaches. His system hypothesizes that the prediction of what a person will do in future assignments is already written in the record of his or her past behavior. Determinism is the underlying assumption here. If people have been job hoppers in the past (have held five jobs in the past five years), they will probably be job hoppers in the future. The goal of the pattern interview, then, is to probe intensively into the résumé, filling in each gap to uncover "patterns" of behavior. It is presumed that these patterns will persist into the future.

The McMurry system, which has been widely adopted and copied by firms and by a corps of consultants who have developed similar plans, delves into attitudes by eliciting verbal reactions to the conditions of past employment. An applicant who states that most past employers have been incompetent, unpleasant, or otherwise deficient may be predicted to adopt similar verbal responses about the new employer after the initial period of adjustment is over. Further, one may predict such things as leadership, creativity, and maturity by asking questions that get at past behavior, from which reasonable inferences can be made. Table 15.1 shows how such questions might be devised in this behavioral approach to managerial selection.

Table 15.1 Using verbal responses to obtain predictors of future attitudes or capacities.

TRAIT	QUESTION THAT WILL HIGHLIGHT THE TRAIT
Creativity	Has the applicant ever created anything?
Leadership	Has the applicant ever led anything?
Loyalty	Does the applicant speak well of former employers, schools, parents, and associates?
Maturity	Has the applicant been dependent upon others? Destroyed things that were his or her responsibility? Has his or her behavior been excessively oriented toward pleasurable activities?

The assumptions in the line of questioning are that people's behavior does not change or that it may be costly to change it. That being true, the time to find the undesirable behavior patterns in applicants is when they are still applicants. One might even hire persons with less than desirable behavior patterns, knowing what the defects are and allowing for them.

Clearly more scientific than some of the more esoteric methods of personality and aptitude testing, McMurry's system nonetheless shares the limitation that it is deterministic and is more apt to achieve conformity in hiring than any other outcome.

The distinctive feature of this approach is that it presumes that a *pattern of behavior* is the key ingredient in hiring. Reference checks, intensive attention to past behavior, and the reports of past observers about the behavior of individuals are coupled with the probing into every aspect of the applicant's past results in order to create an extensive dossier that gives the interviewer the equivalent of many years of personal acquaintanceship with the applicant. The interview that is vital in this approach may be nondirective when it will manipulate the individual into revealing things he or she might not otherwise divulge. Telephone checks of former employers are larded with probing questions to strip aside the amenities that former employers customarily drape over people they have fired.

The method's most important shortcoming, although it has fewer than many other approaches, is that it deals mainly with behavior and not with the effects of that behavior in results.

4. The Background Approach

One of the fastest rising in popularity, the background approach has resulted in a dramatic increase in campus recruiting in recent years. In fact, much of the pressure upon the campus-recruiting process has grown out of an unstated and sometimes unconscious assumption that a college degree is needed for most managerial and staff positions. There are some interesting assumptions here.

1. It is assumed that people who have a degree learned something in college. It is further assumed that this learning is something that they will carry to their first and subsequent positions. It is also assumed that the learning will convert into behavior on the job and that the behavior in turn will produce results that could not be produced by noncollege graduates.

2. Much of the drive to garner degree holders was caused by studies that show that 75 percent of the present crop of chief executives of the largest firms are college graduates. The studies of sociologists Warner, Abegglen and others, it is held, comprise predictors of the promotability of college graduates.[19] To some extent, this has become describable by the favorite cliché of the psychologists—"a self-fulfilling prophecy." Companies that presume that only college graduates can do managerial work enact policies that permit only college graduates to become managers. As an example, one utility company for many years recruited at colleges, limiting interviews to those in the upper brackets of their class in grades. Later they found that only high-mark students succeeded.[20]

Where Are the Soft Spots?

There are many studies that show that the most successful automobile dealers, realtors, and successful small business operators are not college trained.[21]

Two of the largest firms in the country in sales and profit have diametrically opposing policies with respect to the promotion of college degree holders into managerial positions. At AT&T, the college graduate enjoys a distinct edge. At General Motors, where results are primary guides to internal selection, a majority of managers are not college graduates, including at this writing the president. GM has an extensive college recruiting program; however, its assumptions are different from those of some of its corporate counterparts. GM assumes college graduates will demonstrate what they have learned once they are on the job and that their learning will be verified by the results they achieve rather than by the degree they acquired before joining the firm. (Ford, number two in manufacturing industries, shares GM's pattern of selecting managers.)

The background approach has the limitations of all the single-cause approaches to selection. It examines a single variable (academic degree) and generalizes this as a predictor. In fact, some combinations of degrees are automatic guarantees of rapid rise in the large corporation. People with a B.S. degree from Massachusetts Institute of Technology and an M.B.A. from Harvard, for example, may never have to really work again. Their rise to the general management post is assured. Admittedly, they have already as youths gone through several screens that many other people fail to survive, but their subsequent progress will not be measured by their results achieved until they reach a crucial position in the firm. Who would dare to give them a bad appraisal? They might remember it when they get on top. Their salary progress will be swift in order that the jump need not be too great when they arrive at the top.[22]

The suggestion here is not that background is not useful information, but rather that as a single predictor it has the limitations of all single-cause explanations for multiple-cause outcomes.

The Goals Approach in Operation

An objectives-results approach does not presume to displace all of the methods presently used. It merely subsumes them to other criteria and shapes the plan for selection in somewhat different terms.

It starts with statements of job objectives for the job being filled rather than with job descriptions, which have been oriented toward skills, experiences and staffing requirements. The method turns, secondly, to a measurement of the candidates' results on past jobs.

It means that the selection process begins by defining objectives for the vacant position in far more detail than was previously thought either necessary or possible. This requires that the firm must have some strategic goals in mind that require talent and must have stated these strategies explicitly before it starts staffing to attain them. Philip Marvin of the University of Cincinnati suggests that there are seven factors involved in preparing a useful position profile.[23]

1. The value added factor: During the next year, what outputs from this position would be regarded as top performance?
2. The frustration factor: During the next year, what frustrations will be associated with this position?
3. The responsibility factor: In addition to value added, what other performance expectations will be required of the employee on this job?
4. The authority to act: What authority should be given the employee to do the job which is expected to be done?
5. The reporting relationships factor: To whom must the employee report in this position and for what?
6. The performance criteria factor: What explicit criteria which explain the value added factor should be defined for this job?
7. The fit factor: Does this employee fit the temperament, geographical culture, and social makeup of the situation for which he or she is being considered?

These seven factors, Marvin concludes, should detail the makeup of the person the organization can digest, and who, in turn, can digest the organization.

While the emphasis in the foregoing material has been upon the employer finding the right person for the right job at the right time, the same materials can be used by the applicant.

This can be shown in Figure 15.1, in which the requirements of the hoped-for position are spelled out and the standards of the applicant are used as criteria for rating alternative employment opportunities.

Your own personal needs and expectations comprise the criteria for making decisions among alternative opportunities. These needs can be matched against the seven factors noted above and decisions of acceptance or rejection made. Abraham Maslow's mix of *needs* comprises a rough approximation of what most people need and might be useful in such decision making:

1. Physical Needs. "How badly do I need the money which I will get from this position?" This is a function of present resources, standard

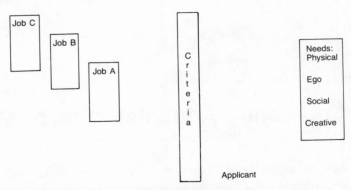

Figure 15.1 How to use selection skill in finding your niche.

of living, family and personal financial requirements, and waiting power.

2. Ego Needs. "Will I find the ego-building sense of attainment that I need in this position?" If you are accustomed to deference or power, you may find that the new job doesn't satisfy those needs and would lead to dissatisfaction on this count.

3. Social Needs. "Are the kind of people I will associate with at work the kind of people I enjoy being with and would be happy to have daily personal relationships with?"

4. Self-Actualization. "Even though the job pays well and the power and associations are good, will I be expressing my highest levels of creativity and abilities in the job?"[24]

If the job meets these four requirements, for most people, the position is highly desirable. The specific symbols by which we fill these needs will vary with individuals, but Maslow suggests, "these are the common needs of normal healthy persons and comprise an ascending scale of excellence for the situation into which one might wander or move by choice."

CHAPTER 16

Relating Salary Administration to MBO

Wealth is not without its advantages, and the case to the contrary, although it has often been made, has never proved widely persuasive.

—John Kenneth Galbraith

A system of managing that does not purport to cope with the practical problems of salary administration really is not adequate as a system. In moving managers to behave in ways that will achieve company goals, the salary administration policies of the firm can function either to reinforce certain kinds of behavior or, on the other hand, to extinguish desired behavior, if they are wrongly conceived or improperly applied.

Salary administration at the managerial level in American companies is not necessarily applicable to companies elsewhere. There are some basic articles of faith about the purposes of management compensation in our country and in our time that differ from the ideas about salary in other countries or in other times.[1]

In modern Europe, for example, it is not uncommon for all wages and salaries to be so closely regulated by the government that any possible incentive effects are minimized. In certain countries such as India, the paramount concept of wage and salary administration is the necessity of the employee. As an Indian employee would say, "The company is my father." Additions to the family or increased expenses are often considered rightful bases for increases in pay.

Salary Administration as Incentive

Figure 16.1 indicates the scope of salary administration under the MBO system of managing.

196

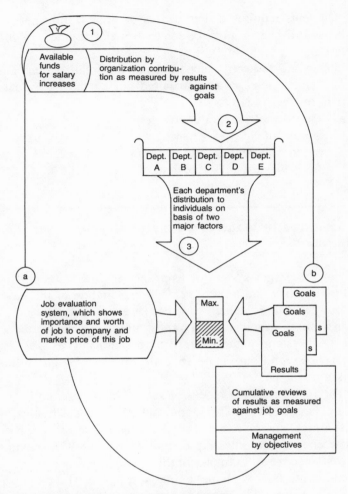

Figure 16.1 Relating salary to goals and results.

1. It begins with the company's achievement of economic success, which generates the funds available for salary increases. Obviously, if the firm is steadily losing money, this sum will be less than if operations have been financially successful.
2. The distribution of these funds among the company's various departments is made by top-management judgment of the relative contribution of the respective departments as measured by their results. This distribution of relative amounts among de-

partments requires that measures of organization performance be established in advance for each major segment of the business.

3. Within the respective departments, the total amount available for salary increases is distributed among the individual members on the basis of:
   a. The formal job evaluation system.
   b. Statements of performance against goals, as worked out between subordinate and superior for the period or periods since the last salary review.

The Procedures in Wage and Salary Administration

Part 3(a) of this larger system of using pay for incentive purposes deserves close scrutiny and a more detailed explanation of the procedures used. These procedures, which have been well spelled out in the literature of personnel administration, constitute a logical sequence that makes it a subsystem of the entire compensation process.

As may be seen from Figure 16.2, the process of salary administration has six major phases:

1. The initial building block for salary administration begins with a person at work. This includes that person's activities, responsibilities, and behavior. The clerk, the machinist, the typist, the sweeper, or the sales representative making a presentation to a customer are all examples of this first figure. Their work is vastly different, but we hope to measure its worth by a standard scale that provides internal equity and also keeps the company competitive with other employers of the same kinds of workers.

2. To reduce this multifarious array of activities to a common dimension of measurement, we prepare *job descriptions* for each position (or for benchmark positions that are typical of a family of occupations). These job descriptions use a common language and common patterns of description to delineate the work performed in each job. Thus, measurable statements of likenesses and differences among the jobs described are achieved.

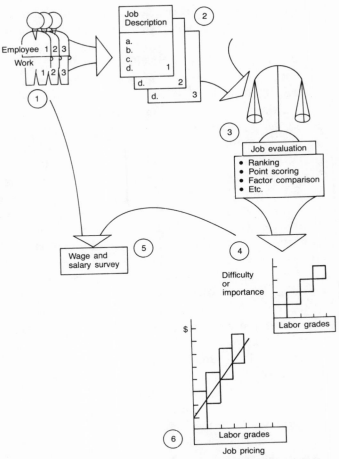

Figure 16.2 The process of job evaluation and salary administration.

3. The next step is to weigh the job descriptions to determine the relative worth of the jobs described. This process, which is known as *job evaluation,* consists of matching the respective job descriptions against certain yardsticks or measures of differences and similarities in content. Among the more common systems of job evaluation are ranking of jobs by subjective judgment as to their relative worth to the firm, use of a point scoring system that assigns numerical weights to certain factors

that have been determined as having worth to the firm, and comparison of the relative weight of factors that might be present in the job. All such methods require two ingredients:
a. Descriptions of the jobs being done.
b. Some kind of measuring scale to determine the relative weight of the content of the jobs as described.

4. After being evaluated, the jobs are arrayed in stratified ranks, called job or labor grades. For example, the labor grades may ascend by modular blocks with all jobs evaluated as having 165–200 points being placed in labor grade I; jobs with 201–235 points in labor grade II, and so on. The aim of this classification system is to ensure equity in pay for different jobs, in different locations, or in different sections of the same location.

5. Internal equity is not the only factor to be considered, however. Our employees may be equitably paid in relation to one another but over- or underpaid in relation to the general market for their skills. Hence, we must see how our rates compare with those prevailing in the labor market from which we hire our people. To make this comparison, we ask other employers to provide us with the dollar rates for jobs that are similar to ours. This industry or community survey assures us that we are not overpaying any single occupation and also that we are not being noncompetitive to the degree that we shall not be able to hire enough qualified people to staff our positions.

6. Finally, labor grades are matched against the market prices for the various jobs in the company and the jobs are priced in current dollars. The community or industry average for these positions is shown as a sloping curve, being considered as a *range* with a minimum and a maximum salary. Whether the firm should pay above or below the community curve, or merely match it, is a top-management policy decision based upon such factors as the company's profit position, the labor market it operates in, or other reasons.

The result of this procedure is a system that offers comparable pay for comparable work done, with due attention to length of service, performance levels, and the firm's competitive posture.

At periodic intervals, employee salaries are reviewed to determine whether they should be moved toward the maximum for their range. The basis for this decision is the performance appraisal system.

*Ordinarily for managers, the system should provide for perfor-
mance to be reviewed more often than salary, with cumulative performance results forming the basis for increases in salaries within the grade
and range.*

Such is the sequence of standard administration procedures. For
higher-level executives, however, some further considerations have to be
borne in mind.

How Much Is an Executive Worth?

The financial rewards of top executives cannot be determined by the
same criteria used to compensate other employees—not even key scientists or other professionals. The executive's job is, in many ways, unique
and thus not susceptible to standard valuation. Essentially, the corporate
manager is a risk bearer who assumes the responsibilities of ownership
without its benefits. The rewards of top executives must stimulate them
to run their businesses with maximum efficiency and profit. Ultimately,
their remuneration should be related to the benefits stockholders, workers, and the general public derive from skillful management.

As we pointed out at the beginning of this book, the old-style
capitalism of Adam Smith has vanished. With it has gone the automatic
reward for risk enjoyed by nineteenth-century entrepreneurs. It was easy
for such people to reward themselves. They took what was left over after
all the bills had been paid. They did not even have to share the profit
with the income-tax collector. If they wanted to spend the money, they
could do so. If they wanted to reinvest it in the hope of making more,
that, too, was up to them.

But in our time corporate managers have taken charge, performing
the functions previously discharged by the owner. Yet, since managers
are not owners, they do not have the free access to the till that the
entrepreneur enjoyed. In fact, it is often argued that the corporate manager is only a highly paid employee. However, if top executives must
bear the risks without hope of attendant gain, they are likely to manage
the affairs of the company with diminished zeal and enthusiasm.

As far back as 1932, Adolph Berle and Gardiner Means pinpointed
this problem in *The Modern Corporation and Private Property.* "If all
profits are earmarked for the security holder," the authors asked,

"where is the inducement for those in control to manage the enterprise efficiently? When none of the profits are to be retained by them, why should they exert themselves beyond the amount necessary to maintain a reasonably satisfied group of stockholders?"[2]

The two economists concluded that if the incentive system is to work, profits must be distributed "either to the owners or to the control" (that is, management). This being the case, in our own time of far-flung corporate ownership, profit incentives should apply only to management that creates the profit, since the stockholders are "merely the recipients of the wages of capital."

Anyone who has attended a stockholders' meeting is aware of the inherent conflicts between the corporate managers and the "owners." Thus, no aspect of corporate life is more loaded with economic, social, political, and administrative implications than the question of executive pay levels.

- When is an executive overpaid?
- Should an executive be paid according to different criteria than lower-level employees?
- How can executive pay become part of corporate strategy?
- To what extent are executive pay levels determined by public needs and interests?
- Is there a discernible relationship between the level of executive salaries and the profits accruing to stockholders?
- How large must executive salaries be to provide corporations with vigorous and skillful leadership?
- How do tax laws affect executive pay practices?

"There are only three problems in executive compensation," a member of a board of directors of a large corporation said recently. "The first is internal dissension, the second is litigation, and the third is public criticism." These three factors provide a useful framework for an examination of the entire problem.

Internal Inequities

In large companies, executive salaries are scaled downward from the salary of the chief executive. Surveys show that if the president gets $100,000, the vice-president in charge of sales will get about $70,000, the vice-president of manufacturing or research $55,000, the vice-president of engineering $45,000, and the vice-president of personnel $35,000. If the president refuses to accept a raise, he or she may compress salaries at the bottom levels of the scale, especially if there are six or seven levels between the top executive and the first-line manager.

The problems don't end here, however. Psychologist Jay Otis of Western Reserve University, who specializes in salary administration problems, points out that within each department or division pay scales are likewise cued to the remuneration of the chief officer of the department.

Consider the sales vice-president who gets $70,000 per year, and the vice-president of manufacturing who gets $55,000. In their respective departments, the salaries of their subordinates will tend to slope downward from their own pay levels. Thus, the manufacturing vice-president may have a manager of a substantial manufacturing plant who will earn, say, $20,000 per year, while a regional sales manager who does not even report directly to the sales vice-president may get as much as the plant manager, though the sales manager has less responsibility and certainly fewer people to supervise. This arrangement extends down through the organization so that the plant manager's secretary is paid less than the sales manager's secretary simply because the salaries are arranged around different clusters. Admittedly, a rational salary administration system would eliminate such inequities at the lower levels of the corporate hierarchy. But, in practice, the salaries usually cluster under the department's top executive, and this may create internal dissension within the company.[3]

The problem could be resolved to a considerable extent, however, if agreement could be reached on a definition of the term *executive*. Some authorities take the view that an executive is someone who formulates plans, reviews the work of others, and integrates the demands of various groups within a business enterprise. Others would classify in the executive category anyone who has professional, managerial, or technical status and makes important decisions bearing on profits. This definition would encompass such individuals as researchers and corporate counsel.

Charles Abbott has proposed still another definition. He concludes that executives are people who act in a way that gives them unique roles in the company and in society. They are the paid risk bearers, which is different from being paid administrators (who are, in reality, high-level employees). Administrators are experts solely responsible for the professional quality of their advice. Executives must make decisions, guide their implementation and bear responsibility for the results.

Risk takers must be compensated for their risk-assuming roles, which were formerly incumbent on the owner. In the large company, then, individuals below the rank of *division general manager* cannot be classed as true executives, according to Abbott's definition. A division general manager is the lowest-ranking official who makes decisions directly bearing on corporate profits.

Under this concept, designers for General Motors, for example, are responsible for the quality of their work, which is vital to the future of the business. But only the company president, the executive committee, and the managers of Chevrolet, Buick, Oldsmobile, and other GM divisions decide which alternative design will be chosen and put into production.

Salary policy for the executive group is quite distinct from that for engineers, market research experts, and others. All the latter are *vital employees,* but their salaries can be arrived at by standard procedures. Determining the salary of a vital employee is a matter of viewing his or her particular job against a set of factors that apply to all jobs—the grade classification, the condition of the labor market at the time, the funds available for salaries, and so on.

It is pointless to follow this standard procedure in determining the remuneration of risk bearers because their functions are unique. *The executive must be paid for the results he or she obtains in terms of profit and growth.*

Let's consider the president of a small company manufacturing envelopes. Under her management, the company makes a profit of $1 million on $10 million in sales and an investment of $5 million. The president's aggregate compensation is $95,000 a year, though the company has only 500 employees. The competing companies in her field are doing one-quarter as well in terms of profit and return on investment.

Now let us compare the envelope company president with the top executive of a company in a different field with annual sales of $300 million and earnings of $3 million on an investment of $150 million; he gets only $80,000.

If we applied the standard job evaluation procedures to both executives, the president of the envelope company would be considered overpaid. Yet the president of the large company may not be worth more, while the president of the small company may actually be underpaid considering the results being achieved in the envelope field.

Or take two division managers of one large corporation. General Manager A runs a highly profitable small division that earns 15 percent on sales. General Manager B runs a division with ten times as many employees, a bigger investment, and a sales volume fifteen times as large, yet the absolute profit is only twice that of the small division and the rate of profit 90 percent lower.

Obviously, we must consider other factors as well in determining the relative remuneration of the two executives in this instance. Is Manager A cruising along in a soft job where any member of average ability could make money because of trade advantages, patent position, or windfall profits? Is the manager whose division shows a lower rate of profits faced with extraordinary problems of competition, costs, declining markets, or other obstacles that would overwhelm a person of ordinary caliber—problems that the manager, through special ability, has partly overcome and, as a consequence, has succeeded in preventing them from causing sizable losses?

The case of many Eastern railroads is a pertinent example here. Amtrak loses large sums of money on passenger traffic, and private railroads earn large amounts hauling freight. Does this mean that a passenger traffic manager should be paid less than the manager of the freight department? Not necessarily. A more realistic approach would be to measure each manager's performance against reasonable expectations under prevailing conditions. If the freight traffic manager does not take advantage of all opportunities, this should be reflected in the annual raise or bonuses. On the other hand, if the passenger-traffic chief reduces losses, even though still operating in the red, this contribution deserves reward as measured against reasonable expectations.

It should be evident, therefore, that no simple formula can be applied in rewarding individuals for generating profits.[4]

The Litigation Problem

Corporation and tax laws provide ample opportunities for legal troubles when a company, especially one with a board heavily dominated by its officers, appears to be self-serving in its compensation policies.

As a rule, the stockholder is a fairly passive animal when it comes to suing the company or its officers for excessive compensation. The stockholder is willing to be treated simply as a recipient of the "wages of capital" and only asks for a fair shake. When dividends are not forthcoming, the stockholders may unite into a militant but for the most part ineffectual organization that badgers management at annual meetings. It is only infrequently that stockholders' ire results in a lawsuit against management.

More often, the dissatisfied stockholders simply sell their holdings and buy another stock paying a higher return. The thought seldom crosses their minds that they have bought anything more than an equity on earnings. Of late, stockholders have seemed to be even a trifle indifferent to this, provided management uses the nondistributed surplus in such a way that the value of the stock increases fast enough.

Another kind of litigation that might confront management is a suit in the tax courts by the Internal Revenue Service. Such suits are brought by the IRS against corporations that don't abide by rulings on executive compensation.

The most important legal restraints, however, are those affecting possible tax loopholes for executives. High salaries obviously provide little incentive if a sizable proportion of them has to be remitted to the tax collector. Accordingly, corporations are continuously devising executive compensation plans designed to mitigate the tax burden.[5]

One answer to the problem of high income taxes is *deferred compensation*. Here part of the executive's compensation is held back until retirement, when the income will be smaller and consequently subject to a lower rate of taxation.

Stock-option plans permit executives to buy company shares at a price below the going market price as of a certain date. Since the executive is granted several years in which to pick up the options, he or she can often wait until a propitious time arises to buy, or may buy the shares and hold them until they can be sold at a sizable profit. Either way, provided the shares are held for six months or longer, the executive pays a capital gains tax instead of the steeper income tax. At the same time, the manager has a powerful incentive to make the company prosper so that the value of the stock will increase and can be sold at a profit. Changes in tax law, however, have reduced the time period over which options may be exercised, thus making this form of compensation less attractive than it used to be.

Public Criticism

Public criticism is another important factor influencing the compensation of executives. This is mainly directed at the practice of granting top managers large bonuses over and above their high salaries. Typical labor union newspapers usually make a point of comparing hefty executive bonuses with the pay of workers. Such comparisons are especially popular at a time when contracts are being negotiated. Such stories impress the public, but how valid are the objections to the managerial bonuses?

The real test is whether the stockholders, the workers, and the public profit or suffer because of such bonuses. Few General Motors stockholders, for example, complain because 12 percent of profits, after deducting 6 percent of net capital, may be placed in a bonus pool and distributed to key officials on the "bonus roll."

Perhaps arguments for rewarding such intangibles as "leadership" can never be fully communicated to the general public. Thus, public criticism can be expected to continue. The true test is whether the policy makers in Congress and the executive branch of the government will have the insight and the pertinent facts to refrain from reducing everyone's rewards to one common denominator.

Some psychologists maintain that people seek other rewards besides money. However, I have not been able to get those same psychologists to expound their theories at a management conference for less than a $1,500 fee. As one wag put it, in motivating people "money beats whatever comes second best by a substantial margin." For more than two decades now it has been fashionable to proclaim the death of the economic mortal and to kick the corpse for good measure. Experience with executive compensation seems to indicate, however, that there is still some life left.

CHAPTER 17

Zero-Based Budgeting and MBO

"But I can't set objectives for my job," says the subor-dinate. "The output can't be measured!"

"Let me test you with a thought starter," says the boss. "Suppose your job were eliminated and your department taken out of the budget. What, if anything, would this organi-zation lose that it might miss? Try putting that in writing for me."

—Anon. conversation

While this conversation has an air of shop humor—perhaps gallows humor—about it, it embodies the basic idea of zero-based budgeting. If your position and/or department were cut from the budget, would your organization lose anything?

Actually, it is very unlikely that any job could be eliminated with-out causing a loss to the organization that someone would miss. The cases where a job could be cut without causing a loss are rare. Even those apocryphal government commissions to supervise extinct Civil War widows and War of 1812 veterans, which somehow never were taken off the books and which still get $150,000 a year in appropria-tions, have some reasonable political patronage purposes that could, in some far-fetched way, have some advantages to somebody. At least the party bosses who keep our political system afloat would miss these pro-grams if they were eliminated.

A more productive conversation can be generated if the boss asks the following two questions:

1. "If your budget were reduced 10 percent, what would the ef-fects be?"

2. "If your budget were increased 10 percent, what benefits would accrue from that addition?"

A valuable scrutiny of objectives will almost surely follow.

The second scenario—asking what would be lost by a 10 percent reduction in the budget and what would be gained by a 10 percent increase—is a realistic, if simplified, version of what zero-based budgeting attempts to bring to what is known as the MBO calendar.

The MBO Calendar

The MBO calendar identifies three key events in the anticipatory year which occur in the best-managed organizations. These are:

First, *financial and program audits* produce clear and objective statements of strengths and problems inside the organization. Such audits, especially program audits, can also introduce from the outside statements of threats extant, risks to which the organization is exposed, and opportunities that lie in all of the above.

Second, *annual strategic goals statements* are prepared to answer four sets of questions:

1. Where are you now in your area? What strengths, weaknesses, problems, threats, risks, and opportunities do you see?
2. What trends are present? If you didn't do anything differently from what you are doing, where would you be in one, two, and five years, and do you like that?
3. What are your missions? What are you in business for? What indicators would best reflect achievement in those missions?
4. What strategies could be considered and what would each contribute to the missions, and what would each cost?

Third, *budget submissions* are made. At this point you are set up for a more intelligible and rational process of budgeting that comes in October (or three months in advance of the operating year that is the subject of this planning process).

The amount of detail involved in producing financial and program audits is relatively slight. Audits are generally based upon sampling of accounts, studies of dramatic incidents, or random inspections. The method here is for the auditor to row out over the huge ocean of fact and information and to dip up a bucket here and a bucket there and then generalize about the whole ocean from that sample.

The amount of work required in preparing the annual strategic goals statement and the annual edition of the five-year plan is greater and the output is more detailed, but it is still broad-brush in nature. The statement doesn't have to be fully detailed, but the major directions should be decided. "Will we still be in the same business five years from now?" is one of the questions it answers.

It is in the budgeting stage, however, where the most explicit detail must be clarified. Here, in asking for funding for a specific program, you should show the hoped-for outputs sought, state objectives, equate revenues and expenses, and break the budget down into precise numerical form. Budgeting is the first commitment in managing by objectives.

What Is Zero-Based Budgeting?

Many experts suggest that the zero-based budget is more than a budget; they see it as a zero-based organization plan.[1] The traditional budget is sort of a bag of money that is replenished annually and from which funds are drawn according to a plan. Under the traditional budgeting system, it is implied that people wait until after the amount in the bag has been determined before making up their minds on what they do.

Traditional budget requests are often stated in terms of incremental sums. This process centers around the additions sought, rather than focusing on the total sum as in zero-based budgeting. The boss may suggest that a budget increase of $10,000 be made for your function next year, while you argue for a $100,000 increase. You haggle like merchants in an oriental bazaar and eventually reach a compromise figure somewhere between the two figures.

Zero-based budgets show two key figures: the amount of last year's total budget, and the amount of this year's total budget. You discuss the whole sum, not just the incremental addition to last year's budget total. This requires you to defend and justify the whole sum, from zero to the top, in terms of objectives.[2]

Thus, I would define zero-based budgeting as *the process of allocating or moving resources to the most cost-effective uses to achieve the strategic objectives of the organization, in response to proven needs, perceived threats and risks, and hoped-for opportunities.*

Zero-based budgeting reportedly originated in the U.S. Department of Agriculture in the early 1960s. It was subsequently employed in industry by Texas Instruments, and today is used in many firms, including Xerox, BASF, Eastern Airlines, Owens-Illinois, Southern California Edison, New York Telephone, Combustion Engineering, Dillingham, and numerous other companies. In government, its most famous user was Jimmy Carter as governor of Georgia.[3] A campaign promise made by Carter was that zero-based budgeting would be the system of budgeting in the U.S. Government upon his election as President. The system had already been adopted by numerous federal agencies, including the Food and Drug Administration, the Coast Guard, the General Accounting Office, and the Energy Research and Development Administration.

The most persuasive use of zero-based budgeting is that which was described by Peter Pyhrr, then with Texas Instruments, in an article in *Harvard Business Review.*[4] This article brought the first widespread attention to the idea. Pyhrr later wrote a book on the subject expanding on these three basic steps:

First, write a brief verbal description of each organization activity's objectives as a *decision package.*

Second, evaluate each of the decision packages on a *six-point scale* to forecast effectiveness.

Third, allocate resources according to the position on this six-point scale as uncovered in the *decision process.*

Displayed in visual form, these three steps of zero-based budgeting might look something like Figure 17.1.

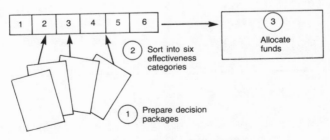

Figure 17.1 The three steps of zero-based budgeting.

Where Zero-Based Budgeting Works

In addition to knowing *how* zero-based budgeting works, you need to know *where* it works.

Zero-based budgeting is a fine technique for staff service, advice, control, and information functions; including such areas as the legal, traffic, production control, personnel and human resources (may be broken down into major segments), credit, and financial management departments. Each unit becomes the subject of a separate decision package.

Do not, for openers, try to apply zero-based budgeting to sales management, manufacturing-plant management (factory operations), or other profit-center areas where profit plans, sales forecasts, or engineered standards can be used to determine budgets. Good, solid profit planning with flexible budgeting will probably work better than zero-based budgeting in these areas.

Capital budgeting is not a likely place to start with zero-based budgeting either. Use cost-effectiveness studies and traditional budgeting methods to handle capital problems.

On the other hand, government operations are quite apt to be a likely place for attempting zero-based budgeting because they consist largely of service, advice, control, and information outputs mandated by law and supported by appropriations.[5]

The major problems you are tackling with zero-based budgeting lie in the area of overhead costs. These are always troublesome because of their generality, lack of measurability, and long-term impact. Overhead costs are a real problem for most organizations where controls are needed to restrict rising costs of general, administrative, research and factory-burden expenses.

Now let us look at the three steps of zero-based budgeting.

Step 1: Prepare Decision Packages

You create a decision package when you create an organizational unit. For example, if you are doing research and development work in a single laboratory, that is a decision package. If you have several labs spread among several divisions, and each is under separate management, then each R&D lab becomes a separate decision package.

The key in deciding what units to consider as a separate decision package is managerial responsibility, not the collection of numbers or classifications.

If, for instance, your personnel department were to experiment with zero-based budgeting, it should collect decision packages from every key function manager under the personnel director's supervision—training, labor relations, compensation, employment, and personnel research. These individual decision packages will later be combined into the total human resources package. Have the manager in charge prepare and submit, in a face-to-face discussion, his or her decision package. A one-page decision package format provided on page 214 in Figure 17.2 provides a guide with the following information:

- Items 1–8 (shown in circles on the form) are the identification and name of the package.
- Item 9 is a terse statement of the purpose, mission or objective of the unit. This answers the question, "What are we in business for?"
- Item 10 shows a general statement of the activities engaged in to achieve the objectives of the unit.
- Item 11 indicates some alternative ways of getting to the same objectives and shows the costs of those alternative means.
- Item 12 states the advantages of retaining the activity.
- Item 13 answers the question, "What would be lost if this activity were eliminated?"
- Items 14–18 show the proposed new budget and the parallel new budget.

Working these very hard-nosed questions out with the boss can be a revealing experience. If it is to be done well and thoroughly, it will ordinarily require more than a single meeting.

The idea of this step is to equate costs and benefits:

- What are we spending now?
- What are we getting for that expenditure?
- What do you plan to spend next year?
- What will we get for that?
- Could it be done better, cheaper, faster, easier, safer, or with greater dignity to people in some other way?

- Should we increase expenditures in this area? Should we decrease them?
- Are there things you are doing that could be abandoned without losing anything valuable?
- Are there things that, if added, would have a high yield? What are they? How much will doing them cost? What yield will they produce?

The format of the decision package isn't the important thing; it is merely a tool to get at some tough-minded discussions. If it works well and if some trust is developed, the subordinate managers will be coming in with hard decisions, not waiting for the boss to be tough.

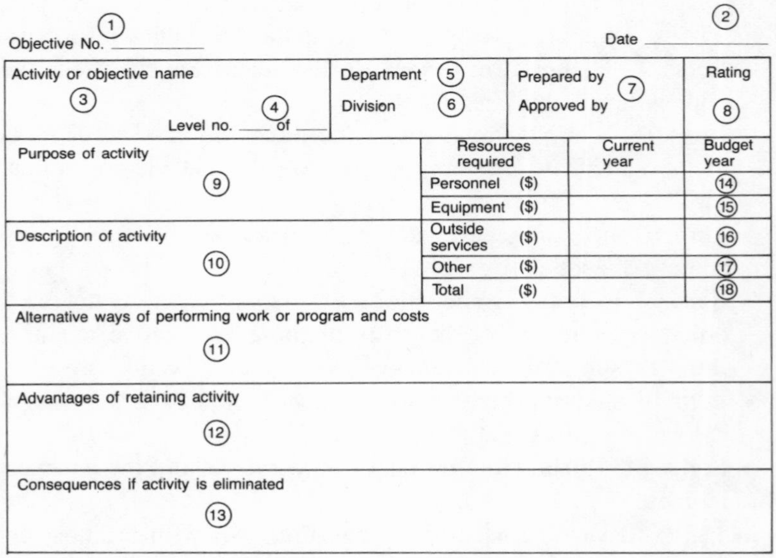

Figure 17.2 Sample decision package format.

Step 2: Sort into Six Effectiveness Categories

Ranking the alternative uses of funds is made easier if the decision packages go upward one layer of management at a time. Here are some ways that ranking could be done:

First, the boss could do it for all of the units under his or her jurisdiction.

Second, the boss might use some kind of participative management method, such as a committee, to perform the ranking. The committee might consist of all the managers involved and might include an outsider or two for objectivity.

Third, the boss might state the criteria and have a committee do the actual ranking, either by vote or consensus.

A six-point rating scale can be used. Under this system, each decision package is scored on a scale of one to six points. An example of such a scale is provided in Figure 17.3. The boss or committee then assigns a numerical value to each of the decision packages under consideration. When there is doubt over what value to assign to a particular package, that decision package should be discussed fully and a decision should be forced.

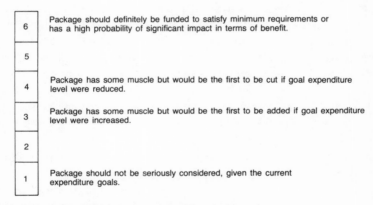

Figure 17.3   Example of a six-point rating scale.

Here are some examples of how some typical decision packages might be rated on a six-point scale:

Continuing to occupy offices rented on a long-term lease would be rated as a category 6 package since no savings would be achieved by moving out. Even if you moved, you'd still pay the bill.

Purchase of a helicopter for use by the research manager in getting back and forth between the lab and the golf course quickly would be rated as a category 1 package. Unless the research manager was in a grass-seed experiment firm (or the research manager owns the company), this would be an obvious and immediate reject.

The key ingredient is using some preestablished criteria for evaluating alternative decision packages. They need not follow the six-point scale described here, but you need to have some criteria to follow. These criteria should be chosen after reviewing the strategic goals of the organization.

Step 3: Allocate Funds

Not every package that is unacceptable at the lower level is abolished. The idea of moving decision packages upward should use the principle of a cut-off level.

Take the case of a research department that submits six decision packages, all with high cost-benefit prospects. Each of these packages should be sent forward, even though some are better than others. Meanwhile, the public relations department also submits six decision packages, three of which are high in cost-effectiveness and three of which are either low in cost-effectiveness or are vague about potential outcomes.

You would surely throw out the three poor packages of the public relations department and rate the remaining nine packages, ultimately, by a common criteria.

Don't eliminate the lowest-ranked decision package if it shows a high cost-effectiveness ratio; send it forward.

If everything public relations proposes scores low on cost-effectiveness, no automatic assumptions should be permitted that public relations will continue to be funded. If funds can be used for other projects where cost-effectiveness is greater, use them elsewhere.

For example, one government agency may write a cost-effective plan for handling hard-core unemployment problems, while another agency produces an inefficient package for hiring migrant laborers. The latter package should be asked to compete with the former. You might even transfer the responsibility for migrant labor programs to the other agency, where the job may be accomplished more effectively.

Conclusion

In management by anticipation, your budgeting should be an integral part of the strategic planning and commitment process. Zero-based budgeting is one of those crunch points in the process where the allocation of scarce resources against unlimited demands takes place. No wonder budgeting is called "the allocation of discontent."

Zero-based budgeting is not only consistent with an operating MBO program but should be made an integral part of it.

CHAPTER 18

Discipline by Objectives

For a large and growing number of people, loyalty to institutions and obedience to written and unwritten laws are no longer automatic. . . .

—Henry Ford II

For a lot of reasons, managers can expect to have discipline problems in their jobs in the eighties. People at work aren't buying old-fashioned kinds of discipline the way their parents and grandparents did. Furthermore, there are new groups in the work force that rebel strongly if the manager tries to enforce discipline. Minorities see traditional discipline as being racist in origin, even if it is imposed equally on all races and cultures. Women will not accept traditional discipline when they see it as having any trace of sexism. Not only that, but because of a higher level of education among employees today's work force refuses to accept unexplained orders and will not stand still for a punishing type of atmosphere.[1]

Two dominant expectations of people at work will require substantially different policies and practices of companies with respect to discipline which can probably best be solved by an MBO approach. These expectations are:

1. People expect to be able to have more control over their own lives and conduct.
2. Everyone has certain human rights that cannot be abridged by a boss on a job.

Modern discipline is remedial rather than punitive, a blending of discipline and coaching with an emphasis on the achievement of objectives rather than the extermination of sin. It requires rules to be reviewed periodically against objectives to see if they are still productive in

218

changing conditions, and it allows the exceptional performer who is achieving exceptional results to be treated with far greater tolerance when it comes to violations. The presumptions of discipline by objectives in the work environment are as follows:

1. Discipline is for the most part voluntarily accepted and, if not, is not legitimate.
2. It is not a punishment system, but a shaper of behavior.
3. The past provides useful experience but is not an infallible guide to right and wrong.
4. Contribution to objectives is a reasonable guide as to when to depart from rules.
5. Rules should be reviewed periodically against objectives to see if they are still productive.
6. The application of individual discipline makes each individual responsible for his or her own output, and individual differences are explainable in individual results.

This chapter discusses the difference between the traditional concepts and the newer approaches, gives some umbrella rules for discipline, and offers advice on handling the nonrule offense (for example, how to deal with a sales representative who offends customers by telling racist jokes).

The Change from Old-Fashioned Discipline

The old-fashioned approach to discipline was that of the Old Testament dictum, "an eye for an eye and a tooth for a tooth." The purpose of such discipline was to exact punishment for sins, maintain conformity to old customs, and sustain the authority of the old over the young. Punishment was defined to fit the crime. Retributive justice drew upon a kind of natural law, which provided that certain actions were forbidden by lower classes of persons and when such offenses occurred and were proven, the guilty party would naturally be subjected to the punishment that had been designated for that crime. In the Far East, theft was punishable by amputation of a hand; in the American West, theft of a horse was punishable by hanging; and so on. Aboard the old British Navy sailing ships, the punishment was generally the lash, with a specified number of strokes for specific offenses, and hanging for another group including murder, mutiny, and cowardice during combat.

While it is entirely conceivable that such a system in its origin may have had some behavior-change objectives, over time such exacting kinds of punishments acquired a character quite apart from the behavior-change effect and became an almost divinely inspired system of cause and effect, as if the crime itself produced the punishment.

Modern discipline is forced to meet a number of new requirements beyond punishment. Modern values tend away from excessively physical forms of punishment. The decline of capital punishment in many states and foreign nations is matched in declining levels of physical punishment for lesser levels of offense as well. Greater protection of the rights of the accused is being developed now more than ever before. The belief that it is better to allow many guilty persons to escape than to punish one innocent person prevails in society at large, in our courts and police system, and in industrial and business discipline.

The decline of arbitrary individual judgments and the movement toward group judgments of guilt or innocence (those requiring disciplinary procedures) is rising, even in the school system, the last bastion of dictatorship. The trial by jury of one's peers, the right to counsel, the right to confront accusers, the right to cross-examine witnesses, and the use of evidence in systematic fashion are now widespread.

The right to protest unilateral judgments is also rising in disciplinary cases. Even in those cases where no labor union exists, the skeletal outline of the arbitration system, the grievance procedures, and the right to appeal, are increasingly being used in disciplinary cases.[2]

Two major segments make up the modern behavioral approach to discipline.

1. A list is developed of actions, regulations, rules, behaviors, or offenses that shall trigger the corrective and remedial process.
2. A set of procedures is drawn up that shall be put into action when such offenses occur. This may also include some of the powers of persons and creation of groups to deal with and apply the procedures.

In all human organizations there will be kinds of behavior that cannot be permitted, for they keep the organization from going toward its objectives, bar individual members from being free to do their own work, or interfere with the personal rights of others. Traditionally, listing such offenses is done in order of seriousness and according to the severity of the ultimate punishments that might be used in the corrective process. These may be noted as falling into categories such as "major," "moderate" and "minor" or some such classification.

Usually lists of such offenses are posted in places where they can be seen and referred to by employees, without flaunting them in a threatening way. They are reviewed at the time of employment as part of the induction process. They are available to every manager and discussed with all supervisors from time to time. Notes or memoranda interpreting them are circulated to all managers who have responsibility for their application.

Traditional Discipline Systems

At this point, we can see little to differentiate between the rules of the modern factory or office from the work force of the Pharaohs in their structure of application. The rules were different and the punishments certainly more severe, but the basic design of the disciplinary system was similar: list the crimes, note the punishments attached to each, and promulgate and apply each. This old-fashioned discipline had several basic assumptions, which require updating in the new climate for discipline. These assumptions could be listed as follows:

1. Discipline is what superiors apply to subordinates and never the reverse.
2. The past is the arbiter of present and future actions.
3. Discipline is punishment for forbidden actions, and the severity of the punishment should, when practical, be exactly proportional to the severity of the offense.
4. The effect of punishment is deterrence of others who have not sinned and who will be halted in their tendencies to do so by the example of those who have sinned, been caught, and punished accordingly. Punishment for *principles* should be more severe than punishment for the act itself.
5. Where the prevalence of wrong behavior increases in the entire group, it may be necessary to accelerate the severity of the punishment for the next person caught violating a rule in order to set an especially impressive example for the others.
6. When a single individual cannot be isolated who will admit

responsibility for the violation, then the entire group should be punished, which will strike the guilty individual's conscience as well as motivating the group to turn in the violator or perhaps even punish him or her themselves.

7. Absolute consistency in punishment should be maintained *at all times* in all cases. If this is not done, the group will protest, feel that injustice is being done, and seek ways of circumventing the disciplinary system.

8. The severity of the punishment for a second offense should always be much more severe than for the first offense, even though identical to the first in nature and severity.

9. The announcement of punishment and its administration should be given the maximum possible visibility and exposure, in order that the deterrent effect shall be maximized.

While there are, of course, many other specific details that could be noted, these are illustrative of the philosophy, format, and structure of the traditional disciplinary system. It has permeated the school system, the workplace, and the life of the citizen.

Discipline by Objectives

While the systems of discipline in law enforcement and in school systems would be worthy of some discussion, here we are concerned with the workplace and personnel policies relating to discipline of people at work. Discipline in such an environment has some special features not characteristic of discipline elsewhere, such as in the home or the church. The difference centers around the objectives and purposes of the business firm. The presumptions of discipline by objectives in the work environment could be listed as follows:

1. *Discipline at work is for the most part voluntarily accepted, and if not voluntarily accepted is not legitimate.* The recruit aboard a whaler out of New Bedford in the early 1800s was subjected to ferocious standards of discipline, which could be considered voluntary if the seaman signed the articles and was fully aware of the strict requirement of being a sailor on a whaler. If he were shanghaied aboard, however, or beguiled by

lies from a recruiter, or forced into accepting such a job because he was starving ashore and could only find a single alternative to starving, he could hardly be identified as a volunteer.

Such a voluntary bargain implies that the person entered it freely and willingly, with full knowledge of the demands to be made and the rewards and punishments for success and failure.[3] Yet if the individual actually understood and accepted the stringent requirements, the need for barbaric punishment is questionable. The discipline thus becomes a harsh reminder of the penalities for trying to escape a trap into which the sailor unwittingly stepped.

Yet, the human memory is fallible, and if you are reminded again and again during the hiring interview that your position with the accounting firm entails extensive travel and long hours at certain times of the year, you cannot expect to remake the bargain after employment, to which the employer has committed funds and time. If after entering the business you see more clearly after the fact that which you did not foresee with such clarity, you cannot selectively break the bargain without penalties of one kind or another.

2. *Discipline is not a punishment system, but a shaper of behavior.* Like B. F. Skinner's operant conditioning, the disciplinary action should serve to provide favorable consequences for the right behavior and unfavorable consequences for the wrong behavior. This means that not only are verbal or physical punishments used in a response, but all of the elements in the system that can be conveniently arranged to produce the desired behavior will be employed, and not merely the judiciallike system of accused, prosecutor, judge, and crime and punishment.[4]

On a military base it was noted that young soldiers were slipping over the fence after hours in violation of regulations. Some officers proposed stiff courts-martial. Others proposed issuing live ammunition to sentries. The wise commanding officer, however, discovered that they were visiting local bars. He ordered that beer be sold in the PX throughout the entire evening. The rate of fence jumping dropped considerably.

While we really don't care about the details of the case,

the principle is important. You find the causes of the behavior and arrange the situation so that it won't occur. Nobody was punished, for that was not the objective. The objective is to keep the soldiers in camp. The difference is the avoidance of "principles" to be upheld, and a concentration upon behavior and results.

3. *The past provides useful experience in defining and changing behavior but is not an infallible guide to right and wrong.* The fact that something has been done consistently in the past is, of course, no assurance that it is the best behavior for the present. While it often is, the greatest uses of precedents are in positions where danger, high cost, or excessive losses could result from failure to use the right principle voluntarily the first time. The boss who suggests "do it my way the first time, then, after thinking about it, introduce improvements if you can" is sensing the importance of using experience, while encouraging innovation. The superior is providing a base point for departure.

4. *Contribution to objectives is a reasonable guide as to when to depart from rules and regulations.* When subordinates are well aware of their own objectives and those of their unit, variation from rules and regulations becomes a part of their professional or occupational skill. The engineer who knows when to depart from rules and when not to is a better engineer than one who adheres slavishly to every rule simply because it is a rule. The breaking of a rule, however, when such violation has the effect of being counterproductive and carries the employee or organization away from the desired objectives, should be the subject of some unfavorable attention on the part of the superior. Equally culpable is the individual who adheres strictly to regulations, when the effect of this behavior is such that the organization is served poorly and its movement toward its objectives is impeded or halted.

The tiny voice of the bureaucrat inevitably cries out to establish the presence and presumably sacred nature of the rule and regulation. When bureaucrats are in charge, they punish or reprimand offenses against consistency, precedent, or rules for rules' sake. Their memory for the details of such rules is formidable. Their belief in their sanctity is impressive. Their contribution to objectives is marginal, perhaps ranging as high as nominal.

Yet people who break the rule or the regulation do so at their own risk. They may have done so without full knowledge of objectives, either their own or the organization's. They might make a change for what seems to be a contribution to objectives when, in fact, they are diminishing the total contribution. They may, indeed, on occasion hash the whole plan. It is this latter unseen possibility that should deter responsible people from casual variation for its own sake, just to be different. Not to worship laws and rules as having a special mystique of their own is excellent. Not to hate them blindly is equally sound.

5. *Charts, lists, and compendiums of rules and regulations should be reviewed periodically against organization objectives to see if they are still productive.* In organizations where the system of management by objectives is being utilized, it makes good sense to review the rules periodically and revise the regulations of the organization to prevent absurdities in behavior being enforced upon employees. Where there are no stated objectives, then, of course, such review against them becomes impossible, and the mere listing of activity guides is perfectly logical. Organizations tend to conduct their affairs in a way that is *activity*-centered, or *input*-centered rather than *output*-centered. For such organizations, it thus seems important to keep all of the activity under control.

If input-centered, organizations emphasize discipline to prevent nonconforming use of inputs. The control of expense accounts is the most common application of an input-centered system of management. The manager who makes a trip to New York City where meals and lodging are higher than in Dodge City, Kansas, for example, will be bound by identical regulations for both locations. The possibilities that the objectives of gain attributable to the New York expenses may be far greater than for the Dodge City trip, and therefore should be treated as having different requirements, is contrary to every traditional rule. To the office manager who would prevent such variances, the ultimate logic lies in the statement, "But we simply can't have people setting their own expense rates, or we would be victimized by excessive expenditures." To which the response might well be, "We expect people to set and achieve their own objectives, otherwise we would not achieve breakthroughs and innovations to new heights of organizational achievement."

6. *The application of individual discipline by objectives makes each individual responsible for his or her own output, and the individual differences are explainable in individual results.* It is reported that Alfred P. Sloan, former chief executive officer of General Motors, used the expression, "Did he get the job done?" in response to ordinary complaints that individuals had varied from customary practices or rules on the job. Abraham Lincoln, when told that General Ulysses S. Grant drank whiskey regularly in large amounts, is reported to have replied, "Tell me what kind he drinks. I should like to buy a case for my other generals. I can't spare this man; he fights!"

The point is clear. The exceptional performer in achieving exceptional results should be treated with far greater tolerance when it comes to violation of rules and regulations. This implies a converse rule. The cavalier treatment of ordinary rules of conduct is permissible only to people of exceptional competence and those whose achievements of results against goals is exceptional. Ordinary and below-ordinary people should adhere to the rules until their exceptional excellence is proven.

Are All Forms of Discipline Obsolete?

The steps of shortcutting to reach a goal can be constructive for one person, destructive for another.[5] Having made this distinction, we now face the procedural matters in dealing with destructive kinds of variation. About two million crimes take place in this country each year. Every day over 300 people are killed or feloniously assaulted. Over 3,000 reported thefts occur in an average day, in addition to over 500 car thefts. Clearly this is destructive behavior, and law enforcement is a growing problem.

While the rates of crime in the workplace are proportionately less than they are in the population at large, where crimes are mainly by unemployed and underemployed persons, there is needed a kind of legal system inside the plant and office comparable to the one outside. At the same time, this system of legal codes should draw sharp distinctions between the customary antisocial behavior and the finely honed requirements of conformity to the will of the boss on the job.

The Requirements of Discipline

To make the disciplinary process into a teaching and behavior-change action, some conditions must be met.

1. Rules and regulations should be devised and made known as outlined in the section above.
2. When an apparent violation has occurred, the action taken should occur as close to the time of the violation as is feasible. Holding off discussions of personal behavioral lapses until the "annual performance review" or some future time lessens the behavior change effect.
3. The accused person should be presented with the facts and the source of those facts. "Mr. Smith of the Eliot Store called this morning and stated that you have not taken inventory in his store for two months."
4. If a specific rule is broken, the superior should state that rule. In the above case, for example, "As you know, our rules call for an on-site inventory every two weeks, with a signed report turned in certifying the inventory."
5. The reason for the rule should be given; for example, "Three things can occur if this rule isn't followed. First, the company could lose money because it puts goods in stores on consignment, and the store could go out of business and leave us a big bad debt. Second, the store managers like to have their billings accurate, based upon inventory and not on estimates. Finally, we need the accurate inventory to schedule our production for the month ahead."

6. Ask the apparent offender if he or she agrees that the facts as they have been stated are correct. Then ask what the objective was in following the dilatory behavior. Asking for an "excuse" or "alibi" or even for the reasons places the apparent offender on the defensive and can quickly lead to a fight. Asking about the apparent objectives in behaving as he or she did opens the door to future improvement. By wording, we turn the context from backward-looking to forward-looking behavior.

7. State the corrective action in positive and forward-looking form: "Given your objective of covering more stores in the territory, how can you do that and at the same time meet my three objectives for getting inventory taken?"

Periodic Review of Shop or Office Rules

A continuing source of discontent, especially among young employees, is the existence and enforcement of rules that apparently have no reason—rules made for objectives long since outmoded and forgotten. Development of sound disciplinary policy requires that the personnel department initiate and maintain a review of rules of conduct for the plant or office. As Figure 18.1 shows, such a review should deal with two specific categories for each rule. In the first column, the rule as it now exists should be stated. In the second column a brief statement of the contribution of the rule to objectives should be listed. Where the rule makes a contribution, or prevents something from happening that could diminish contribution, it stays. Some typical contributions to objectives of work rules could be the following:

- Prevents line shutdown.
- Prevents spoilage and repair costs.
- Prevents customer complaints about quality.
- Protects safety of fellow workers.
- Protects safety of the employee.
- Improves yield of line.
- Prevents tool breakage.
- Prevents overexpenditure for small tools.

The rule stated as it presently exists:	The contribution to objectives which this rule makes:
1.	1.

Figure 18.1 Review of plant or office rules.

There are, however, certain rules that have vast powers of survival, for which only the following responses can be found. They should be eliminated unless further study shows them making a contribution to objectives.

- We've always done it that way.
- It's our policy.
- That rule was made out of many, many years of experience.
- The boss (now retired) installed that one.
- Because I want it, dammit!
- It's generally a good thing.
- You wouldn't really know why, so let's not discuss it.
- Don't make waves.
- I don't have time to explain it to you, just do it.

Further study might well reveal a legitimate reason, in the form of a contribution to objectives. It might even be found that rules that are absolutely necessary in one location or department won't be necessary in another. Smoking is not allowed in the plant where volatile liquids are used but may be allowed in the office.

Creative development of discretionary and selectively applied rules is evidence of good management, not bad management. Just as was the case with the no smoking rule, there may be discretionary application of rules affecting attendance, starting and stopping times, time cards, and other matters.

There is no inherent and automatic virtue to consistency when the making of rules is concerned. *Consistency of application* among all of these employees covered by the same rule is, however, necessary to avoid charges of injustice and disputes among employees. You might, for example, suspend the attendance-keeping rules for engineers by eliminating time cards, if it is done for all engineers. You can't selectively single out Jim and make a rule for him alone (unless he or she is a Steinmetz, Shockley, or other genius).

Using Progressive Discipline

For certain kinds of offenses, such as murder, rape, felonious assault, major thefts, deliberate damage to company property, and the like, the first offense is the last, since it is a cause for immediate discharge.

Another category of offense which is worthy of disciplinary attention is less than a cause for immediate discharge, and here the use of progressive discipline applies. Progressive discipline means that the employee is subjected to several stages, each one moving closer to the separation stage, but each one in turn designed to effect a behavior change prior to that move. The stage system used at General Motors, Ford, Chrysler, and numerous other large firms has grown for the most part out of successive tests of its success, as reviewed by arbitrators for equity and fairness to the employee.[6] These steps generally include:

Step 1: First Offense. Instruct the employee in the proper method, explain the rule and its reasons, and explain what the next level of discipline will be for a reoccurrence. *Write the incident in his or her personnel record.*

Step 2: Second Offense. This could be a repeat of the first, or it could be a different offense of a similar magnitude. If a repeat of the first, summarize the instructions, tell the individual that this is a second offense, that this is a reprimand, and that the third step will be a temporary layoff without pay. Explain the reason for this rule. *Write the incident in his or her personnel record.* If the offense is a second offense of a similar magnitude but different in specifics, instruct the employee in the proper method and give a warning of the step that will follow a third offense. *Write the incident in his or her personnel record.*

Step 3: Third Offense. The first-line supervisor should at this stage consult with his or her superior and the personnel department since the issue might become arbitratable. Having verified that the stage is clear, the supervisor instructs the individual and gives him or her a layoff of two to five days without pay, with the warning that a repeat of any similar level offense will result in discharge and the personnel record marked to prevent reemployment. *Write the incident in his or her personnel record.*

Step 4: Discharge. Following a confirmation from the supervisor's superior and the personnel department, the supervisor should discharge the employee. *This should be written up in his or her personnel record,* with recommendations for rehiring or not rehiring.

This brief description of the stages of discipline is based upon successful experience of employers in unionized and in government supervision who have discharged employees and been upheld. Throughout the entire process it should be borne in mind that each move may be subsequently subjected to close scrutiny of an arbitrator, a review board, or a top manager.

Some Umbrella Rules for Discipline

In addition to knowing the general stages, the supervisor should now apply certain rules that hang over the entire disciplinary process itself like an umbrella.[7] Failure in any of these rules could result in the action being reversed.

1. Be certain that a stated rule exists, is clear, and that the employees know the rule.
2. Use a statute of limitations rule for writing up disciplinary incidents. If, for example, an employee breaks a rule and has this entered in his or her record, after six months of good performance without further incidents, remove the record from the file and clear the slate. Do not carry minor incidents over from year to year. Layoff reports could be kept for periods of two to three years.
3. Avoid behavior that creates further incidents. Using profanity (even where it is the ordinary language of the shop) in disciplinary proceedings or physically touching a person invites explosions, anger, and physical responses.
4. Don't apply the procedure inconsistently to individuals, such as

adding a step between steps 2 and 3 or shortening the layoff period for one person, unless the facts are sufficiently different to permit toleration.

5. *Listen* carefully to what the other person says at all times, and note the substance of his or her remarks in the record.

6. *Be certain of your facts* before making your decision. In the rushed life of the business world, wrong perceptions, garbled information, and errors in fact will come easily. Dig as deeply as is necessary to get all of the necessary facts before moving into action.

7. Don't jump the stages for less than discharge offenses because of emotional pressures. This is the most likely cause of reversal by an arbitrator, who will reduce the penalty to the level at which the offense should have been handled. To discharge a person for spoiling work twice would probably result in the employee's being reinstated with full pay, since ordinary practice would call for this stage first.

8. When laid-off employees return to work, don't continue the punishment. They have been instructed, warned, and seen the effects of their own behavior upon themselves. Treat them like any employee. Don't spend any special amount of time checking on them. Be businesslike, neither clubby nor aloof.

9. Avoid entrapment. Setting snares to encourage employees to violate rules in order that the boss may administer the next stage of discipline is bad business. It breeds distrust in the equity and justice of the whole system.

Handling the Nonrule Offense

Certain kinds of behavior requiring supervisory attention do not fall clearly into the rule book but need correction. Say a sales representative habitually tells racist jokes which offend certain customers, and the president of one large company calls to tell you of your subordinate's behavior.

1. If no rule has been broken, don't invent one to cover the situation.

2. Treat nonrule violations as behavioral problems that need coaching and training rather than disciplining.
3. Use feedback and discussion of objectives to effect a behavior change.

In the case of the sales representative the dialogue might go something as follows:

> "Joe, I received a call from Mr. X, president of the Apex Company this morning. He said that you have offended several of his people because you tell jokes about Jews, blacks, and Italians while you are on their premises. He says, further, that they have many such employees and that they are insulted by what you say."
>
> "I don't mean anything. They're just jokes. Where's their sense of humor?"
>
> "I wanted you to know that Mr. X had called, and exactly what he said."
>
> "They're only jokes."
>
> "What would you say your objective is in calling upon Apex?"
>
> "To get orders, of course. But you know you have to have good relations with people, and a sense of humor and being cheerful is part of getting good relations."
>
> "Given your objective of getting orders through being cheerful, using jokes, how would you say your action is working in getting you to your objectives?"

Notice what the boss didn't say or do:

- He didn't teach about racism.
- He didn't lecture Joe on his stupidity.
- He didn't use satire or sarcasm.
- He didn't agree or sympathize with Joe.
- He didn't prescribe, "Now here is what you must do. . . ."

The emphasis here is upon behavior change, through concentrating on responsible behavior in the future. He presented the facts as he heard them, avoided generalizations and sweeping charges, and used a socratic discussion to permit Joe to obtain insight through seeing his own problem. Once Joe sees the objective and the problem, he can start discussing some *optional plans* for solving the problem.

> "What do you think you should do next, Joe?"
>
> "Well, I guess I'd better quit using jokes, even become a sourpuss if that's what they want."

"All jokes?"

"Well, at least the ones about race and religion. I guess I could also apologize over there to some of the people I run into. Maybe I could get a new stock of jokes, too."

"Sounds as if you have a good plan, Joe. Now is there anything you think I can do to help?"

"Sure, Apex is a big account and makes up a large chunk of my business. If you could call the president and tell him you talked to me, and I was startled and plan to apologize and lay off the bum jokes in the future, that might help. Tell him I appreciated the call, too."

The details of the case are, of course, more complex, but it illustrates the principle. What appears to be a discipline case becomes a teaching and coaching incident. There is no useful purpose to writing up this incident. The personnel-centered manager who builds subordinates through coaching has hundreds of such incidents each year. They comprise the ordinary fabric of management and should not be treated as disciplinary incidents.

This blending of discipline and coaching, or remedial rather than punitive discipline, is centered around the achievement of objectives rather than the extermination of sin.

CHAPTER 19

The Problem of the Annual Performance Review

A thick skin is a gift from God.

—Konrad Adenauer

There is no special significance in managerial performance being reviewed *annually*. The underlying value of performance appraisal is the opportunity it affords to feed back results against goals in order to improve performance. This does not necessarily have to take place at year's end, as if it magically coincided with the rotation of the earth on its axis, like a pagan holiday. It is merely convenient for some purposes.

For example, though budget and profit statements are made annually to stockholders, they are also released quarterly to stockholders, and monthly to officers. Similarly, budgets for coming years and estimated sales forecasts are made up by the year with quarterly estimates as well. Even tax bills are no longer annual events, now that payments of estimated tax have to be made quarterly.

Salary reviews are more and more likely to come at times other than at some period based upon the rotation of the earth around the sun. At higher levels, salaries may be reviewed only every eighteen months or two years. By contrast, the salaries of new hires in the clerical ranks are reviewed after three months. Some salary reviews do fall annually, but this practice is being dispensed with in many firms.

Annual Reviews and Management Superstitions

A year seems to be the customary time interval for performance reviews, but there are some definite dangers to be skirted in adhering to this schedule.

Many annual reviews as presently conducted lead to managerial superstitions, which have a distracting, or positively damaging, effect upon people's performance. That is to say, they lead subordinates into unnecessary and irrelevant acts based upon the false supposition that such behavior will bring about better reviews. This is the same pattern of behavior as that exhibited by small boys just before Christmas, and may be called the "Santa Claus" effect.

In Figure 19.1, the line represents a chronological pattern of events involving feedback to a subordinate of the boss's satisfaction or dissatisfaction with results. At point A an action that the boss expects occurs (or fails to occur). At point B the boss does the annual review of performance, at which time he or she takes the opportunity to lash the subordinate for the failure back at A. To the subordinate, however, recent event C, which is quite unrelated to A, immediately comes to mind as being the real reason for the boss's outburst. Here's an actual example:

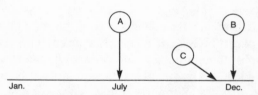

Figure 19.1 How employee misunderstands cause of boss's dissatisfaction.

A department head casually asked one of his subordinate managers to investigate a problem and write him a report. "No hurry," the boss said. "I'd like to have it in a month or so." The subordinate got caught up in some emergencies and wasn't able to turn in the report. By the time he thought of it again, several months had gone by. His boss waited to mention the matter until the end of the year, about eight months after he had asked for the report. Then, in his annual review, he stormed at the subordinate for his laxity, his carelessness, his indifference, and other personal inadequacies.

What was the subordinate's reaction? "I'll never forget an order again"? No. The first thing the subordinate did was to race back over the events of the past few days and try to figure out what had happened to trigger such abuse. He finally fastened upon a minor episode two days before, when he had stepped aboard an elevator ahead of his boss and the door had immediately closed and left the boss standing in the corridor. He recalled that his boss had been a high-ranking army officer. He went back over the interview and singled out several references to his "desire to get to the top too fast." Putting all these clues together, he wound up firmly convinced that his boss had administered the tongue lashing simply because of the elevator incident. He thereupon determined never again to beat the boss to an elevator and proceeded to pass this superstition along to his peers.

Now, as it happened, the boss had not even wanted to board the elevator in question. He was headed down, and the available car was headed up. What he could not figure out was how the subordinate could have missed a message as clear as the one he gave.

This story underscores an important point about the timing of the performance: *Prompt feedback is far more important in changing behavior than intensity of feedback.*

In other words, if the goal is to change behavior, the feedback of evidence of success or failure in reaching goals should be instantaneous, not deferred until some procedural or ceremonial moment.[1]

Under such a system, the annual review becomes a *cumulative* summary of the specific results previously fed back. Cumulative is simply another way of saying, "No surprises in the annual review." If your subordinate failed to deliver by some specific date in May and you never mentioned it, then forget it at the review time as well. Not only will there be no improvement as a result of your comment, but there is also a distinct possibility that you will trigger a superstitious change of behavior that you cannot predict.

Yet, adhering to the principle of instantaneous feedback poses two questions:

1. Does this mean that you spend all your time feeding back information about success or failure?
2. How do you avoid nagging and overly close supervision?

The Best Way to Measure Success

The answer to the first question is no—we should not assume that the only kind of feedback that changes behavior is the kind that comes personally from the boss. Even better is the feedback subordinates can *give themselves* through measuring their own rate of progress and their own goal achievement. This they do by having their goals clear, and the many variables that comprise success, such as time, cost, quantity, quality service, and results, under their own control.

For instance, if you are an isolated plant manager who must read the daily results of your plant's output and other measures of plant performance, you should be able to know whether you are running a successful plant or not at the very moment you get your reports together to forward to headquarters. If you must wait for a return letter or wire to know whether you are doing a good job, you are being denied a real opportunity for growth in the job. Self-measurement against predetermined standards is superior to the boss's measurement of results.[2] Self-measurement may, however, have a diminishing effect if there is no cumulative review at the quarter, half year, or annual period.

Such a system makes the job itself a teaching and learning situation for the manager, using the known principles of learner participation and immediate confirmation of correct responses. If, at first glance, it might seem to some managers too much of a release of control over operations for them to permit this self-measurement, closer scrutiny will show that it is, in reality, a more coherent and controlled approach to learning.

How to Avoid Nagging

It is futile to nag people into changing their behavior. *Nagging,* in the sense used here, consists of punishing subordinates for failure to achieve results they did not know they were expected to deliver.

You are nagging, for example, when you await action, then descend either heavily or merely steadily upon those aspects of it that are bad, without having told your subordinates that such measurements were going to be made.

For the boss personally to pronounce success or failure judgments without having first established goals and measures of their achievement is nagging. It has only a slow and tortuous effect in changing behavior. Nagging can change behavior only to this extent: it punishes behavior people didn't know they were being measured by. Hence, they feel cheated and unjustly punished. They resent the injustice and may rebel against the boss or the organization that placed them in such a situation. To the extent, however, that they stop doing whatever it was that elicited the punishment, they have acquired a new kind of measurement and a guide to behavior. This effect can be achieved without primitive methods, however, and the resentment and emotional upset that accompanies this upside-down teaching method can be avoided.

The most favorable context for this melding of appraisal and discipline is that in which the superior views discipline as a teaching or behavior-changing process rather than as a form of retribution. This process is identical with the procedure followed in using appraisal as a means of management development:

- The standards of behavior are spelled out specifically as a guide to action in the future.
- The individual's behavior is weighed against the standards that have been amply communicated to let him or her know the results expected.
- When an error occurs, the severity of the feedback is commensurate with the seriousness of the lapse and should always, within practical limits, follow immediately upon the discovery of the error.

The Case for the Annual Review

In the business strategy of management development, the set of procedures known as *appraisal* is an important technique. It is also a difficult one, as many of us have found out. Briefly, the rationale behind the appraisal of subordinates by their superiors is that this procedure, well carried out, will improve the subordinates' effectiveness.[3]

In procedures that aim at discovering the worth and capacities of other people and spurring them to greater effort, we know some things for sure, and in some areas we are flying blind. Perhaps it might be good to begin with the ideas that experience in administrative organization has shown hold up. After this, we can explore some of the areas where we are far less certain as to the outcome of what we do.

On our list of accepted facts are the following:

1. In motivating people to be productive and creative in their work, we cannot rely on money alone. This conclusion is based not only on psychology but also on economics. If we hire young people fresh out of college at age twenty and plan to employ them until age sixty-five, there is a forty-five year span during which we must raise and maintain a satisfactory pay level for them. This level of pay has as its floor sufficient productivity or creativity to recoup the costs of salaries and fringe benefits paid to them and the other expenses of housing them at work, equipping them with tools, and providing them with materials. Simple arithmetic tells us that we shall quickly run out of money to recharge their motivational batteries. For example, if we tried to give them a 10 percent increase in pay each year until they retired, they would each wind up with an annual salary of six figures.

2. While it might be possible in individual cases to maintain such a steady and large infusion of cash, this would be patently impossible for the company's entire work force. What then serves to motivate the individual who cannot be rewarded or spurred by money alone? This question becomes the important problem in motivation, and the economic fact that underlies the necessity of this seemingly sentimental question forces us into considering the feasibility of nonfinancial incentives.[4]

3. In times of prosperity and full employment, we must rule out the negative motivation supplied by the employee's fears of being laid off or of economic reprisal for less than excellent performance. In dealing with skilled employees, the emphasis moves toward some *positive* means of nonfinancial motivation, and it is within this environment that most of our modern systems of appraisal have been developed. Of course, these nonfinancial motivations must be combined with economically feasible financial motivation as well, but the nonfinancial motivations cause us more difficulties in management than do most others.

4. In good and bad times alike, we must face the fact that neither fear of economic punishment nor desire for economic reward

can explain the full scope of human motivation. We may further assume, as Douglas McGregor does, that most people do have a desire to succeed, will work to achieve this success, and in so doing will exercise self-control, will accept and seek out responsibility, will exercise their creativity and productivity, and will work diligently to achieve corporate goals when these provide them with social and ego satisfactions. Assuming such things about people requires that we look again at our systems of appraisals to be certain that they are rooted firmly in the best understanding we have of human motivation.

5. Finally, we probably all know by this time that the appraisal process is just as much a reflection of the manager making the appraisal as it is of the person appraised. What the judge considers right and wrong is probably more important in many respects than the qualifications or actions of the defendant before the bar.

The theory of appraisals is that employees can be positively motivated to a considerable degree by their superior's following two basic precepts:

1. He or she lets subordinates know what is expected of them—what constitutes good performance and what constitutes unsatisfactory performance.

2. The superior uses these standards of good and poor performance subsequently to let employees know how well—or poorly—they have performed over a specified period just completed. This appraisal is both continuous and cumulative. The superior does it constantly during the day-to-day course of administration, and also accumulates these observations and sums them up in a periodic review.

On these things, all those who have thought about the subject are probably fairly well agreed. On many other matters, they are not in agreement at all. Nevertheless, this disagreement itself is important, since it lays bare the fact that all is not perfect in the systems presently used for appraising subordinates and that much more research and experience are needed before we can rely upon appraisals to do all the motivating of people we'd like to have them do.[5]

Just how serious is this disagreement over appraisal methods?

The Battle over Appraisals

Many years ago some colleagues and I were preparing materials for a filmstrip on management development. The film was designed to explain to a company how management development worked and could help it in conducting its business. The third section of the film was to be on the subject of *management appraisal*. To ensure that the best and latest techniques were incorporated in the film, we invited a number of authorities on management development to sit down and confer with us on the subject and set us straight about what was right and wrong in management appraisal.

The result, of course, was chaos. Nobody could agree with anyone else—and this disagreement over philosophy and method in appraising the performance of subordinates continues without much letup among other spokesmen in the field. All these experts, it should be noted, deal with performance reviews as *annual* events.

In the modern corporation—the dominant economic institution of our time—this conflict is especially important. Thus, it is more essential than ever that we choose the successors to top management positions from among able and proven people possessing a sound sense of values. Practically all the people who will be running the great corporations in the future will be from the ranks of outsiders—that is, from the people who do not own the property they manage.

Most managers and top executives will work their way up the corporate ladder according to how effectively they comply with the demands of the appraisal systems that rate them. In our zeal for developing ingenious systems of appraisal, we must never forget this fact. Such conferences as these, in which "professionals" in appraisal rethink their systems of rating people, are vitally important simply because the resulting appraisal systems will be the vehicles through which some people rise in the organization and others do not.

The real test of appraisal, then, is not whether it makes people uneasy or whether it has full regard for the sensitivities of those who are chosen or not chosen; the vital test is whether the system allows the right managers to rise and prevents others from doing so. Assuming, as we must, that the managers of the corporation in the future will be principally wielders of "power without property," as Adolph Berle has labeled them, the basic scale of rightness or wrongness of appraisal as a method of managerial selection will look something like this:

1. Appraisal must identify able employees who have proven themselves competent and qualified for leadership in our business institutions through *performance* on lesser jobs, and have shown evidences of ability to assume bigger jobs.
2. The systems must be simple and the people must be easily *recognizable* as being the best.
3. The people chosen for leadership must have a high degree of *acceptability* to those who are left behind, since the latter will be ruled by those who were successful. As Gordon Rattray Taylor puts it, leadership today means that *"leaders must have the ability to prove their right to rule."*
4. Those chosen must have a proper *value* orientation for leadership in our society. In other words, their qualities as total human beings, apart from those traits described on a form, must be suitable.

What Are the Technical Flaws?

We have all read and reread those volleys and thunderings about the problems appraisal presents. Many of them seem to center on the fact that the annual interview between employee and boss, during which the subordinate is told how others assess him or her, is difficult, if not impossible, for the average line manager to carry out. Trained psychologists and counseling experts, who after years of experience have failed to counsel people effectively, have honest uneasiness about what happens when "talented amateurs" try to tell their subordinates about their shortcomings—and, more importantly, what they should do to improve. Yet the ticklish process of one person's telling another about his or her inadequacies is not the vital flaw in the whole procedure. The basic technical flaw in most appraisal systems is the lack of adequate *standards of performance* for the management job.

Let us look first at the subject of technique, and the four ways now most commonly used to set standards of performance:

1. Measure of a Person Against a List of Personality Traits

Perhaps the weakest of all methods of measuring and appraising a person is the use of a predetermined list of personality traits against which the manager is expected to rate subordinates. For one thing, as this book has frequently emphasized, we aren't at all sure what traits are necessary in a manager. For another, it's impossible for nonexperts to identify, let alone attach relative values to, the traits they are supposed to use in rating their subordinates. No doubt a trained clinician might be able through interviews, tests, and so on to ascertain whether or not a person is trustworthy, loyal, helpful, friendly, courteous, kind, obedient, cheerful, thrifty, brave, clean, and reverent. Most of us, though, aren't sophisticated enough to grasp precisely the meaning of such adjectives, even with the help of the handy glossary attached to the chart, to say nothing of measuring these things precisely. Moreover, we can not do it much better in a committee than we can working alone. And even if we could, none of us is competent enough to be able to fasten upon the weak personality traits and then, in a private interview in the executive office, express our views to the subordinate with sufficient persuasiveness and clarity to induce any significant change. Because the standards are unclear, the appraisal will probably be faulty.[6]

2. Highest-to-Lowest Person-to-Person Ranking

Still another technique of rating is that of sorting out a group of people according to their worth and ability and ranking them from highest to lowest. Here, too, the flaws are of sufficient magnitude to cast doubt upon the system's efficacy. The standards again are unclear. For one thing, we know that in a sizable group of people only the very good and the very poor can be clearly discriminated by this ranking system. The vast majority will fall into the middle ranges, leaving us with no option but to say to most people, "I can't find anything seriously wrong to complain about or wonderfully great to praise you for."

Another flaw in this system arises when we try to match up the ranking of one group with the ranking of another. We can never know whether the best person in Group X is better or worse than the best one in Group Y. In fact, it's possible that the best in Group X isn't as good as the worst in Group Y. The graduate school at Princeton, for example, is open only to the top 2 percent of those in undergraduate school. As a result, their poorest graduate student is probably superior to the top student at Podunk U. Yet, Princeton reports that there are vast differences in abilities even among the members of its select graduate group.

In any case, you cannot expect to improve Mr. Adam's performance when all you have to report to him is, "You aren't quite so good as Mr. Baker, but you are superior to Mr. Charles." Parents learn quickly that invidious comparison is a poor method of stimulating their less accomplished children. Nor does it work with mature employees. If, therefore, you cannot use it for improvement, it is certainly not a suitable instrument for evaluation. For certain purposes, ranking has value—in merit rating for salary administration, for example. But its limitations are great. Because the standard is "alikeness," it may result in a triumph of mediocrity in management.

3. The Master Scale of Managerial Performance

This is a scale that describes the general qualities required on management jobs or staff positions against which the performance of employees is matched. Once again we run into standards that are very shifty in nature. The hitch here is the assumption that we know what good management is. Thus, we find master charts requiring people to be rated on their ability to organize, to plan, to control others, to motivate and inspire employees, to conceptualize, to integrate, to be productive, to be creative, and to delegate. It is a fairly safe assumption that these things are what successful executives do. We are less certain that the boss has sufficient discretionary ability to judge a person's ability in each of these areas.

Perhaps there may some day be a master scale of things that every successful manager does. As yet, however, there is no full agreement on this point among companies or among managers. This system also requires that people who are perhaps not themselves good managers rate the managerial competence of others who may have more real executive ability than they do. As more able people are hired from the colleges or from competitors and placed under the supervision of managers selected under earlier and less rigorous standards, the chances are that most ratings of subordinates by superiors will be inadequate because of the inferior knowledge of the boss as to what constitutes good management.

In short, master scales of "what successful managers do" are often constructed by people without genuine knowledge of the management job for use by inferior people over superior ones. One suspects that such a system can hardly produce much that is very good.

It will probably be generally agreed that some progress has been made in the selection, placement, and training of managers over the past twenty years. This improved utilization of staffing must have placed many people of superior aptitude for the job under the supervision of many who have less aptitude for it. In short, in all too many cases today, experience and seniority alone are the accidental causes for one person's being the boss and the other the subordinate. Yet we persist in asking this boss to appraise as if he or she were just as competent.

This improvement through the passing on of accumulated knowledge is evident in the colleges. A former dean at Harvard University told how he once received a frantic call from the father of a boy who had been rejected by the university's admissions committee. "Why," the father protested, "I graduated from Harvard and this boy of mine is much smarter and more able than I ever was."

"Let's face it," the dean replied. "Neither you nor I could be admitted to Harvard today, if we applied on the basis of our records through prep school."

In fact, a high percentage of college graduates might have a tough time today gaining admission to the colleges they graduated from in their youth.

4. Mixing Appraisal of Performance and Potential

The rating of potential will be discussed in more detail in the following chapter. Here it may be said that in appraisals designed to serve this dual purpose, there is an overwhelming tendency to overlook present performance and rate employees high or low on the basis of an estimate of how far they will go in the organization.

Take the case of Dr. X, who is a researcher. Dr. X has a high IQ and a brilliant mind. Nobody can deny that he has potential. Yet when we come to rating him for an increase, we should ask, "What has he *done?"* Often this is an embarrassing question to ask about such a brilliant person, especially when, on further examination, it appears that he has not really done a darned thing. At this point, we slide our system away from performance into potential and reward him for hoped-for things to come.

In some instances, the reverse of this is true. Take the case of old Jim Smith. Jim is a solid citizen who managed to pull off a couple of deals that made the company a lot of money last year. Do we pay off during the appraisal time for these accomplishments? Only in part— because Jim isn't going anywhere in this company. We don't want to push things too hard, so we fudge a little on the appraisal and take off some points for his lack of potential.

Some Common Flaws in All Systems

Whatever appraisal system is used, if the standards are vague, the procedure will suffer from one of two main kinds of flaws:
1. The halo effect.
2. The hypercritical or "horns" effect.

The Halo Effect

The halo effect is the tendency of the boss to hang a halo over the rating of a favored employee. This can happen for a variety of reasons:

1. Effect of Past Record. Because people have done good work in the distant past, their performance is assumed to be O.K. in the recent past, too. Their good work tends to carry over into the current rating period.

2. Compatibility. There is a tendency to rate people whom we find pleasing in manner and personality higher than they deserve. Those who agree with us, nod their heads when we talk, or, even better, make notes of our words get better ratings than their performance justifies.

3. Effect of Recency. The person who did an outstanding job last week or yesterday can offset a mediocre performance over the rest of the year by this single act.

4. One Strong Asset. The glib talker, the person with the impressive appearance, the one with advanced degrees, or the graduate of the boss's own alma mater gets a more favorable rating than the subordinate lacking these often irrelevant attributes.

5. The Blind-Spot Effect. This is the case where the boss does not see certain types of defects because they are just like his or her own. The boss who is a big thinker may not appreciate a detail man, for example.

6. The High-Potential Effect. We judge employees' paper records rather than what they have done for the organization.

7. The No-Complaints Bias. Here the appraiser treats no news as good news. If the subordinate has no complaints, everything is terrific. The employee who pesters the boss but gets the job done is rated lower than the silent, solitary dud.

The Hypercritical or "Horns" Effect

This is the reverse of the halo effect—the tendency to rate people lower than the circumstances justify. Some specific causes of this are the following:

1. The Boss Is a Perfectionist. With expectations so high, the boss is more often disappointed and so rates people lower than they deserve.

2. The Subordinate Is Contrary. Here the boss vents private irritation with the employee's tendency to disagree with him or her too often on too many issues.

3. The Odd-Ball Effect. Despite all the lip-service to nonconformity, it all too seldom finds its way into practice when appraisal time comes around. The odd ball, the maverick, and the nonconformist get low ratings simply because they are "different."

4. Membership in a Weak Team. A good player on a weak team will end up with lower ratings than one playing on a winning team.

5. The Guilt-by-Association Effect. People who are not really known will often be judged by the company they keep. If they hang out with a frivolous crowd or work for the wrong boss, they are due for some reductions in rating.

6. The Dramatic-Incident Effect. A recent goof can wipe out the effect of years of good work and give a person a low rating on the latest appraisal.

7. The Personality-Trait Effect. People who are too cocky, too brash, too meek, too passive, or otherwise lack some trait the boss associates with "good" subordinates will suffer in their rating accordingly.

8. The Self-Comparison Effect. People who don't do the job as their bosses remember they did it when they held that job will suffer more than those whose jobs the bosses are not too familiar with.

In short, ratings, founded as they are on human perception and judgment, must naturally be inaccurate. In industrial engineering, where greater precision can be attained, judgment is held to be impossible for closer than differences of 15 percent in rate of effort. How much more imprecise, then, must be the judgments on the performance of staff people, supervisors, office employees, and executives?

Over and above the problems inherent in the rating process, there are other complications making it difficult to construct foolproof or even workable systems of appraisals. To name but a few:

1. In large, decentralized companies, a high percentage of appraisals must be done *in absentia*. Plant managers are rated by a person who may only see and talk to them once a month or less.
2. With company growth and job transfers proceeding at such a high rate, a substantial number of managers being appraised at any one time are likely to be working for people who have not had sufficient time to observe them in order to make good judgments about their performance.
3. Many ratings have to be made on indirect information or insuf-

ficient observation. Except where close, daily, personal contact is possible, rating is often done on the basis of perfunctory knowledge, hearsay evidence, or results that cannot be directly related to the efforts of the person being appraised.

It seems to be abundantly clear that the solution to the appraisal problem is to devise better standards of performance for each job. The boss must sit down with each subordinate and work out an agreement about what conditions will exist if the subordinate's job is well done. Then the two of them can develop some objective standards of performance. At the end of six months or a year, the mutually agreed-upon objectives are reviewed and the results the subordinate has accomplished are matched against them.

This eliminates the confusion over measuring traits. It obviates the necessity for boss-subordinate rating because the subordinate's work results are measured against his or her agreed-upon objectives. There is no need to define what makes for good "managerial ability." Nor is there any attempt to measure potential. Moreover, the system simplifies the problems of counseling because both persons are discussing work results rather than the subordinate and his or her shortcomings as a human being.

The Limitations of Management by Objectives

Yet despite its obvious advantages over other appraisal methods, management by objectives is not perfect—or even close to it.[7] As a rule, those who install and develop the system understand it quite well, but this is not so true of those to whom it is applied. To the subordinate, it often looks and smells quite like old-fashioned merit rating. And it has no clear-cut name that marks it off from other methods of appraisal. It has been called the "management by objectives" method of appraisal. It has also been called the "results approach," "performance budget and review," and so on. Moreover, at its best, it has certain limitations:

1. It cannot appraise nor completely identify potential. The system deals only with performance on the present job. *Appraisal of potential must be done separately.* To establish that fact, and to show how it contributes only part of identifying potential, see Figure 20.1 on page 259 of the next chapter.

2. The system presumes that subordinate and boss will together establish suitable standards that will serve the company well.
3. It implies that the boss understands the strict limitations on what he or she is supposed to do and will refrain from playing God.
4. In action, it often aggravates a problem that appraisal should help to solve. It stresses results alone and does not provide for methods of achieving them.

What Values Belong in Managerial Performance Standards?

All the above problems and pitfalls in performance appraisal are, of course, familiar to anyone who has studied the subject. Time and again, however, this whole business of establishing standards of performance comes up against a problem that nobody has successfully solved as yet. This problem is how to set fair and accurate standards that do not result in conformity. *The fact of the matter is that most appraisal systems used in industry today are based on standards that merely make it easy for the boss to fill out a checklist and recite the results back to the hapless subordinate to force him or her to conform.*

This can hardly be called adequate for free people living in a free society. The result is often the creation of *neutral* systems of appraisal. Neutrality toward some of the basic values upon which our business and social system is founded means that our appraisal systems labor mightily to measure one major quality of people—their *alikeness*. This is sometimes labeled conformity, and the product has sometimes been called the "organization man." Perhaps, then, we should think harder and better about how to achieve appraisal systems that will identify people with the human values and lift them out of the ranks into positions of responsibility, while at the same time carefully but surely preventing conformity-creative systems from gaining control of our business institutions.[8]

Using value systems as a standard for executive appraisal is admittedly an uncomfortable step but one that seems to be necessary if business is to overcome the deadening effects of conformity and repression of the individual. A system that merely polices alikeness and conformity does not take account of values. Its standards are neutral ones and deal only with performance. This could be dangerous.

Recently a manager, discussing his company's appraisal system, remarked to me, "The whole system is Machiavellian." Intrigued by this statement, I looked into Machiavelli's *The Prince* and found that he had indeed touched on the subject of merit rating:

> A prince must show himself a lover of merit, give preferment to the able, and honor those who excel in every art.

Though Machiavelli gave no hints as to how this was to be done, there is substance here about which every manager might think. Obviously, from our knowledge of Niccolo Machiavelli and his philosophy, we can read this statement as advocating the manipulation of people by the autocratic leader. Robert McMurry advocated the same thing some years ago in an article in the *Harvard Business Review* entitled "The Case for Benevolent Autocracy." Machiavelli's phrase suggests, too, that simply rewarding performance is no indicator of greatness of spirit on the part of a manager and that many appraisal systems today, even those which purport otherwise, are but thinly disguised means of manipulating people. It also points up the fact that rewarding performance alone through devising a clever system of appraisal does not accomplish all the ends we could desire from modern personnel management in choosing business leaders. If appraisals become mere systems of biological quality control designed to reject those who have lesser qualities of physical bearing, mental capacity, and social adjustment, they are as dangerous as Aldous Huxley's Fertilizing Room.

This love of merit, which gives preferment to the able and honors those who excel, is a minimum requirement, but it is essentially *neutral*. Achieving this first step is hardly worth praising oneself—even if it is being done effectively. The second step is the building of *value systems* into the appraisal of people for leadership positions. This, of course, is far less tangible, systematic, or possible to measure. Yet it is probably the essential ingredient in the whole process.

The point of all this is that *technique* is always neutral, even the techniques of social science. Many appraisal forms used in industry today could be applied just as effectively to the dedicated Communist manager of a steel mill in the Urals as to the manager of a steel mill in Pennsylvania, and would rank both equal on the same things. Yet if we look at the value environments in which these respective institutions operate, we become uneasy that such an equality of rating could exist. It occurs to us that perhaps there should be some further standard for being a manager in a free world rather than in a regimented one. The value environment in which the executive operates is not neutral; it stands for something. Speaking of this value environment, Professor David Moore has said:

> The most important environment in which the executive operates is what we might call the *value environment* of our particular society. An executive is a creature of our society; he operates an institution which is a segment of our society; he is part of our ongoing history. . . . The decisions which he makes will have important repercussions throughout society even though he may see his decisions as affecting only his own business.

The question here, of course, is *where do these values come from?* Can they be built into appraisals?

Can We Get Value Standards from Top Management?

If we study the appraisal systems in most large companies, we see the values of adjustment, compliance, and conformity strewn throughout the procedures whereby managers are measured, paid, and promoted. How do you suppose store managers or the plant superintendents adapt their value systems to the speeches of a board chairman whom they have never met or to their regular face-to-face contacts with a local boss armed with a checklist that puts a premium on not sticking one's neck out?

Can We Look to the Colleges to Build These Values into Management?

Not for long. How much nonconformity may we expect so long as companies come to colleges looking for "adaptable" young men? Once a group of campus recruiters was asked what trait they most often sought in a college graduate. "Maturity," they said. Pressed to define the term, they explained that it meant that the student was "at ease with the recruiter, talked as an equal, and had no eccentric habits."

"I liked that boy," one recruiter remarked. "But he had a beard, and I just couldn't bring him into the office for an interview because I knew what our executives would think."

Is Public Relations Our Best Source of Values?

The speeches so many executives read are written by a committee of public relations ghosts. In one large midwestern corporation I happened to be present when a young Ph.D. was instructed to prepare a stirring speech, in favor of individualism and deploring group behavior, for his president to deliver at a conference. "Remember," his PR boss told him, "make enough copies so we can circulate it and get reactions from all around. Most of the group heads will probably have some edges they want knocked off, so don't let too much *pride of authorship* cause you to be disappointed when it's amended."

Is the President the Best Source?

In some organizations the president who sincerely feels the need for more individuality and nonconformity in the ranks is persuaded to take part in the appraisal system, even to the extent of doing an appraisal of the vice-presidents. Sometimes, this is a purely ceremonial act, like that of the President of the United States throwing out the first ball at the beginning of the baseball season. In some cases, though, it is a genuine example of the use of appraisal techniques by a dominant chief for the purpose of bringing lieutenants into line.

In such cases, though, it is more probable that the president is following staff advice and using the form they have devised. Persuaded to use the appraisal system under these circumstances, it is most unlikely that the president will swim upstream against it and arrive at any conclusions different from those built into it by its designers. One of the heroes of our time is the vice-president of a large retail chain who was invited into the boss's office and informed he was about to be subjected to a periodic performance appraisal. Leaning coldly over the president's desk, he grated: "Look, Max, if you don't like my work, just say so right now without fooling around with any form. I'll get on that telephone and in ten minutes I'll be merchandising vice-president for the store up the street."

The president beat a hasty retreat, and appraisal was henceforth limited to those in lesser ranks, who had no such freedom to give vent to their tongues and their souls.

Does Management by Objectives Build in Values?

Do we find less conformity when subordinates themselves set their standards of performance, working jointly with the boss? It must be admitted that no such favorable effect is likely to ensue if the plan merely provides a new design for the annual review. Rather than being democratic, such plans are often merely sophisticated forms of manipulation that become more acceptable to the governed because they have an air of democracy about them. Yet self-expression is more likely to occur where appraisals are based on results than upon subjective opinions.

This leads us to the conclusion that annual appraisals are too often part of the control mechanism by which a leader secures conformity from the lesser ranks. Their sole advantage is that, through more sophisticated techniques, the harness chafes a little less.

The biggest flaw in the annual appraisal interview is that the essential humanity of the person being appraised is, in almost every system, minimized or eliminated. Here's how Alan Harrington described the process in his satirical book, *Life in the Crystal Palace:*

> How can you come to know a man by means of the standardized interview, or nondirective question? The first pours your talk into a predetermined formal order; the second is designed through artful phrasing to *bring out* the job seeker, make him talk. Well, he will follow your order and he will talk, no doubt as you want him to. But curiously enough, with all these psychological maneuverings directed toward the discovery of a human being, an element of humanity is missing. You, the interviewer are the missing element— for the interviewer naïvely expects to receive honest personal answers to contrived impersonal questions.

The most damning thing about the annual appraisal interview is that the human qualities of both parties are set aside for its duration. It is not a communication between two human beings. It is *method* interviewing, a *collection of attributes*. When it becomes nondirective, superiors must pretend a concern they do not feel. If they do feel a concern, they must hide it. This sham must ultimately become apparent to the subordinate, so that the faked concern or faked neutrality of the boss is met by faked experience and faked attitudes on the part of the subordinate. Superiors who conduct many such interviews soon lose their personality—along with that of the subordinate—when they are engaged in the process. After several such sessions, you find two actors talking past each other at the Psychological Corporation.

Take the common appraisal question that asks the subordinate to list for the boss his or her principal weaknesses. Who but a fool would hand the boss on a silver platter any *real* weaknesses? The question practically demands that anyone with any wits at all lie like Judas.

Or consider the frequent recommendation, "Praise first, then tell the subordinate the weaknesses as you see them." How many times do perceptive persons have to go through this process before they learn to discount as sheer manipulative fluff the one thing they have a right to expect—honest appreciation of a job in practicing their professions? As one man told me, "During the appraisal interview I just shrug off all the tripe he's putting out about my good work, and wait for the part that follows the BUT. . . ."

Within the framework of the management-by-objectives system, the annual review offers the hope of avoiding these damaging effects, provided it is identified as a goal-setting meeting instead of an appraisal interview.[9] Such an approach is positive in tone, looks forward rather than backward, yet at the same time requires a summarizing of past events to lay the groundwork for establishing goals and standards for the future. Thus, the cumulative feedback of results attained is not eliminated but takes place within the context of a meaningful behavioral purpose.

A goal-setting meeting must naturally take into account the significant events of the recent past that have brought the two to the position they are now in. Thus, the context becomes behavioral in the true sense of being concerned with "activity that can be seen or measured." The outcome is a learning situation; that is, aimed at "changing behavior." There are no sociopsychological discussions of such matters as personality, motivation, and perception. By starting with measurable activity and digging into its causes, the discussion evolves naturally along the lines best calculated to enable all managers to find for themselves the answer to the key question: "What can I do, do differently, or stop doing that will get better results in my management job?"

Setting Standards for Social Responsibility

During the seventies a whole host of new laws, regulations, and customs emerged governing the behavior of the corporation and business firms. Affirmative action, occupational safety, consumer safety, product liability and safety, and environmental laws are now part of the standards of performance for managers. *A set of objectives for managers that omits social responsibility indicators will not stand the test of the eighties and beyond.*

There are values that society has placed upon itself and its institutions, and if objectives and appraisals aren't kept in tune with those social values through internal techniques and systems, then the government and its regulatory agencies will come in to force management to change. For most managers this means that the following value-laden objectives must be included in every manager's goals and appraisals:

1. The organization and its managers must obey the law.
2. The major threats and risks of the future may be in the area of changing values, and thus the firm must respond to such changes quickly. Each year's goals should be reviewed to bring them up to date with changing requirements from the outside.

Value changes will require more environmental scanning by managers to find out what the prevailing values of society have become, for it is in the social environment that values are formed, not within the company ranks.

CHAPTER 20

Six Factors in Assessing Potential

Every soldier in my armies carries a marshal's baton in his knapsack.

—Napoleon Bonaparte

One of the most confusing aspects of appraisal is how to estimate a person's potential for advancement at the same time as one is rating current performance for the purpose of improving it in the future. The belief that both these things can and should be done at the same time leads many firms to construct a form that is designed to serve both aims and is communicated to the individual at the same session. This kind of form often sets forth down the left margin a list of items to be checked. Some of these are clearly measures of present performance and others are personality traits or generalized character descriptions whose purpose is to aid in predicting the ratee's future behavior. This predicting of behavior on the basis of personality traits and generalized characteristics is usually regarded as constituting appraisal of the person's potential.[1]

As a general rule it may be stated that appraising performance and potential at the same time is a mistake.

How Performance and Potential Relate

The relationship between performance and potential in the appraisal process is indicated in Figure 20.1. Performance of a more than satisfactory nature is ordinarily considered necessary for promotion to a higher level of responsibility. We tend to trust proven people. Moreover, the policy of promotion from within could hardly be applied without some

258

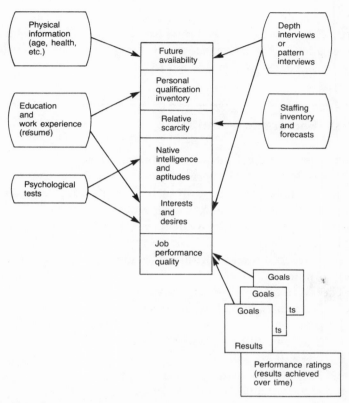

Figure 20.1 Factors in rating potential.

reference to a person's achievements of the goals that are presently under his or her control—achievements that are recognized by peers as genuinely resulting from his or her own efforts and abilities.

Yet we know that simply being a sound performer at a particular job does not necessarily qualify one for promotion to a higher post. Nevertheless, this error is often made. The best worker becomes a supervisor, with little or no consideration given to the question whether the same qualities are called for in the higher job or if the worker has the capacity to acquire the new skills that will be demanded. Quite often, no provision is made for him or her to acquire some of these skills before taking over. Similarly, people in managerial positions are thrust into higher-level posts only to find themselves in over their heads. If discharge or demotion follows, this is a painful process for all concerned. But even worse is the situation where the manager sputters along at a level of performance that is far below what the position could use, but isn't incompetent enough to justify removal.

The Six Factors of Potential

In determining whether a man or woman has the capacity for promotion to the next higher level, or for several promotions above the present position, a number of factors must be considered. These comprise the equivalent of long personal knowledge of the individual. The predictive process is inescapably one of managerial judgment—the judgment of one person about another. No single measurement has been discovered that will infallibly reveal whether a person has potential for greater responsibility or not.

The six factors on which prediction is based are:
1. The person's performance on his or her present and previous jobs.
2. Native intelligence and aptitudes.
3. Interests and desires.
4. The relative scarcity of candidates.
5. The individual's future availability for promotional opportunities.
6. His or her personal qualifications inventory.

Let's look at each of these six factors in detail. For convenience we'll consider No. 1 first, followed by Nos. 4, 5, and 6, leaving the knotty problem of personality assessment (Nos. 2 and 3) to the last.

Job Performance

The performance record of the individual still ranks high among the factors identifying people for promotion. Poor performance in a series of positions may be some kind of predictor that a person will not perform well in a higher job.

One large firm has a policy of rotating its younger managers from time to time, so that a variety of managers can observe their performance. A single bad rating may only be an indication of a personality clash, or even that the individual is better than his or her rater. A series of adverse ratings, however, might suggest an inability to please any boss. If job rotation is to provide meaningful assessments, however, it must meet two major conditions:

1. People being rotated must be given more than token work or observation duties. Rotation assignments that don't test them or threaten failure if not performed well are likely to be illusory because they never reveal the employees' mettle in the face of real tasks that test their capacity to perform independently.

2. The objectives aimed at and the results expected should be explicitly spelled out and placed before the employees as the major measure of their performance.

There can be no accurate measurement of actual performance without some standards in the form of statements of expectations.[2] These statements must be given to the person before he or she commences a measured course of performance. The presumption that "really good managers will discover for themselves what the job is," simply doesn't work and places a premium on clairvoyance or a similarity of temperament between subordinate and boss. While such a similarity is fortunate for both, it doesn't especially serve the company to base its policy on the chance of its happening, since there will often be many duos whose personalities don't harmonize. If every such mismating results in the subordinate's being judged incompetent in performance, a tremendous waste of talent is likely to ensue.

For example, in one company there was a chief engineer who differed greatly in temperament from his engineering supervisor. The boss was a genial, outgoing, affable person, and the subordinate a tense, withdrawn sort of man. The chief often declared that he "didn't understand" his subordinate, and furthermore didn't think he was an especially good engineer. They seldom discussed the man's work, he said, because he felt that a "smart" manager would figure out what the situation was. The subordinate acted in accordance with his perceptions of his job, with the results that his performances differed widely from his boss's expectations. Then a formal program was set up. Together, the two reviewed the subordinate's technical program and his major areas of responsibility and then agreed upon the ways in which he would be measured. The result was a marked improvement in the subordinate's performance as his boss measured it. This the superior attributed to "a change in the fellow's attitude." In fact, his attitude had changed little. What had happened was that he now knew better what was expected of him.

In still another company, difficulties were encountered when young people regarded as having high potential in the field were placed in positions where they could be tested against actual job problems. Some of the young men and women were rated high by their bosses; others were rated less favorably. A restudy of the results showed that where superiors had defined the responsibilities in concrete terms and had informed subordinates in advance how they were to be measured, the newcomers received better ratings than did those placed in departments where the boss had failed to take these steps. Accordingly, the company instituted the practice of informing each trainee of the job's goals and how performance would be measured before he or she was assigned to a department. As a result, ratings rooted in the actual skill and effort displayed were obtained.

Relative Scarcity

The suitability of a candidate for promotion may also be a function of the other possible candidates, as well as the virtues or shortcomings of the individual himself. During a period when young people between twenty-eight and thirty-five are in short supply, promotional requirements for people in this category may be less stringent than at a time when there is an abundance of candidates. If only three persons are available for consideration, selection standards are likely to be lowered, and there will probably be a corresponding decrease in the quality of selection decisions.[3]

Relative scarcity cannot be estimated by looking at the candidates alone, though each should be measured carefully on all factors. The orderly construction of staffing inventories and forecasts of demands, matched against the total available supply, is of equal importance.

The company's posture in affirmative action programs will have an important bearing upon supply, as well. It may be harder to staff key positions with women or blacks than desired where the company's track record in the past has been weak in this regard.

The subject of planning staffing requirements is itself a most complex one, which cannot be dealt with at length here. Yet it is an essential part of the process of estimating relative scarcity or the demand for talent against which potential must be estimated.

As diagrammed in Figure 20.2, the method of estimating an individual's potential as a function of the need for his or her talents is similar whether the planner is estimating no change or growth in the organization or foreseeing dramatic growth and change. Obviously, the condition of growth alone does not determine the relative scarcity of certain types of persons, since that must also be considered as a function of quality changes in the organization. The firm that intends to move into new lines of business—perhaps with a more technical orientation than its present operations demand—may find that more technically educated persons must be brought along into management positions.

Availability

The general factor of availability is used here in its broadest sense. Under this head are considered such aspects of the total situation as the following:

Age. This is important in that it defines how many years the candidate can be expected to put into the proposed new job. Thus, a candi-

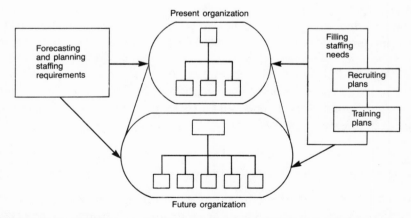

Figure 20.2 Estimating an individual's potential and organizational needs.

date for president aged fifty, with presumably fifteen years more service ahead, might be considered young. The trainee of twenty might be considered ideal if there is to be a long vestibule period before he or she assumes managerial responsibility. The length of future service of the younger candidate is an economic consideration, since the cost of hiring and training is amortized over a longer period of time.

Health. Availability may depend on this element also. The victim of a serious heart attack, for example, may have unfortunately diminished potential simply because he or she is no longer able to undertake certain kinds of work. A person with asthma might have to be ruled out of consideration for promotion to a plant location where the manufacturing process could aggravate the condition. This condition could be ignored, however, if all the company's work is done in an air-conditioned office. Diabetics are sometimes limited by their inability to travel without full meals or by the risks of traveling alone.

Willingness to Relocate. Here is another element in assessing a person's availability for higher positions. The employee who insists upon living in a particular region has a perfect right to do so. But this insistence limits his or her availability in companies that need to transfer their managers at will.

Likes and Dislikes. Marked preferences or distaste for certain types of work ("I'd never take a factory job under any circumstances!") may also prove to be a limitation upon a person's availability in some instances. Here again such people are within their rights, but their prospects for promotion may be restricted in consequence.

Sex and Race. If the company has an affirmative action plan, it is required that some facts about the supply of qualified blacks and women in the labor market be obtained and a specific plan for improving opportunities be created and followed.

The Personal Qualifications Inventory

The record of a person's education and work experience may be an important factor in judging his or her potential. For example, in certain chemical companies it has been decided that only chemists or chemical engineers can hold management positions in process plants and divisions. Without a chemical degree or its equivalent in experience, the person's potential is limited by the fact that his or her qualifications don't match the requirements of the situation.

Such a record is usually prepared when the person first joins the firm. Often, though, it is not kept up to date. It should be supplemented by records of the successive positions held and for whom the person has worked and any incidental special assignments. As each of these positions or assignments is listed, it should be accompanied by an additional line or two indicating the person's major likes and dislikes about the job. This provides a record of interests and inclinations that may also have a bearing upon his or her potential for higher responsibility.

In short, the personal qualifications inventory should be more than a bare statement of personal data, educational background, and work history. It should include details of the work performed, where it was done, salary progress, and so on.

Personal Characteristics

Finally, comes the problem of assessing a person's suitability for promotion in the light of his or her intelligence, aptitudes, interests, and desires. Here psychological tests, combined with all the other sources of information and conducted under professional guidance, may be of some help. Some of the commonly applied tests for assessing people are those that measure the following characteristics:

Intelligence. This is usually a test of general information as measured by IQ. This test is often strongly oriented toward middle-class persons with a marked scientific or mathematical bent.

Interests. Such tests show what tendencies the individual has toward certain kinds of activities that cluster around certain occupations.

Specific Skills. Tests in this category measure achievement in such individual skills as reading speed and comprehension, vocabulary, verbal reasoning, or number relations.

Personality. Such tests, usually felt to be the least reliable of all, deduce from the executive's responses possession or lack of certain personality traits. If the test purports to measure specific traits, this is because the test designers have a feeling or some evidence that these traits are important for executive success. But as we have seen, the evidence that certain traits are necessary or, alternatively, highly unsuitable for executives is rather inconclusive.

Usually, a test should possess two major characteristics before it can be relied upon as a measure of executive potential:

1. *Validity.* This means that the test measures what it purports to measure. Another way of putting this is that success on the test turns out to be predictive of success on the job.
2. *Reliability.* This means that the responses cannot be faked and that each part of the test is so consistent with all the other parts that any attempt by the testee to try to "look better" than he or she really is readily becomes apparent to the experts interpreting the results.

One common use of tests is to identify what kind of intelligence the testee possesses. Some people have great number relations ability, whereas others have nonnumerical or nonverbal reasoning powers. If one of these kinds of ability is germane to the position under consideration, it can be uncovered and measured through such tests.

Tests themselves are always subject to testing, and the use of psychological testing scores in assessing potential is limited by several considerations:

1. Tests should be administered and interpreted only under the direction of a qualified psychologist.
2. Raw test results should not be handed out indiscriminately to lay managers, who might misinterpret the technical language in which they are expressed.
3. The measures of validity and reliability should be known by test users to interpret the results.
4. Tests comprise only one facet of the process of assessing an individual's qualifications for promotion, and should be regarded accordingly.[4]
5. Tests must be culture-free and not discriminate against sex or color.

Potential versus Performance

The danger in discussing potential and performance in the same performance review is that the question of potential is likely to become so large in the discussion that it may never get down to the urgent matter of improving present performance.

Where potential is discussed, the following caveats should be observed.

- Don't discuss personality, especially those weaknesses over which the person has little or no control. "The trouble with you, Joe, is that you stutter," said one man to a fine subordinate. This curt comment caused the subordinate needless distress, since his speech defect was incurable.
- Center the discussion on specific changes persons can make in their behavior and thereby enlarge their potential. For example, you can say, "You might do well to learn more about the shipping operation," or "Perhaps if you spent more time with the accounting people, you would be better able to make cost judgments, Mary."
- Don't make promises you aren't sure you can deliver on, and if you make one, keep it.
- Don't compare one person's potential with another's in the hope that the comparison will improve or energize latent energies in the laggard.
- Be honest and realistic in telling the person where you think he or she might go in the organization, without being especially gloomy or negative when you have to say, "I don't know."
- Always return to present performance and the necessity for doing an excellent job in the present position after any discussion of possible avenues of advancement.
- Avoid stereotyping, especially with women employees. Don't generalize standard "female" characteristics to all women employees just because they happen to be women nor "Negro" characteristics with black subordinates. It's against the law.

PART 5

The Hard Part of MBO: Making It Work

Management isn't an automatic process. Many people have been disappointed in MBO programs because they held such an expectation, but like any good idea, MBO is not self-executing. It works in proportion to the amount of energy and wisdom poured into its implementation. Its rationality makes it appealing to rational people. Its humanistic portions make it difficult. In this section, we will look at the political aspect of MBO, how it relates to resistance to change and to the behavioral sciences, and its findings in such things as job enrichment. Some case study material comprises Chapters 24 and 25.

CHAPTER 21

The Politics of Implementing MBO

There are several approaches to implementing management by objectives, but no matter which one is chosen, the political constraints cannot be ignored. They must be dealt with as realities.

— Gerard F. Carvallho

It is not likely today that many managers will object to management by objectives as a concept or philosophy. The question of available alternatives seems unanswerable in the face of such an eminently logical developmental system. Why, then, do people seem to have reservations about committing themselves to it? Why, indeed, do some find it impossible to make it work, while others report great success in its application and enthusiasm for its effects?

One of the major reasons for the failure of MBO in many organizations is that those in charge fail to recognize the *political* character of the implementation process. MBO is indeed logical and systematic, but it also must deal with a number of factors, including power and authority, the organization form, and the values and expectations of people. The MBO implementer, therefore, must recognize the reality of political constraints and manage them during the process of implementation.

If this is not done, MBO may start off with a flourish but gradually fade away; begin well, reach a certain level, and stall; or start well but produce a dramatic failure and be dropped, becoming a taboo subject thereafter. Success, on the other hand, results when MBO begins at a sound level of acceptance, gains from its own successes, continues to flourish and expand its influence and contributions, and is widely appreciated and supported.

270

Case studies of successful and unsuccessful implementation plans show that there are three major avenues currently used for implementation of MBO and that all three must be modified by political constraints characteristic of every organization. This chapter will briefly illustrate the three approaches and then describe the political considerations that must guide them.

The Three Approaches

Methods of implementing MBO may rely on the use of (1) persuasion, (2) education, (3) raw power and direct orders (see Figure 21.1). Case studies indicate that no one route is best: instead, analysis of the organizational climate and the situation will indicate the best approach—one alone or perhaps a combination of all of them. A specific set of steps in linear form would be highly desirable, but such a method would probably miss the mark and lead to an implementation that fails in one or more respects.

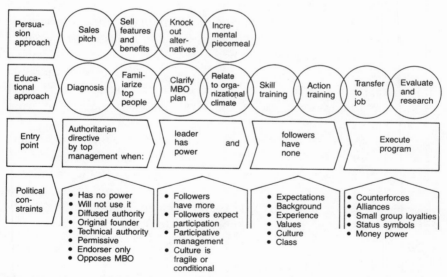

Figure 21.1 The three approaches to implementing MBO, and the political constraints.

1. The Persuasion Approach

One reason for the failure of MBO to achieve its full potential has been the misguided reliance upon persuasion as a means of implementation. The guru or inspirational speaker comes to a meeting of management and through hortatory lectures persuades everyone that MBO will be beneficial. Persuasive methods ordinarily can be distinguished by their content:

1. They appear to be balanced—that is, they explain all of the advantages of MBO, then turn and judiciously explain the disadvantages of not managing by objectives. This is clearly an advocacy approach designed to persuade.
2. Features and benefits are grist for the persuader's mill. A description of the features and a discussion of the usefulness of each are persuasive tactics.
3. In the debater's form of persuasion, all of the alternatives for solving some chronic problems are noted. Then each is knocked out in turn, except the MBO solution.
4. Incrementalism, probably the most risky form of persuasion, consists of starting with a simple segment of the whole program and selling it. "You simply sit down once a year with all of your subordinates and talk to them about their objectives" would be an incremental approach. Many instances of MBO failure have been caused by incrementalism in the introduction. The concept began as a change in the company performance-appraisal system or as a salary-review plan but lost favor when the full implications of the time and effort demanded were realized.

Persuasion is the favorite method of hortatory speakers and consultants. It is detested and avoided by academics, who prefer an approach that relies almost wholly upon education, particularly in the underlying theory. As a complete method of installation, it obviously leads to disillusionment. Yet it has a useful part in implementation in the early stages, if only to get people to submit to education.

2. The Educational Approach

One of the most successful patterns for installing an MBO program is a continuous educational effort that teaches the concepts, philosophy, and procedures of MBO in detail.[1] As a training subject, MBO has many excellent features:

1. Training should produce behavior change, and training in MBO is measurable. It can be readily determined if the training worked: did the trainees set objectives or didn't they?

2. The quality of the results can be noted clearly. The course may suggest, for example, that a manager should establish three classes of objectives. The effect on the manager can be checked by examining sample goals statements.

3. MBO comprises a sound basis for relating training to the job. Some training sessions require students to set objectives on their job as part of the course; they learn by doing what they are being taught.

4. MBO provides a vehicle for teaching more general management education. It can be the framework for teaching motivational methods, management functions (organizing, planning, and controlling), and such interpersonal skills as coaching, counseling, and listening.

5. MBO can teach interpersonal skills that can be applied on the job, rather than skills the boss will not permit or endorse when the trainee returns to the desk or plant floor. This is especially true if the boss attends the session or is used as a trainer.

6. MBO can reinforce company objectives rather than become, as it does in many behavioral courses, an internal reform movement to overcome the organization's autocratic or bureaucratic tendencies or to produce some new kind of organizational form.

7. MBO is capable of maintaining a high level of trainee interest, since it deals with the real world of work and world problems, and with interpersonal and group relations problems.

8. Conceptually, it is easy to learn, for MBO training courses ask people to "talk shop," and they have a tendency to do this whether they are in training or not. Except for courses in which the trainers have worked hard at obscuring the obvious, the language is operational and practical.

9. The basic framework of MBO permits it to take a behavioral or logical systems direction without appearing contradictory or mutually exclusive. This means that it can appeal to the per-

sonnel and training people in the organization as well as to the engineers, controllers, and dollar-centered managers.

10. Both insiders and outsiders can be used as trainers. The insiders have more knowledge of the business and can deal with real-world problems, but the outsiders can be briefed sufficiently to relate to the world of the trainee.

3. Authoritarian Directives

It is an article of faith, supported by some research evidence, that the installation of MBO must start at the top.[2] In part, such a beginning is justified. The purpose of the business flows down and the methods of getting there flow up. The strategies of the business are chosen by persons with high-level responsibility, whereas the operational objectives are the responsibility of lower levels. This might lead to the conclusion that the power of the higher ranks must be invoked to direct implementation. This approach, which Joseph Juran has labeled the "king's ear" approach, is founded upon the assumption that, if the staff person can get the president's ear and get the right directives issued, everybody below will obey. The concept is that of the self-executing order, a rare phenomenon.

Behavioral scientists deplore such autocratic methods, but they are used in some organizations where tight technical organization and discipline are the mode of operation.[3] Where the following conditions exist in the organization, such authoritarian methods will indeed work:

1. The leader has absolute power and is willing to use it.
2. The followers need the leader more than vice versa, because the leader has—and can withhold—knowledge, skills, or resources that they need.
3. The followers have lived under unexplained orders for some time, perhaps for their entire working lives, and have learned to expect them, even when the subject is MBO.[4]
4. The situation requires autocratic orders. The leader is in charge of a ship at sea in a storm, a plane in distress, or a temporary work force, and is expected to give orders quickly and clearly.

Under proper circumstances, autocratic implementation of MBO has been successful.[5] That is not to say that all situations demand it;

many are not suitable for autocracy—the college faculty or the volunteer group, for example. The major limitations of the use of force to implement MBO lie in the situation in which it is applied. Where the boss has no power or has power and will not use it, the followers expect to be consulted and have something important to withhold (and will do so). Under these circumstances, the authoritarian directive will produce counterresponses that block MBO.

The Politics of Implementation

The constraint of organizational politics is a formidable barrier to implementation. Unless it is taken into account, it will outweigh the logical and behavioral efforts that go into directing, persuading, or educating people to accept a new management system. Several political factors must be considered.

The Power Structure

An often overlooked political factor affecting the implementation of MBO is the power structure of the organization. MBO is rightly seen as having the potential for shifting the locus of power inside the organization, and accordingly will meet political resistance from those who might be affected adversely.[6]

The resistance of such persons as corporate attorneys or other executive staff members is frequently rooted in the probability of shifting power. A person who has developed a strong personal relationship with the top officers in which they draw upon his or her counsel in all sorts of matters beyond law or some other specialty is clearly threatened by systematic management. In one large firm, the corporate purchasing director had performed numerous personal favors for the president and his family and had attained the status of a family favorite. When MBO was suggested, this family retainer saw immediately that his status could be threatened, and he greeted the proposal with a flurry of cluckings and exceptions. He noted its flaws and limitations, insisted that it was nothing new, and adopted other delaying and obstructive tactics familiar to the MBO administrator.

In another firm it was the tax manager who headed up the political resistance movement against MBO. The manager had helped the family with the controlling interest to minimize their personal estate taxes over the years, and he hoped to retain his personal position of favor.

The Diffusion of Authority

In many modern corporations there has been a blurring of the decision-making power. Starting at the top, where the charismatic leader or dynamic chief has been supplanted by "the office of the president" generally occupied by two or three people, it is difficult to identify a single channel for decisions. This has some advantage in gaining acceptance for decisions, but it also generates political maneuvering in order to get objectives decided upon. In other organizations, the key committees of the board may produce some mutually exclusive objectives which they are pushing. These require some political pulling and hauling in order to make a particular position dominant.

In government, of course, the basic motivator of the system and its servants is political power, and the diffusion of power is well understood by most of the people who share in it. Cabinet members know that bureau chiefs ostensibly under their control can lobby Congress to protect a job or program. Letters from the congressional representatives can always sway the bureaucrat. At the same time, the large departmental public relations departments in government can swing public opinion to press Congress for increased space or increased military and welfare appropriations.

Such a political climate requires more patience, continuous effort, and persuasion to get a management style change such as MBO into effect. Even some trading of favors and arm twisting may be necessary.[7]

The Fragility of Participation

Even in those organizations where participation of the lower levels has been designated as the mode of operation, it is possible that it can be withdrawn. Where the possibilities of power exist, there is a possibility that power once withheld will be reasserted.

Take the case of the governor of a state who was enthused about MBO and employed a participative style of management. He delegated extensively and pressed decisions down to the lowest possible level, which produced high morale at these low levels. But after the governor left office, his successor immediately suspended all the mechanics of participative management and centralized everything in his office. In the process, he declared his support of MBO, but in fact he killed it by locating total control in his office.

A similar experience has been found where a humanistic president of a corporation installed a participative MBO program. Upon his retirement, a four-star general assumed his office and promptly applied autocratic controls, eliminating certain policy committees; scuttling meetings, which had been the major vehicle for MBO; and ordering the appraisal form abandoned and training programs stopped. The reason he did so was plausible: the company had been in market trouble, and a lax style of MBO had made the corporation easygoing but unprofitable. After a turnaround, he retired, major promotions were made from within, and the earlier participative management style of MBO restored with excellent results.

It is a hard political fact about organizations, public and private, that MBO that is inextricably tied to participative management may be damaged if an autocratic boss gets on top. MBO that is top-down and somewhat autocratic to begin with suffers no such setback. On the other hand, it never had the developmental and humanistic benefits of participative management in the first place.

The Problem of Countermoves

A strong move to produce an MBO program that would change the behavior of people or the arrangement of the organization and how it does its work can be counted on to produce an equal and opposite reaction somewhere. It may be expressed by scoffing and wisecracks, by satiric definitions of the acronym MBO ("Massive Bowel Obstruction" or "Mr. Big's Obsession," to name two), or by overintellectualizing of the obvious.

In other cases, the reaction produces some fairly stiff fights, scuffles, and corporate infighting. This is not peculiar to MBO but is characteristic of political response to changes that will shuffle the power structure and power alignments in the organization. Changes in cost accounting or market research, a new salary system, or simply reassignment of parking places will trigger the counterresponse.

Predicting the reaction and pinpointing its source is one of the arts of organization politicians. They are then able to take corrective, remedial, or ameliorative action before the problem arises. In some instances, they find these sources of reaction by testing their ideas in tentative form, sending out position papers, and holding discussions in order to elicit such responses. If the trouble spots surface after installation, they can be patched up through trading or arm twisting or by changing the program.

Even though most politically aware persons realize the advantages of option B over option A, it is often impossible to get complete support. Therefore, the need to modify and amend the MBO program after it is under way—for example, in the second go-around—should be considered one of the political realities. Running roughshod over those who would resist a new idea not only stiffens the backbone of the resistors but makes all changes less likely to be accepted.[8]

Unit Loyalty

An often overlooked rule of allegiance is that people center their loyalties around the smallest unit of which they are a member rather than the overall organization. The basic unit for the soldier is the squad, not the service branch, the armed forces, or the Free World. For the engineer it is the engineering project rather than the entire firm. The personnel expert is often more centered in his or her staff department's goals than the corporation's.

This fact has great significance for implementing MBO. It means that the objectives must be related to *this* person, *this* job, in *this* unit, *this* year. Expecting people to be motivated by grand designs and overall global strategies is unrealistic and contrary to political realities.

In one large oil company, for example, the MBO program met poor acceptance in the engineering and development departments, even though it was a smashing success in the refinery and in the marketing department. The resistance in the two departments was not only embarrassing but threatened to weaken the program in other areas as well. A wise MBO administrator suggested a conference in which the people in engineering designed their own MBO system, with special salmon-colored forms and a different kind of calendar of events. The program immediately began to operate smoothly.

Diversity in applications of the MBO program may be necessary for the political reasons of unit loyalty. Permitting variances in details, in application, in timing, and in sequencing of events may assist implementation.

The Individualists

One of the greatest potential sources of political opposition to an MBO program is the uniformity and conformity imposed by some systems. When the MBO program is seen as a set of forms to be filed, a cookbook set of procedures, it will run into individuals who resist.

The reasons lie in the value systems of technical, managerial, and professional people, who possess primarily middle-class values. They are most often the educated professionals, although a degree or college experience is not necessarily the sole criterion, since people without degrees who have associated with such persons at work have often acquired their values. In any case, these people cherish professional individuality, and while an objective observer might see this individuality as insignificant, it has an important bearing upon the behavior of the person. The desire to participate in decisions is strongly held by the middle-class employee, and denial of the wish will produce political effort contrary to the whole idea.

Sometimes the individualists will object to the name of a program. Administrators have found it necessary to adopt another label for the MBO program, calling it "goals management" or permitting major subunits to use their own names or acronyms. The fetish of maintaining a single unified program with a common label, often adhered to by corporate staffs, can work to the disadvantage of the program.

The image of being "unprofessional" or of requiring unprofessional behavior can be the kiss of death to any kind of new procedure. The unexplained and seemingly pointless order or the cold memo not accompanied by a dialogue increase the likelihood that the program will be seen as an indignity or as unprofessional.

This perception can be extended to the specifics of the standards of performance produced from the goals-setting process installed. If it seems to be enforcing conformity and attacking present eccentricities, the whole program becomes suspect.

One of the major features of MBO, which makes it politically palatable to professional people, is that it is indifferent to activities but is deeply concerned about output.[9] This assurance of the protection of individual idiosyncracies is important to professionals.

Status Symbols

Attention must be paid to the effect of the new system on the present structure of status in the organization. Status symbols are the subtle indicators of a person's standing in relation to others.

In some instances, there are the physical symbols of office— uniforms, desks, office fittings, parking places, and the like. In other instances, more probable in an MBO program, it will be the reduction in influence or authority for some, as the center of decision making moves to a lower level. In one bank where MBO was installed, the power to make certain equipment purchase decisions was delegated. Yet when the new equipment arrived, the president was shocked. "My feelings were hurt that they hadn't consulted me," he reported later.

Social and status significance is attached also to certain prerequisites or roles. If an MBO system robs people of such status symbols as authority to conduct the annual performance review or to award raises, resistance from the deprived can be expected. In their own minds they are forced to downgrade, depreciate, or even attack MBO, although the true reasons for the opposition will not be revealed.

Such an attack is not conducted openly, of course, for the losses would appear to be a trivial, and perhaps even an immature reason for attacking something as logical as MBO. Thus, the attack will be couched in terms that are eminently logical and rational in language, even though the basis is far from being rational.

Organizational Form

Among the more sophisticated approaches to political maneuvering to get an MBO system in operation is that of organizational planning. Decentralization, for example, may be ostensibly an organizational structure change, but it can also force MBO into being. Decentralization is also a political action, for it represents a shifting of power within the organization. It is a blending of the bureaucratic form with centralized control with the humanistic form in which lower-level persons make more independent decisions.[10]

The dispersal of profit responsibility in many places simply makes it impossible for the top executive to control all the activities of all of the subordinate profit centers. Accordingly, higher-level managers must satisfy their domineering tendencies by defining results expected and measuring those results, meanwhile keeping their hands off the operations. This is far less a matter of being persuaded of the virtues of delegation and participative management than a simple inability to see everything. When you run out of eyes, hours, and ability to see everything, you are naturally required to manage by objectives whether you like it or not.

Such exemplary managerial practices are likely to develop in organizations like conglomerates where the new units have been acquired in one bite. It is especially imperative when the acquired company was purchased on some kind of payout plan over the years, with strict contractual arrangements allowing members of the founding management to retain their positions as long as profits are satisfactory. Far better than a sophisticated training program is an installment method of acquiring new firms which promote MBO; the result is almost inescapably MBO. The idea, for example, that a corporate president can manage 100 divisions autocratically rather than by objectives is, on the face of it, impossible.

MBO also results in firms that are nationally dispersed (the Prudential Insurance Company, for example), with all but a few managerial functions distributed among the five or six large regional offices, each with a complete, functional staff. The bank with 350 branches will probably manage them by objectives, even if it does not realize it is doing so. The alternative is an exorbitant computerized management information system (MIS) and communications system. It is far more economical and sensible to find good people, place them in jobs, get them committed to objectives, and control them by exceptions.

On the other hand, a centralized organization form with functional departments usually means that the MBO program is often a form of artificial or arbitrary choice. Bosses who are in the same room or even the same building with all of their employees may declare that MBO is their official style. However, they often are playing house with the employees and in fact do not manage by objectives at all, even when they talk a great MBO game.

The Effects of Alliances

Two or three divisions or departments, connected by a network of alliances, joint programs, mutual support, and interdependencies, can make or break an MBO program at will. The credit and sales departments, which share the task of keeping receivables under control, can make a shambles of capital management goals or they can make achievement seem effortless and natural. The industrial engineering department can team up with production to make MBO easy or difficult.

Alliances can be formed among groups that fear they would be weakened, and their joint resistance will benefit both. Hospitals are replete with examples of groups that might ordinarily find themselves in competition but are instead joined in coalitions in the face of threatening objectives. The surgeons and medical staffs competing for personnel and technician time will stand together against the administrator whose objective is to reduce technician costs.

Take the case of the controller who was committed to a computerized management information system. It was his intent to have an on-line, real-time, alphanumeric tube in every manager's office. Thus, he would have daily, even hourly, control over every important input or resource to be employed in every part of the business. The personnel department at the same time was pushing MBO, suggesting delegation, freedom of action, and goals management rather than control of detailed activity.

In another office, the corporate attorney had built up a "Merlin the Magician" relationship with the president. The counsel was in and out of the president's office, reporting little stories and advising on all sorts of things. He, too, recognized MBO as a threat to his position as high counselor. He teamed up with the controller to condemn MBO as a spurious and probably risky adventure that was probably not fully thought through and perhaps basically unsound, if not downright illegal.

MBO never stood a chance. Power is not something voluntarily relinquished, and those who have it may see MBO as a shifting of power downward and will accordingly employ alliances and political power to fend it off.

Money Is Power

Those who control money or produce it in large amounts have power and can sway all kinds of decisions. In one large electronics firm with ten divisions, for example, one division produced 80 percent of the profit. Thus, the general manager of that division had far greater power over corporate policy than his rank would indicate. If he disagreed with or could not use a corporate policy, he would simply ignore it. Because he produced most of the profit, he was sometimes gently admonished but never severely crimped.

People in such a power center are able to block new programs that do not suit their mode of operation. On the other hand, if the general manager of such a center can be persuaded or educated to adopt MBO, it will probably become a corporatewide system.

In other instances, power resides elsewhere in a single function. Marketing is king in many firms where the "marketing concept" determines the basic strategic goals. In others, it is the technology center or the financial group. In highly unionized firms, the labor relations manager will have considerable influence and often determine whether MBO will be given a hearing, to say nothing of its being implemented. Power is often rooted in the ability to affect revenues, expenses, or pricing.

Dealing with Conservatism

Economist Kenneth Boulding has pointed out that change agents, liberals, and innovators are often characterized by high-intensity behavior, while conservators and persons opposed to change are low-intensity in behavior. The change-oriented person may have to be dramatic, shrill, strident, persuasive, and even flamboyant to get a full hearing. The best response for conservatives is to lower their voice and be rational, cautious, and meticulous.

It is the strategy of conservatism and calmness to propose that the change be examined in detail, that it be tried only in part, and to suggest that perhaps certain aspects have not been fully revealed. In the face of such a strategy of delay and obfuscation, the change agent must act with skill. He or she may upon occasion take the organization by storm or persuade the top manager, get a directive from on high, and proceed with a vigorous combination of advocacy and education to build a plurality in the organization.

The true merits of education as a vehicle for change are seen here. The conservative critic can thus be isolated and quietly permitted a change of mind without engaging in high-intensity tactics, for it should be realized that the strength of a countermovement is often related to the intensity of the attack on the status quo.

In some instances, the value of the outsider is that he or she can provide the decisive voice of change to break the deadlock of inertia created by the low-intensity opponent. When the outsider is gone, then the less intense movements can begin. Once the silence has been broken, insider MBO advocates can restore quiet, deplore the excesses which they themselves introduced, and quietly proceed with their educational and persuasive efforts.

Conclusion

MBO has failed in many organizations because those in charge ignored the political considerations included in the implementation. MBO is logical and systematic, but it must deal with various problems and influences. This does not mean that politics are contrary to the management systems known as MBO and that, where politics are present, changes and a new system cannot be expected to flourish.

Political behavior itself has purposes, and goals are the beginning point of politics as well as of business or administration. However, the MBO implementer must not ignore political realities, and the choice of methods of implementation must discriminate among alternative approaches and recognize that the political constraints are realities that must be managed.

CHAPTER 22

How Much Subordinate Participation in Goal Setting?

The only purpose for which power can be rightfully exercised over any member of a civilized community against his will is to prevent harm to others.

—John Stuart Mill

Among academic students of management, there is much controversy over the question of how much autonomy subordinates should have in shaping their own goals, as well as those of the unit in which they work, and how strongly the boss should impose his or her views when it comes to goal setting with subordinates. This chapter deals with some of the key issues and ideas on this question.

Because participative management has been extensively studied, parts of this chapter will be supported by citations from research on this subject.

In essence, at one extreme is the position that subordinates should be asked to set their own goals and those of their work unit. The rationale for this approach, according to its advocates, is that it motivates subordinates to do more or be more productive. At the opposite pole are those who take the view that if the boss doesn't know what to expect from subordinates, he or she shouldn't have them on the payroll and therefore should *tell* people what to do, and when and how to do it.

Actually, neither extreme is a universally applicable style of management, or of goal setting. The research evidence indicates that the use of participative management is a discriminatory skill. In short, it shows that participative management works with some kinds of situations and followers and does not work with other kinds of situations and followers.

Which kind of situation will probably call for participative goal setting, and what kind calls for tight technical organization, tight discipline, and effective control from above?

MBO has been hailed by the advocates of "power equalization" because of the possibilities it holds for the exercise of participative management. Now it is true that participative management is perfectly acceptable as one method of goal setting in the MBO system. As a system, however, management by objectives works also by autocratic or top-down goal setting. The choice of which method to use, or when to mix them, is determined more by the demands of the situation, especially the *expectations of subordinates,* than by the basic nature of the system itself. In fact, the system is really neutral to such value judgments.[1]

Let us look more closely at the system as it might demand either participative or autocratic methods, or mixtures of the two. Let's go back to our old friend, Manager M, with three subordinate Managers, A, B, and C. The organization run by Manager M exists for a purpose: the accomplishment of certain objectives for which the members of the group were hired. These people are aware that this purpose exists, though its exact specifications may have become blurred by each individual's preoccupation with the mechanics of his or her specific task. Ultimately, somebody will evaluate the performance of the group by comparing how closely its results match the goals it was formed to achieve.

Here we have a type of system commonly found within administrative units. In fact, it could be argued that it is a basic system. Schematically it resembles Figure 22.1.

1. In *common goals* we find such things as organization purpose, policy, objectives, plans, and aspirations common to the whole unit. These include budgets, standards, programs, projects, PERT, networks, and so on.
2. In *manager-subordinate relations* we find such matters as review, control, appraisal, management by exception, the annual business review, closing statements, budget reviews, periodic cost statements, production reports, volume reports, and the like. We will look at this whole area in some detail.

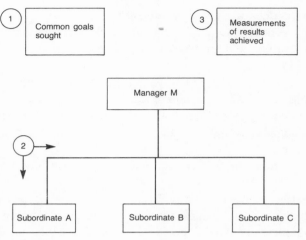

Figure 22.1 Schematic of basic system.

3. *Measurement of results* provides feedback, which produces behavior change.

The Research Findings

Social scientists have done extensive research in the subjects of leadership, organization, and communications. Some of their discoveries have been widely hailed as breakthroughs in management, or new patterns that will eventually supplant existing methods of managing. Most of this work has been extended to the prescriptive conclusion that participative goal setting is better than nonparticipative goal setting.[2]

Actually, what have the social scientists learned from their research? One provocative idea they have suggested is that participative management obtains better results than autocratic control and dictatorship. This question will be dealt with in this chapter.

Perhaps the leading exponent of participative management has been Douglas McGregor. In describing how management by objectives works he says: "Genuine commitment is seldom achieved when objectives are externally imposed. Passive acceptance is the most that can be expected, indifference or resistance are the more likely consequences."[3]

Just what does the research tell us?

Gurin, Veroff, and Feld conclude that participation is really a middle-class value, and grows out of the prior expectations of those being supervised.[4]

Vroom has pointed out two distinctions in the definition of participation. The first he calls "psychological" (you think you are participating in the decisions that affect you), and the second, "objective" (you actually participate strongly in the decisions that affect you whether you know it or not).

Vroom's study throws some interesting light on how follower personalities affect participative management.

"The effects of participation in decision making depend upon certain personality characteristics of the participant," Vroom says. For example, independent people perform better when they have high participation, his research shows.[5]

Highly authoritarian personalities, on the other hand, perform better when they don't have any participation, but are simply told what to do, when to do it, and how to do it.

Most people *like* participation, however, even though their productivity may not be favorably affected by their getting it.

How can we explain these conflicting data? According to Vroom, it is because we like things that meet our needs. If we like participation, participation is what meets our expectations and needs. But some people, unfortunately, have never been led to expect that they will be asked to participate in the decisions affecting them.

The difference in the effects of tight or loose supervision, of participation or nonparticipation, is shown in studies by Martin Patchen of the University of Michigan, who found that close supervision, combined with high rewards or exercised in a situation of high group cohesiveness, resulted in high production. In still another study of a Swedish railway system, Rubenowitz also found production-oriented supervisors rating high on overall performance, whereas "person-oriented" supervisors rated lower. The findings of these two studies are thus diametrically opposed to those of earlier studies using comparable methods on similar kinds of workers. At least a dozen more research studies during the seventies reveal that participation of subordinates in goal setting is not the essential feature of MBO.[6]

The conclusion to be reached is that neither tightness of supervision nor looseness is a sole controlling variable, and that participation of itself has no claim to being the core of a new pattern of MBO that will guarantee high productivity if universally adopted by managers. There is some evidence, however, that a strong orientation toward goals, coupled with leader enthusiasm, ample rewards for achieving the goals, and the uniting of people in moving toward them do have a beneficial effect.

Advantage of Participation in Managing Managers

In dealing with a system such as MBO, designed to cope with the problem of managing managers, it would be erroneous, however, to brush participative management aside. It is most useful under the following circumstances:

1. Where subordinates expect that they will have an opportunity to participate in the decisions affecting them or in setting their own goals. To bar such participation would clearly be unproductive.
2. Where subordinate managers already have shown themselves to be of independent temperament. Such people will expect to participate in establishing their goals.
3. Where one member of the group has proved to be habitually inattentive to the work, careless in his or her relations, or productive only of foolish suggestions. Here the influence of the peer group can be brought to bear on the problem of changing that person's behavior by confronting the offender with the surrounding organizational or cultural value system. The values of peers comprise standards by which the individual will usually measure his or her own behavior and, if necessary, adapt to them.

One way to raise the standards of back-sliders is to confront them with the group standards in a situation staged by the superior or by the circumstances of group management. Cues, reinforcers, and other stimuli to changed behavior come from the group, the boss, and from within the individuals themselves. Usually the inward forces are importantly affected by the outward ones. These outward stimuli to excellence may be internalized if they are made apparent to the individuals. Their goals will rise to meet the expectations of the boss, peers, or the organizational culture.

The Social Values of Participative Management

In the early days of the movement toward more participative management, social scientists were often heard proclaiming the democratic values of permitting workers to take part in shaping the decisions affecting them. But this particular line has practically been abandoned by the new "behavioral scientists" who have steered their studies in the direction of proving that participative management increases productivity.

To many managers, it has seemed that this change in direction has been rather fruitless, and all the more so because the democratic argument did not deserve to be dropped anyway. For the company making a profit or in a sound market position, the idea of using participation for the purpose of creating a stronger society is not perhaps so outlandish as many social scientists apparently expected business managers to think. The modern corporate manager, in fact, is often the leader in such matters as race relations, participation in governmental and civic affairs, hiring of the handicapped, and the strengthening of the free institutions of our society.

Since research evidence shows that participative management probably does no harm, and often helps, especially in managing people from middle-class backgrounds and similar value systems, the appeal that there may be long-run social value in participation has not fallen on deaf ears. In this sense many business managers lead the social scientists in their confidence in the values of participative management, even though they may doubt its efficacy as an infallible spur to productivity.

Does Participative Management Raise Productivity?

Since it is the behavioral scientists who have argued the case for a universal style of participative management on the grounds that it leads to increased production, their position calls for careful examination. Because their data can be interpreted as showing that, in most cases, participative management probably does no harm, coupled with the fact that it offers social values in which business should be interested, it can be assumed that it is wise for the manager to try it first, in preference to more dictatorial methods. It should be recognized, however, that this is hardly a strict application of science in the modern sense.

1. It is heavily weighted with values. Values such as power-equalization and democracy-at-work are ethical and normative, rather than scientific.

2. It is heavily weighted with abstract classifications. The abstractions may be Theory X or Theory Y, autocratic versus participative management, permissive versus dictatorial, and similar hot-cold, black-white opposites.

3. It relies on dubious generalizations. Studies made in research laboratories and insurance companies have been extrapolated to apply to infantry platoons, foundries, automotive assembly lines and machine shops, even though the evidence may not justifiably be thus extended.[7]

In order for this new behavioral science to be completely relied upon as scientific in the modern sense, it should meet some of these requirements:

1. It should constitute a system that takes due account of the other phenomena commonplace in the management of job and function. For example, most behavioral-science theories of managing exclude the economics of the firm. In one of the leading works in the field, the word *profit* is not mentioned at all.
2. Such polar opposites as good and evil, X and Y, should be enlarged into genetic concepts that would eliminate rigid classes of behavior on the part of managers. It should be recognized that management practice is never all black or all white, but multihued, and may be classified according to the conditions that determine the dynamic relations of the manager or his or her environment.
3. Behavioral science research should be more concrete in terms of the company studied, who was involved, at what time, what transpired, and what actions were taken with what effect. Well-prepared, detailed case studies are more scientific, in the

modern sense of the term, than surveys in which the subjects are isolated from the concrete realities of their situation.

Measured against the above criteria, the school of behavioral science that views motivation in terms of need fulfillment emerges in many respects unscientific. How can the tests of modern science be applied to such concepts as the "needs" of individuals? A commonly held viewpoint of this school is that these needs comprise a hierarchy that ascends from physiological and safety needs through social and ego needs to the needs of self-fulfillment. But once scientists move away from physiological needs (which can certainly be measured), how do they measure the remaining needs in the hierarchy with any degree of precision and certainty? The questionnaire and interview (perhaps checked by adroit design, or even the polygraph) may possibly furnish crude measurements, though these are likely to be distorted by ignorance, self-interest, or other bias. Nevertheless, a certain circularity of logic entraps the scientists and the subject.

The ego needs of subjects are reflected in the answers they give to questions. The questions also are used to measure these needs. No further objectivity is possible.

At the other extreme are the behavioral scientists represented most typically by B. F. Skinner, principal inventor of the teaching machine. Skinner's definition of behavior is activity that can be seen or measured. If there is no observable change in activity, then no behavior change occurs. Since learning means changing behavior, learning can thus be measured by measuring the rate and direction of behavior change.[8]

This position implies that the behavior of persons is a result of shaping forces in the environment, including other people and teaching. While there is room for some theoretical dispute here, as a practical approach to management this approach meets business demands for theory (proposed explanations of actuality) better than the needs concept.

- Behavior is what is asked for and rewarded in business.
- The internal workings of attitudes and motivations, along with individual personalities, are left to their own management, together with their privacy and their right to refuse to succeed or fail.
- The presumption that individuals will respond situationally to the shaping influences in different environments leaves them free to

seek out the kinds of situations outside the displeasing job where their behavior is more personally suited to their attitudes.

- Measurable behavior is consistent with the measurable rewards basic to the business system.
- Attitudes often *follow* behavior where such behavior is attended by feedback of success and adequacy at the time it emerges.

In short, individuals at work can do their jobs well, and be paid and promoted for doing so, and retain their personal privacy into the bargain. They are paid for the result of certain behavior, and their behavior can be controlled on the job.

Is a Person a Machine?

This bald statement of the Skinnerian position as it might be considered in business strikes many as rather cold. Is there no validity, then, to the *needs theory* approach to management? To be sure, there is. The fact that the Skinnerian type of behavior measurement is the epitome of modern science while the needs theory is more Aristotelian and speculative doesn't rob the latter of its usefulness or even of its necessity. The world is not a godless, materialistic sty, and matters of the spirit and personality are still considered to be relevant to the work situation.

Thus, the needs approach is of the utmost importance in the overall management of business enterprises. It should be the basis of the total management posture toward the organization. Policy, procedure, and rules and regulations rooted in soundly thought-out, if scientifically imprecise, theories, have great value. The pursuit of equity, justice, fairness, and ego support, and the style of personal direction that Rensis Likert has called "supportive" (that is, ego building) may be impossible of measurement by many scientific standards, but they have an epidemiological value in treating the gross ills of organizational behavior. Managers who assume the hard-nosed posture because of dissatisfaction with the lack of precision in the needs theory may find themselves failing to achieve organizational objectives as they become bogged down in union troubles, turnover of key personnel, excessive attention to squabbles, and the diversion of management and staff attention from organizational goals to personal vendettas.

Once such policies and procedures have been applied, however, performance can be sharpened by the shaping processes of Skinner and the more precise measures of individual behavior.

CHAPTER 23

MBO as an Antidote to Future Shock

The world was all before them, there to choose their place of rest and Providence their guide. . . .

—John Milton, *Paradise Lost*

Alvin Toffler coined the term "future shock" in a 1965 article in *Horizon Magazine*. Subsequently expanded into a best-selling book, *Future Shock* has gone through fifteen hard-cover printings for Random House and another twenty-one in paperback printings for Bantam Books, plus mass sales for the Literary Guild and Psychology Today book clubs. Clearly, Toffler struck a popular nerve, not just with the term, but with his devastating exposition of what all of us feel as we look at the rapid changes taking place around us.

When events occur such as occurred in 1973—with Watergate, Agnew's resignation under fire, the dissolution of the Nixon Administration, and another Arab-Israeli war all tumbling upon us one after another—we grasp what Toffler meant when he described the "dizzying disorientation brought on by the premature arrival of the future." Nor are corporations fully ready for change.[1]

The consequences of an inability to cope with rapid change, Toffler suggests, are the death of permanence and the emergence of an age of transience. We are more surrounded by novelty and diversity than with stability. What we need are some new strategies for survival.

If Toffler's brief were that we really don't do a good job of managing change, we could accept it wholly. J. K. Galbraith makes this point admirably in *New Industrial State*. Corporate planners themselves concede the general inability of formal planning to forecast the future.[2]

Marshall McLuhan would suggest that the rate of change affects us because our modes of communication have speeded up and changed in character to involve us in the change more personally and immediately. The world of discovery from Columbus through Byrd might have been equally staggering to the people of Europe had they been able to share the experience of the explorers as this generation has walked on the moon with Buzz Aldrin and his friends. Professor Clare Griffin makes a most persuasive case for the nineteenth century's having been the one with the most revolutionary change, while the twentieth century is relatively docile by comparison—in the rate of change, at least.

How True Is Toffler's Perception?

If you have ever spent time studying the administrative arrangements of a hospital and have seen the management there attempt to change admissions, nursing, or dietary procedures, you might conclude that Toffler doesn't understand the situation. Like many other bureaucracies, the hospital, university, and government agency move toward progress at the pace of a tortoise with gout.

The U.S. Postal Service, despite herculean efforts from top management and loud shouts of encouragement from its clientele, still plods through bureaucratic procedures, untouched by winds of change. "Neither snow, nor rain, nor heat, nor gloom of night stays these couriers from the swift completion of their appointed rounds." Thus goes the slogan. "Then," one asks, "what in heaven's name *is* doing it?"

George M. Cohan wrote the song, "Forty-five Minutes from Broadway," in 1904. He was alluding to New Rochelle. If you aren't derailed or if some idiot hasn't run out of gas on the westside highway, you might make it in seventy-five minutes today. To the 42nd Street exit, that is.

Toffler's examples prove only what he was looking for. As befits a brief, he conveniently does not present contrary evidence.

The most important conclusion to be reached from Toffler's well-documented evidence of people, places, organizations, information, and life is that it all adds up to a new science called "futurism" which he has become identified with. The fact that he is pushing hard for this new discipline, using the advocacy of the missionary to do so, is not as easily recognized as it might be. He does not, for example, tell you outright, "I'm plugging a new discipline called futurism." If he did, you might become suspicious that his brief isn't always objective and well rounded. After all, what good is an advocate if he tells every side of the story?

Futurism is a relatively current intellectual movement. It is a form of latter-day Jules Verne fan club or a kind of applied science fiction association of ideas and people which has attracted an increasingly respectable audience. Its high priest is Herman Kahn, whose tome, *The Year 2000,* ranks as a bible of the movement (along with Toffler's book), and suggests that our society suffers from a new kind of vertigo growing out of the rapid rate of change itself.

As an escape from the present, futurism ranks well up there with raising American Beauty roses, collecting Early American antiques (authentic or fake), or watching the Washington Redskins on TV with a Budweiser in hand. Futurism is much more important in the questions it raises for the future of society than for its answers to any of those questions. While the basic literature and language of the movement is scientific and scholarly, the effect is reminiscent of other "wave of the future" movements.

Organized science has found the futurist theme extremely productive in obtaining ever-increasing appropriations for scientific research. It is not uncommon to see gale force "winds of change" blowing strongly to emphasize the inevitability of the "onward sweep" of science, which, translated, often means that the annual rate of expenditure for research buildings, doctoral grants, and new projects will rise by at least 10 percent again next year.

As an intellectual movement, futurism may be unique in that it has its own song—"Blowing in the Wind" by Bob Dylan. Quite germane for the futurist, it never gets specific about what those answers are that are forever blowing around out there in the wind.

A further indication of the strength of the futurist movement might be demonstrated in the increased attention corporations are giving to long-range planning. As practical professionals interested in the future, top managers have steadily advanced the art of planning into something resembling a science, with obscure new tools ranging from linear programming, queueing theory, and extensive use of computers, to MBO.

Among the population at large there is a rising interest in or curiosity about what the future holds. Horoscopes and astrology are big business, and self-proclaimed prophets like Jeanne Dixon find their every word caught by a vast audience.

Apparently, futurism is mildly addictive, does not lead to escalation to harder stuff, and will not have degenerative generic effects on future generations, but will, on the other hand, undoubtedly improve the breed. It also deals with managing change.

The movement that is counter-futurist, however, is far less well organized but is probably far more deeply entrenched in the fiber of society. To date, the futurists have limited their discussions solely to the features and benefits of their own wide-eyed cause and have not acknowledged the existence of these counter-futurist forces, which, I would propose, are formidable.

Presumably there is a vast middle group somewhere between the futurists and those who seek to march us forward into the past. What do we know about the majority and how change affects them?

For one thing, people are finding it harder and harder to obtain reliable facts.[3] Despite mass-media coverage of events, we aren't really, it seems, staying abreast of what is happening. Marvin Bower, long-time chief of the McKinsey & Co. management consulting firm, in emphasizing the importance to managers of making "fact-based decisions," has stressed the difficulty of taking the crucial first step and getting facts in hand.

For another, once we have the facts, it is increasingly difficult to infuse meaning into them. More raw facts, more hard data, more information and closer scrutiny of first-hand evidence don't seem to produce natural meanings.[4] Instead they call for human judgments that are harder to make about goals and objectives.

Finally, we discover that people and their behavior comprise the most obstinate area in which to uncover facts and add meaning to them. Changed social relations and changed forms of organization defy the new tools of behavioral science to define them clearly and bring meaning to the facts.

The Reality-Based Person

Midway between the futurist, who sees the revolutionary changes coming, and the antiquarian, who would return to the golden glow of the kerosene lamp, is the "reality-based" person. This person is not a rebel who would change everything, then immediately discard it all in favor of even more change. Nor is the reality-based individual desirous of abandoning the things of the present that comprise the good life in favor of the more primitive styles of the past. Though this person understands the discontent of the intellectuals and the young and the radical conservatism of those who move backward toward the rebirth of some form of landed aristocracy, the reality-based person's problem is wanting desperately to hang onto those things that are good while taking those steps that promise a future benefit or avoidance of unfavorable consequences.

Is reality today a computer printout? An IBM advertisement in *Fortune,* picturing a lonely executive wandering with head bowed across the balcony of a glass palace, promises the reader that IBM sells "not data—but reality." If IBM could deliver on this promise, overnight the demand for its product would certainly make it larger than ever. Reality isn't an object. It is an idea, a perception, or a commonly held opinion.

People don't work at making steel and automobiles as much as they produce services and spend their lives manipulating information and ideas that become more and more obscure. Planning became the fount of reality when land, which was the basis of classical economics, was unseated. Enterprising bosses, robber barons, and owners were replaced by what Galbraith calls the "technostructure"—a swirling mass of committees and task forces that make decisions. Knowledge workers saw reality as numbers, theories, symbols, and probabilities, rather than people or things.

The reality-seeking person of today has lost satisfaction in the performance of the task for its own sake. Pleasure no longer lies in the seeking and the attaining, for one has learned that the opportunity for setting a goal and achieving it is all too rare in the real world. The reality-based person is the one with the highest tolerance for ambiguity.

If Toffler were correct, MBO would probably not work, for MBO presumes that people can create, invent, and will their own future.

Odiorne's Law: "Things that Do Not Change Will Remain the Same"

In MBO it is presumed that we will not be swept into the glowing future on a wave of inevitability. Somebody will have to make it happen. If we suffer from future shock, it will only be because somebody changed things badly.

Murphy's Law that "Things left alone get worse" is false. Things get worse because we don't start with reality (which includes some actual and potential problems) and take action to solve our problems. Things get worse because we don't know that they are getting worse. Refusing or being unable to face reality, we can't see the regression.

We won't even move backward into better times unless someone makes it happen. The ecology movement, the zero population growth movement, and the preservation-of-something-or-other societies won't succeed unless they start with reality and define explicit goals of where they want to be by a specific point in time. The lesson to be learned from the Students for a Democratic Society of the sixties, which collapsed from unclear objectives and a wrong perception of reality, is that change requires managing. Lamentably, there is a trap that ensnares the managerial mind that prevents things from going places we would like them to go and permits them to deteriorate into courses that are unsatisfactory to us.[5]

Odiorne's Law that "things that do not change will remain the same" doesn't mean you *should* want change, either into the magic land of science fiction or backward into the last century. It doesn't even suggest that you *must* want to solve the problems that are killing you. But if you *do* want to do any of these things, Odiorne's Law must be taken into account. Somebody has to make it happen by starting with reality and setting a goal.

Odiorne's Law has three major postulates and thirteen theorems that are induced from the postulates (see Table 23.1).

MBO as an Antidote

Most major corporations today have adopted some form of goals-oriented management system. Sometimes called MBO and just as often by some other name, the basic idea is that *every responsible person will sit down with his or her boss and make some specific commitments to future results*. In many ways this forward projection of new ideas and commitments to achieving them would seem to be a vehicle for imple-

Table 23.1 Odiorne's Law: "Things that Do Not Change Will Remain the Same."

POSTULATES

1. People get so enmeshed in activity they lose sight of the purpose of their work. This is called the Activity Trap.
2. People who haven't any idea of where they are have difficulty in deciding what their goals are.
3. Reality consists of having a clear perception of where you are and where you would like to go.

THEOREMS

1. People caught in the Activity Trap diminish in capability rather than grow.
2. The Activity Trap originates at the top of organizations and extends to the lowest levels.
3. Organizations that have become Activity Traps kill motivation of people working in them.
4. Most problems don't get solved in activity-centered organizations, and some problems get worse.
5. Facts go into hiding in activity-centered organizations and often stay there.
6. Managers in activity-centered organizations systematically kick facts under the rug in order not to see them.
7. Production of data in activity-centered organizations is inversely related to the knowledge of reality.
8. After a decision has been made on an activity, managers resist new facts that might change that decision.
9. Reality means learning to live comfortably with ambiguity.
10. Activity-centered managers avoid reality by converting it into something else.
11. Managers in activity-centered organizations are more likely to see a reality that isn't there than a reality that is there.
12. It is easier to create reality that opposes change than to create reality that favors change.
13. Reality is found when face-to-face transactions are commonplace and is lost when face-to-face transactions are not commonplace.

menting change. At the same time it is a means of controlling such change and making it a conscious act of people rather than an implacable tidal wave independent of people and their ability to control it. That which people themselves conceive and accept prior to its being achieved should hardly frighten us nor produce vertigo, for it is we ourselves who will the changes or will their delay.

In order to be more than a system of relentlessly whipping the horses of change, however, MBO should begin with reality. It requires that four questions be answered in the goal-setting process:

1. Where are we now?
2. If we didn't do anything differently, where would we be in one, five, or ten years? Do we like that answer?
3. If not, then where would we like to be? (This is the beginning of the customary procedures of MBO.)
4. What are the optional courses open to us, and which one shall we choose?

Things do not happen solely because of inevitable social forces. There is still time to go backward into antiquing for those who choose. There is likewise ample opportunity for other people to accelerate toward an artificial and disposable plastic world of fast foods and shopping malls if they so desire (and many must so desire or it would cease).

If we realize where we are and perhaps how we arrived there, we might then see where we are trending and thus avoid some of the undesirable collisions which lie ahead. Such collisions are not fated by inexorable trends, and can be averted by foreseeing them and setting new courses. This presupposes, however, that we figure out where we want to go, or the road we are on might not carry us there. The antidote lies in a keener attention to purposes and their definition by more of the responsible people. MBO is a program that expresses that attention to purposes.

CHAPTER 24

MBO—Systematic or Mechanistic?
Nine Cases with Nine Precepts

An historical concept must be gradually put together out of the individual parts which are taken from reality to make it up. . . .

— Max Weber

Much of our formal education doesn't equip us to live in the real world. This is not because teachers themselves are particularly separated from life's affairs, but rather because so much of the knowledge taught is *mechanistic*—mechanistic in the sense that knowledge is divided into artificial compartments. In a traditional high school or college curriculum, the students start by studying algebra for fifty minutes. A loud bell rings, they close the algebra book, rush down the hall and start studying history for another fifty minutes. When that period is concluded, a bell rings again, and the pupils slam shut the history book and hurry to another room, meet another teacher, and study chemistry for fifty minutes. Thus, knowledge is bunched into neat fifty-minute bits, all different, compartmentalized, segmented, packaged, and bound for discrete wrapping and limits.

The trouble with this is the impression it creates, sometimes lasting for life, that the world of work is actually compartmentalized in such a mechanistic fashion. Out in the world of life we do, in fact, work at specialties and defend our turf against intruders from another compartment. We work at posting accounts receivable but never payables (that's another department). Purchasing is a different compartment from sales. Lunch hour is another compartment, and out in the suburbs is still another compartment called home and family.

303

The Meaning of Systematic Thinking

Systematic thinking recognizes that there are many phenomena in life and knowledge, but it starts from a new assumption: It recognizes all phenomena are related to one another and all are part of a whole.[1] A mechanistic approach, on the other hand, treats such things as being unrelated and encased in bubbles, and drives people toward atomistic thinking. Mechanistic thought forces us into the mode of seeing advancement in learning as consisting of more rigorous and detailed or expansive viewpoint which asks how things are related one to another or are variants of the same thing. This intense specialization is not without its advantages.

This shortcoming of mechanistic thinking is nowhere more apparent than in many MBO programs and certainly has dominated much of the academic research about MBO. Typically the researcher starts with the assumption that MBO consists of a simple act; usually this consists of a single set of interviews between a boss and a subordinate. The first is the *goal-setting interview* and the second is the *performance review interview*. Thus, research and training in MBO have concentrated heavily—far too heavily—on the bubble of the *two-interview model,* pressing deeper and deeper internally into the mechanics of the interview process (transactional analysis, nondirective, the coaching process, the dialogue-memo process, and so on) or into the internal characteristics of the goals produced from such interviews (make them tough, realistic, measurable, attainable, and the like). Debates about details proliferate.

The missing viewpoint is a *systematic* viewpoint, which reveals how that MBO process—or orthodox MBO—relates to the rest of the work of managing and of life in the organization generally. *Most of the failures of MBO are a product of this mechanistic viewpoint, for MBO isn't an addition to anyone's job, it is a way of running an organization. It's a way of life.*

While it is true that plain competence and technique in steps, such as setting goals, can count for something, I'm sure you now realize that MBO is more than a cookbook procedure.[2] Take the case of the manager of an accounting firm who decided to "install" MBO. He had read several useful articles and was convinced of its value. Accordingly, he sat down and dictated a memorandum to the effect that all hands were now notified that MBO was in effect. They would respond, the memorandum added, by sending him in writing in five days a complete set of their objectives. These would be the basis of future pay raises, and perhaps more ominous things.

It was not long before the manager concluded that there was no magic in MBO. The reports that were returned were perfunctory, terse, and noncommittal. Furthermore, there was barely a flicker of evidence that anybody had changed their behavior one iota as a result of what they had received in writing or what they had written in return.

Simplistic approaches often produce turbulent and undesirable effects when any new program is "installed," whether it be automation, organizational development, MBO, or merely a new payroll system. But the nine short case studies that follow illustrate clearly how MBO can work when treated systematically rather than mechanistically. Each case leads to a precept.

Case 1

A large consumer products firm with some 10,000 employees sought to draw upon the benefits of MBO. Upon the advice of a large consulting firm, the organization of the company was decentralized. Rather than a president and several vice-presidents in charge of various functions, such as manufacturing, sales, and engineering, the company was divided into ten major profit center divisions according to product lines, with a grocery products division, a basic commodities division, a feed division, and so on. A general manager was placed over each division with responsibility for total operations (except for certain central staff functions such as research). Within two years, the company could clearly be identified as operating under an MBO system and was widely written about as a model for MBO.

Precept 1: If you would like to implement MBO in a centralized company, decentralize it into profit center divisions, and you will inescapably have management by objectives. Structure and purpose are interrelated.

Case 2

A large insurance company had traditionally operated under a compensation plan for its sales agents which paid everyone from sales representatives to agency plant executives on the basis of personal sales volume produced. The result was that none of the agency plant managers did much managing. After all, if you could make a high income by personal selling or a low income by diverting your time to managing others, which would you do?

After some in-depth studies, the compensation system was changed so that managerial bonuses were paid to general agents and agency managers who achieved certain managerial objectives, but no payments were made for personal selling. Personal selling by executives stopped and the attention to management that then emerged centered around the attainment of marketing strategies as well as sales representatives' objectives. The managers' outputs were measured in terms of their subordinates' contributions but not their own. Total sales leaped impressively. The organization could be clearly identified within two years as one in which MBO ideas were firmly implanted.

Precept 2: You can modify the job behavior of people if you can change their objectives and tailor the system of rewards accordingly.

Case 3

For more than five years a middle-sized research and development laboratory was a source of concern to its owner, a major corporation, because expense budgets had been going steadily upward, but nothing was forthcoming in the way of new products, new processes, cost reductions, patents, or any other tangible output. A study showed that morale was poor because employees spent an inordinate amount of their time in organizational infighting, petty feuds, professional backbiting, and similarly unproductive and disruptive behavior. People seemed to fritter away time on nontechnical matters. There were reported instances where one group had deliberately downplayed and disrupted another's progress on a badly needed project by making an organizational end run around the lab director to higher management at the corporate headquarters with tales of mismanagement. Some facts were considerably embellished by the journey. Some of the best young people were leaving, and the more highly paid senior employees were less and less productive.

A new outside director came into the lab as chief, and immediately pressed everyone hard to define some specific important technical objectives, to make commitments to their completion, and to write off the least productive projects. There was considerably more feedback from peers and superiors, and frequent meetings were held to report progress and even failures to corporate personnel, such as marketing and production. With proper strategies sharply defined, the battles and bickering disappeared almost as suddenly as they had arisen, and a new sense of purpose emerged. The lab became a stimulating place to work. It also began to produce project results that paid off handsomely.

Precept 3: A goal is an acquired motive. Much of the explanation about motivations (inner tensions in groups or inside the individual) could be better explained as lack of common goals which unite people.

Case 4

Budgeting in a large school district had always been a predominantly political process rather than a managerial one. The superintendent and the school board had for years mounted major political and public relations campaigns, with the support of the teachers and parents groups, to attain an ever-increasing level of funding. In some years, they had been so successful that it had required great imagination and energy to figure out how to spend the money. Indeed, in one case, they made an error in calculation for a school tax election, and subsequently produced more than a $1.5 million surplus, which they didn't know how to spend! They decided to add a new building, but only after it was dedicated did they finally determine its purpose. After much private brainstorming and consulting, it was decided that, to be utilized, the edifice would require a new adult education program. The superintendent and school board then had to politic to get the support personnel and money to operate the new program. It was a moderate success, but privately many observers considered it to be something that could have been better done elsewhere by using existing schools nearer the residential areas for evening classes.

Unfortunately, the costs overburdened the economy, the town nearly went bankrupt, and the voters began to defeat every school funding proposal. Eventually, a new superintendent arrived on the scene. He announced a new system requiring the filing of statements of program plans and objectives three months in advance of the budget submission period and the need to defend the programs on their merits. Furthermore, he said the major emphasis should be on moving resources from obsolete uses to more urgent current ones. This was a radical change from the past, when every new idea was funded without any effort to abandon the dead ones. Under the pressures of a new budget system and the procedures to match (without calling it MBO), the school board and school system began operating toward objectives in order to obtain resources to do the job.

Precept 4: If people are required to state objectives in order to get funding for their jobs, they usually discover that statements of clear objectives are perfectly possible after all.[3] If they can get unlimited funding without stating objectives, they will not state them.

Case 5

A large corporation was losing market position because its employees and managers were viewed by angry customers as being arrogant, cold, impersonal, and hostile. The corporate training department decided that a special training program applying transactional analysis to customer relations was desirable because if everyone behaved in what the TA experts call an "adult-adult" mode, the relations would improve. At the completion of the course, measurement studies showed that employees were using the course skills and indeed the customers were less dissatisfied with the quality of service received at the counters of the firm. There was also a heartening upward surge of repeat business by satisfied customers.

Precept 5: When training is related to a business objective, it stands a better chance of succeeding and of its successes being noted than if it trains for the sake of training.[4] *Thus, training should be training by objectives.*

Case 6

A large corporation gave considerable autonomy to its twelve divisions. Accordingly, one division would select and hire people by one set of procedures and other might not use any part of the same system. For example, one large division used psychological tests for personality and intelligence measurement; other divisions flatly rejected such a technique. But one division seemed to have a far better track record than most in retaining and producing managers who went on to higher-level positions in the firm.

The personnel research director of the corporation did a rigorous study to find out what they were doing differently. He discovered that the major difference lay in their methods of selecting people for initial employment and their system of selecting people for promotion. The first step in their selection or promotion was to make out a complete and detailed set of objectives for the first year of the vacant job. The goals statements replaced position descriptions. Recruiting, interviewing, screening, and hiring proceeded in terms of these objectives.

The other divisions did not use this selection-by-objectives approach. They used descriptions of activities, skills, and experience required, or psychological tests but relied mainly on interviews and collected impressions of the candidates by the interviewers. The results varied and seemed to be related more to luck than design. The corporate personnel director concluded that selection could be an important application of the MBO idea, especially if objectives were used as criteria for screening candidates.[5]

Precept 6: Objectives have many uses in making managerial selection decisions. Some of them are far more valuable than the conventional uses in appraisal.

Case 7

The purchasing department of one organization was frequently embroiled in conflict with other departments, especially the engineering and development departments. Charges of ineffectiveness and slow delivery, wrong quality, and inflexibility were often aimed at the buying group. In turn, its members charged the technical people with being uncertain about specifications, vacillating on specifications, making endless changes, and being too adamant on single sources. The vice-president of administration was assigned to study the situation and find some remedies.

After hearing both sides, he recommended that a modified MBO relationship be created between the two groups. Every purchase order for materials or services being acquired for the first time would require a dialogue and written commitment, which both departments would agree to in advance. The purchasing people were told that in every initial order of any significance they were required to meet face to face with the requisitioning person or group to clarify all questions and to confirm agreements and understanding with a draft memo that would be filed with the purchase order. Both departments would have copies. In the event of disagreement about performance, the memorandum would be the basis for resolution.

After some initial discomfort among people whose only communication in the past had been the company mail system, an almost magic improvement took place. On several occasions, because the parties were busy during ordinary working hours, they used lunch hour for the discussions. Face-to-face discussion led to closer acquaintance, the quality of service leaped dramatically, and bickering was reduced to cheerful badinage and banter. Each group agreed that the other group had shown considerable improvement in behavior.

Precept 7: The basic idea of MBO is not limited to the ordinary superior-subordinate relationship. It can be used for the important relationships between people who serve one another in a staff-line relationship.

Case 8

One large organization decided to make MBO its basic managerial philosophy and system. In addition to conducting extensive training from the top down in MBO theory and practice, they started a new supervisor course. As the first step in induction into management, every new staff and line supervisor or manager was sent to this course to define objectives for their newly received assignment. After completing the course, each was required to meet immediately with his or her boss and agree on the objectives of the new position for the first year and the first quarter. This required that each new manager set objectives for mastery of the new job, for learning and development plans, and for implementing a goals program for subordinates.

Overall the MBO program in this company had mixed results because of some reluctance among experienced people to change their ways of doing things. Among the new supervisors or newly promoted persons, however, MBO became a way of life. Over a five-year period in which a number of new supervisors were added due to growth and promotions, and as replacements were made up the line, MBO became firmly cemented into the supervisory structure. With over 15 percent of the managers new in their jobs each year, within five years over 70 percent of the managers were solidly committed to practicing MBO.

"I think it would take as much effort to obliterate MBO in this organization as it takes in some organizations to install and implement it," said one executive. "The younger managers here started out from the first day on MBO and they simply don't know any other system."

Precept 8: Inducting new managers and supervisors into their first management position by formal introduction to MBO will in due course produce the most successful implementation of MBO.

Case 9

A manufacturer of consumer durables marketed almost all of its products through dealers who comprised a large and hard-to-manage group. One of the major problems in the manufacturer-dealer relationship was the independent character of the dealers. They had a substantial personal investment in inventory, plant, and cash and were important to the manufacturer, but they also serviced the product, and when their service was bad, the main manufacturer's image suffered. Control over the performance of the dealers was often tenuous, and when the dealers ran into financial or profit problems, they were apt to engage in behavior that cut their costs but also angered customers.

The parent company invested considerable time and effort in developing an MBO-centered management system tailored to the dealer-distributor. Sample objectives were researched, methods of implementation were devised, and, at corporate expense, the dealers were invited to attend a one-week seminar on managing their dealership by objectives. The training period for all dealers extended over several years, and not every dealer attended. But those who did reported excellent results, better management of the departments within the dealership, and more effective marketing and management strategies. Soon it was an article of faith that every dealer benefited from the course, and MBO became orthodox behavior in managing dealerships. Results for the corporate sponsor were extremely heartening in terms of improved market position and profitability.

Precept 9: Management by objectives can be used with business affiliates as well as with direct employees by providing it as a business service to franchises, dealers, distributors, or clients.

Conclusions

Much of today's research into MBO has to do with the narrowest construction of the idea. Such a perception usually treats MBO as if it were related only to the superior-subordinate relationship in a line organization, typically part of a large corporate or institutional environment. That, in fact, may be an overly mechanistic and constructed view. As the precepts suggest, MBO is more a philosophy and system of relating people who work together than a system of managing superior-inferior relations.

Management by objectives isn't an additional company program appended to or layered over the existing structure. It forces a relationship between all units and becomes a way of life.[6] The attempt to treat it as a mechanistic program encased in a twice-a-year interview bubble is probably the greatest cause of its misuse and failure. But seen systematically, MBO can change the character and direction of the organization for the better.

CHAPTER 25

MBO in State Government: A Case Study

The state like every other community exists for an end.
— Aristotle, *Politics*

A constructed case study probably provides the best object lessons on managing public affairs by objectives. This is a composite of experience with MBO in three different states compiled into a single illustrative case example.

Recently the State of Old West opted in the direction of MBO, with decentralized management of the state tied to MBO. It broke itself into a half dozen or more "ministates." Each area was headed by a professional public administrator, quite similar in education and experience to the other administrators. Most had MPA degrees; most were old enough to have had some solid experience but young enough to be energetic and ambitious. All were informed that they would be in charge of their own area of the state in all respects except higher education and one or two other areas. All were solemnly informed that they would be managed "by objectives" and that they were admonished to do likewise with their own responsibilities. Extensive training in MBO accompanied the program. The basic pattern of MBO as it was defined consisted of a five-part program:

Precept 1: Goal Setting. Each administrator would strike agreements with his or her superior about what was expected in terms of results, and such statements would be made in advance of the period.

Precept 2: Budgeting. The objectives would be related to resources that would be released to achieve the job. That is, the budgets would be

314

forthcoming for the tasks to be achieved, or the results would be amended if resources were for some reason not forthcoming.

Precept 3: Autonomy. Each person would be left alone to make decisions affecting his or her territory or responsibility, except that reporting periods and forms were agreed upon in advance. It was also agreed that each would obey the law and the policies affecting the various responsibility areas.

Precept 4: Feedback. Since the managers would know how well they were doing in their work while it was going on, they were expected to know when their results were faulty, to initiate corrective action upon learning of such shortcomings, and to *notify or ask for help* if things went clearly beyond permitted exceptions in a serious fashion.

Precept 5: Payoff. There would be rewards in proportion to achievement. For one thing, the merit system would reflect achievements rather than personality or political affiliation. Furthermore, performance reviews would be related to achievements against goals. A proposed incentive plan for managers was not strong enough to survive the political buffeting encountered and was abandoned before birth.

As a theoretical example, Old West's MBO had much to commend it. Yet it was not without its troubles, most of which comprise a cautionary tale to those in public administration wanting to use this most useful and stimulating method of management. In each of the five basic precepts which comprised the system, problems and lessons emerged.

1. Goal Setting: "Tell Me What's Expected in Advance"

From the beginning, when the area managers sat down with their boss to discuss objectives, it was apparent that the superiors and cabinet ranks did not really have a clear fix on what they expected from such line managers. "When I find out what we are here for, I'll try to let you know" was one kind of response. This, of course, was not a defect in MBO but in the existing state of management, for it described what had been going on for some time. In areas such as conservation the results sought were clearer than in the prison system, where nobody could agree on what prisons were supposed to produce. In environment the law was reasonably clear, but the development of strategies for getting compliance was not all that lucidly defined. A major corporation and large employer in one region stated baldly that having to live with the state's air-quality laws would put the organization out of business. It was agreed that more thought would have to be given to this case, since unemployment in that sector was already above the national average. The state unemployment service, the welfare chief, and the director of economic development of the state broke into a rather noisy argument over what the environmental objectives should be.

This led to the conclusion that each ministate must have a person responsible for shaping and recommending objectives in each functional area for its own geographical area. The bureaucracy in the state office building resisted this flowing away of its power and personnel out to the field. This battle came to a head when the state chief of mental health services went to the press over an unfortunate death of a mentally retarded child in a program initiated at the ministate level. MBO had killed this child, he charged. The governor backed the decentralization system in this case, and the MBO program survived.

Object lesson: Decentralization, or the moving of important decisions to lower levels in the organization, is not a natural phenomenon in political organizations, and when it occurs will meet resistance from those in the bureaucracy whose power flows away from them.

There are other important lessons that were learned about goal setting in this case. First, while operational objectives must be measurable, many of the best strategic goals were not reduced to measurement but to verbal statements of conditions that would exist if the goal were attained. Strategic objectives require criteria, but not all criteria will be measurable. This distinction between strategic and operational goals is an important one in government.

The patent and staple argument against MBO in public administration that "my most important responsibilities can't be measured" is, of course, true, not only in government but in business. The similarities between strategic staff work in corporations and government are startling. Neither relates to the production of things. Neither, in fact, directly and immediately relates to profits. Neither is free of unexpected changes in the world. Both work in multiyear time frames. Both produce software rather than hardware. Both entail judgments of small groups of experts and professionals rather than short-term leadership of large corps of workers.

Yet all of these conditions have not prevented the best-run organizations from using staff MBO superbly well. Service organizations, it was discovered in the ministate's case at hand, can state their goals if they abide by some guidelines that have evolved in practice:

1. Anticipate strategic missions as much as possible in defining objectives, but adjust as often as necessary.
2. Developing indicators to be watched is a means to improving output and should not become an end in itself. The indicators themselves should be changed if needed, and no manager should have more than a dozen key indicators and probably less than that. If there are more, there should be somebody helping watch and respond to them.
3. It is important to answer the question "Are we doing the right things?" prior to answering the more explicit questions of measurement and "doing things right."
4. Timing is of the essence in goal setting. Those objectives that are multiyear in character (to clean up the pollution in the Cupcake River to federal standards by June 1985) need to be stated before the budget allocations are decided, not after. Those of an operational character can be stated at the beginning of an operating period after the budget allocation and not before (to buy a new patrol boat for the Cupcake River by June 1, 1980).

   The best MBO programs in government will probably have two sets of objectives—one long-range set stated prior to budgeting or resource movement and the second or short-range set after the budget is decided.
5. Any operational indicators should be related to some kind of important output and should contain some element of time (such as park visitors per month).
6. It is a mistake to expect too much precision in operating objectives. The most exact science consists of approximations, and goal setting is far from an exact science. This need for reasonableness in goals can be achieved by stating them in *ranges*

("between 22,000 and 23,000 violations processed during the coming six months"). If some precision-obsessed soul insists upon a single number, pick the middle of the range and state it as the target.

7. Despite the special character of government objectives, which often makes them difficult to measure, a *rule of rigor* can be applied: Measure that which is measurable, describe that which is describable, and eliminate that which is neither.

8. There is a division of labor in goal setting and management. A final lesson is that higher-level people who constantly are interfering in operational management will cause the MBO program to abort. The proper function of cabinet or policy-level positions is to define strategic goals. The function of operating heads is to be responsible for operations and commit to short-term (one-year) goals. The case of the cabinet person who insists upon knowing every operational detail is commonplace in government. In addition to being a serious handicap to management by objectives, it is also easily recognized as bad management in general.

2. Budgeting: "Give Me the Resources to Do the Job"

Precept 2 of the case study at hand was the provision of resources to do the job. This meant that the manager at the lower level was given budgetary resources. But it meant more than simply getting *more* resources, it also meant some latitude in moving resources. Many state and local governmental accounting systems are labyrinths of regulations which prevent such movement ("01 funds can be spent for 01 purposes only, but 03 funds may be spent for personnel or for any other purpose exclusive of travel and entertainment").

A strategic planning system within the MBO system provided much flexibility in moving resources, for it required that for each program four questions be answered:

1. Where is this program now—statistically, factually, and in judgments about strengths and weaknesses?

2. What trends are apparent? If we didn't do anything differently, where would we be in five years?
3. What mission statements could be shaped for this program?
4. What would be the financial consequences of each mission?

These budgetary-mission statements were prepared about January of each year and forwarded upward to the state level where they comprised working papers for the compilation of the immediate budget requests and for multiyear budget planning.

The most successful application of this plan was executed by one ministate area manager who moved personally and individually with each of the key subordinates through an interview using these four questions as an agenda. Each manager prepared some notes, but the process was operated basically on a face-to-face basis. The superior then dictated the results of the interview with the subordinate and the resulting memorandum became the strategic goals position paper for the two to make their budgetary-allocation decisions upon. The questions are not simple. For example, in one discussion the superior raised these kinds of questions: "Let's look at the first topic: Where is your program now? What statistics are generated for your program? Who creates them? Are we well enough informed about the present situation? Do you have enough information to know what your strengths, weaknesses, and problems are? Do there seem to be any impending threats? What risks are we exposed to in your area? What are some opportunities which you see that might be pursued in the coming year or five years?"

Note that these are probing questions that force the subordinate to dig deeply into his or her own business before sitting down with the superior. It requires judgments about threats, risks, and opportunities. It also requires that people begin to think about new and original things as well as thinking about unthinkable possibilities.

Among the more interesting questions overheard in one such discussion were the following:

- Imagine that your budget were suddenly cut 20 percent. What would you be forced to stop doing? Then imagine after that move were completed that budget was restored again. What would you then add? Is it the same as the thing you dropped? If not, why not? Why can't you just do the new things within the existing resources?

- Are there skills in your organization or even that you yourself possess that aren't being fully used? Is there any way you could use them more fully, given the existing resources?
- What resources could be used well in your job that you don't now have? For example, what could I do, do differently, or stop doing to help you succeed?

The most important single reason for failure of MBO in government is the tendency to treat it as a paperwork system rather than as a face-to-face management system.

Memoranda are essential to verify and follow up on agreements made face to face. When used in the absence of such face-to-face dialogue, they can be poisonous. The MBO system becomes bogged down in a morass of forms, memoranda, and unintelligible evasions. The logic of MBO alone won't carry it off if the system is depersonalized and mechanistic. This is especially true in the movement of resources, for such shifts often require human ingenuity, managerial support, and some confidence, which comes with personal assurances that risks are worth taking.

This is even more valid when the manager in state government must interface with local and county officials. For them, there is no compulsion that requires that they cooperate, and only personalized and face-to-face discussions have any hope for getting mutual information, cooperation, and commitment. A random sample of the relationships that system people call *interfaces* shows that in most government agencies they are not interfaces at all but a crossing of memoranda.

Object lesson: The allocation of resources and their movement should always be done on a face-to-face basis.

---

3. Autonomy: "Leave Me Alone as Much as Possible to Do My Job"

Because steps 1 and 2 are necessary, step 3 is not possible until 1 and 2 have been completed. If subordinate managers know what is expected, and what resources and help are available, they can then be relied upon to show self-control, and govern their actions to achieve the commitments they have made. People who make commitments to somebody else whose opinion is important to them are practically obliged to do something about those commitments. This is especially true if those commitments have been made in face-to-face discussion, and have been confirmed in writing.

The power of commitment is what makes MBO work, and the absence of such commitment can cause it to fail.

The objectives and constraints are known in advance. Thus, the subordinate knows that he or she is to "achieve my commitments and stay within my constraints" and so can operate freely within these boundaries. This is significantly different from "doing what you are told to do." Under such a constraining rule, innovation and variations in methods require lengthy requests for permission, funneled through the hierarchy, and producing three effects:

1. Decision making is slowed down.
2. Innovation is dampened and ultimately dies.
3. There can be no excellence at lower levels.

The problem of managerial control remains, however. The higher-level official is always responsible for the actions of subordinates, and it would be unrealistic not to expect that higher-level persons will be concerned about lower-level performance. Yet, through the completion of explicit goals, stated in far more detail than ever was thought necessary or possible, managerial control through subordinate self-control is possible. The tightest form of control is self-control.

The exception principle requires four major rules for subordinates if it is to function as a tool of managerial control in an MBO system:

1. The subordinate must be clear on the goals and know when they are not being met, and know earlier than anybody else.
2. The subordinate should know the reasons those goals are not being achieved.
3. The subordinate should be able to initiate corrective action as soon as a deviation appears and he or she knows its reason, even before the boss learns of the problem.
4. The subordinate should be able to call for help, and thereby notify the superior early enough. Most bosses do not favor unpleasant surprises, and should be protected against them.

In the case study in the state of Old West, one manager described his rules for deciding whether to call the boss for help for notification purposes: "If the boss could hear about it from some third party, I make sure I get there first. The third party could be a peer, a higher up, or simply an indignant client."

In one instance, a highway patrol team ran into a dispute with the air police from an Air Force base in the area. On the supposition that the commanding colonel might call the state capital, the regional manager called his boss and explained the situation. When the complaint arrived in due course, no adrenalin flowed at the higher levels.

The boss, on the other hand, must show some restraint when receiving a single isolated report from a citizen. Such letters to the governor or a legislator should be bucked down through the channels for more grass-roots information, and not become a basis for tearing down the management system and recentralizing all decision making.

In one highly publicized incident, the entire decentralization MBO process was nearly scuttled because a state truck ran over a cow. The owner wrote an indignant letter to the legislature, and the state office bureaucracy attempted to use the incident as proof that MBO produced reckless and irresponsible behavior at lower levels, implying that every cow in the state was endangered by MBO. Fortunately, the director of administration for the state was able to resolve the question quickly. One of the major influences was the fact that a speedy response was forthcoming. Within an hour of the report's reaching the state capital, a responsible official from the region was on the scene, viewing the bovine's remains and making specific arrangements with the farmer for fair reimbursement from local funds. Under a more centralized system the payment would have been years in coming, for the state capital was more than a hundred miles from the cow.

MBO should produce a more personalized responsive system of government for citizens by placing decision making over small matters affecting citizens in the hands of lower-level organizations.

Delegation and leaving lower-level subordinates alone once their objectives are established clearly and resources defined accordingly produces a more localized decision system to allow for local variances.

---

4. Feedback: "Let Me Know How Well I Am Doing in My Work"

Objectives, properly defined, should comprise an instrument panel of vital signs of the organization. These vital signs are analogous to the pulse, body temperature, blood pressure, and other vital signs of the human organism. Such a vital sign as body temperature could be "normal" within a range as follows:

normal at rest, 98.6

after exercise,   99.9

in cool climate, 98.0

The physician doesn't demand that every temperature be identical with the at-rest norm. Nor should managers expect precision in measuring their own performance, nor should their superiors demand such uniformity. Take the case of the park system in Old West. Records of park use per month by summer months for four earlier years showed the following:

1976: 7,601

1977: 7,950

1978: 8,310

1979: 8,734

For planning purposes it was noted that a secular trend upward in excess of 300 to 400 a year was observed. Thus, it could be anticipated, "other things being equal," that a rise of another 400 to 500 could be expected in 1980. This became the *normal* objective. This meant that the preparation of staff assignments, preparation of park sites, tons of refuse disposal planned, and similar demands upon the park management and staff could be anticipated.

Yet the purpose is *not to forecast nor to predict*. The prediction is that park use in 1980 will be at a rate of about 9,200 persons per month, and the *prediction itself is a means to better management*. It affords the management a vital sign. If it goes above 9,500, then some kind of response is indicated. If it goes below 8,700, then some kind of investigation and possible response should be made by management.

The idea of measurement is not to punish the people for being poor forecasters. The forecast is created to provide vital signs for management to make managerial responses.

Thus, when an energy crisis came along and cut sharply into the park use (motorists could not obtain gasoline) the use of the park went down to 3,165 per month. The park manager used this opportunity to move personnel from planned services to other approved projects within the park and to other projects that had not been thought feasible outside the park.

5. Payoffs: "Reward My Accomplishments"

Perhaps the major distinction between government and business applications of MBO is not in the profit motive for the firm but in the willingness of industry to relate achievement to pay. This is achieved in several ways, and the experience of those municipalities who have developed and installed performance-payment systems has been sufficiently good that it proves such incentive compensation is viable for government.

Clearly, managerial or professional compensation in government cannot be related to *profit*. But it can be related to *performance* if these performance objectives exist.

1. There must be a norm or standard of performance related to the public purposes of the organization and the specific performance objectives of the job.
2. Such standards must be related to *output* for a period of time, usually a year.
3. The standard should be written as a form of performance contract for that year, which requires objectives to be carefully negotiated.
4. There should be statements of special conditions under which the incentive pay will not apply. If the job holder is penalized for hard luck, or rewarded for windfalls not of his own doing, the system can fail.
5. Provision for review at the higher levels must be made, both of the goals used as standards and of the results actually achieved. This assures uniformity of treatment among equals and prudent use of public funds.
6. Selective application of incentive payments is possible without destroying the system. For example, in one city the incentive-pay principle was applied to revenue-producing positions. Where the revenues went beyond historic normal standards, an ascending scale of compensation was awarded, provided certain other kinds of objectives were also met.
7. Incentives for innovative objectives can be managed through suggestion-award plans. Under current systems, it would seem to be more prudent to relate the award to the achievement by rewarding only proved savings, or demonstrated innovations that increase yield from resources.

8. Relating rewards to achievement requires a change in many performance reviews or appraisal forms and procedures. The old form of adjective-rating of performance against a list of personality traits, if related to pay increases or merit ratings, will compete and perhaps extinguish achievement-centered behavior.

In an MBO management system, performance review and merit rating must be directly related to goals and results statements, and adjective rating systems must be abandoned.

Summary

MBO in government is confronted with the same kinds of bureaucratic and political traps that every new program runs into. Strong administrative overtures are met with equal and opposite countermoves. When power flows from one place to another, people from whom it is flowing will resist that flow away from themselves. The political leader tends to seek ever-increasing amounts of power, in contrast with the economic sector where leaders operate on a principle of acquisition. It is difficult to say which is loftier. Procedures that were once important, perhaps even noble, persist long after their useful life has ended. Activity for its own sake becomes a false goal, becomes firmly embedded, and ultimately becomes a religion. Changing the behavior of bureaucrats is not easily done, for their security lies in doing what has worked in the past. There is a general reluctance to invest heavily in training that is innovative in character, for it promises to produce an unwanted change, and perhaps new centers of power. Finally, the culture of government, especially state government, is more *affiliation centered* than achievement centered. Ideology seldom dominates state government, nor is there a strong culture of performance on behalf of the constituency, with some notable exceptions.

These are the lessons of MBO in Old West's program of applying MBO. It does not prove that MBO has procedural nor logical flaws, nor that government is evil. It does demonstrate, however, that some special efforts are required to make MBO work. Turning a government into an achieving organization is never easy.

CHAPTER 26

MBO in the 1980s: Will It Survive?

The reports of my death are greatly exaggerated.
— Mark Twain

The above statement, which Twain cabled the Associated Press from Europe after it had mistakenly reported his demise will be applicable to management by objectives in the next decade. For more than 20 years people have been falling in love with the MBO idea, adopting it as their own, only to turn unfaithful in the long haul of marriage. Straw-man killings surrounding MBO have occurred ever since it became popular and useful. Yet, despite a decade of obituaries, it continues to grow more pervasive and has become almost orthodoxy in management.

What accounts for the reports of MBO failure? Why do so many observers enjoy berating MBO and announcing its end?

At least three main reasons can be cited:

1. MBO requires changes in the way things are done. This characteristic is disturbing to many, especially those who might be required to substitute output for activity and achievement for time consumption. It also requires shifting from an autocratic power basis to one more widely shared.

2. Many knowledge workers—such as staff people, engineers, and high-talent people—enjoy "winging it," shifting their goals with every new bit of knowledge they acquire. MBO requires that you make some advance commitments.

3. Many people simply don't know how to make MBO work. Many agree with MBO theory but are deficient in its technique.[1]

We have conflicting evidence on the extent to which MBO is used in management. One study by a consortium of consultants surveying general managers and executives found the system used in 80 percent of the major firms covered by the survey. Still another survey of personnel managers in the same strata of firms found only 20 percent using the MBO technique. A recent study of hospitals with more than 300 beds showed that more than half are operated by an objectives system of management and that half of the remainder plan to move toward objectives management in the near future.[2]

Several conclusions can be drawn from this evidence.

- Where the objectives are financial (profits, ROI, sales costs), MBO has persisted. Where goals are nonfinancial it is all too easy to let things slide back into older, more traditional modes.
- The functional aspects of MBO are easier to see and therefore are readily defined. Those that require a behavioral orientation have never really been fully accepted. The idea that a face-to-face discussion or group-participation method of goal setting is essential in MBO has not been nearly as well accepted as the idea that budgets, program plans, and problem-solving goals should be committed in advance.

For these reasons we often hear speeches by general managers, line executives, and chief executive officers firmly espousing MBO while behavioral scientists, psychologists, and personnel experts in the same firms declare that MBO is totally absent from their organizations.

It is readily predictable, however, that during the 1980s use of MBO as a means of managing profit center divisions and managers will grow. Pressures to improve the functional effectiveness of the organization demand a more rigorous style of analysis and commitment of all key executives. The charismatic, intuitive manager's days are numbered. The costs of failure are becoming higher, and the necessity of advance planning has become more apparent to most firms.

Making Management More Functional

Many tough problems lie ahead for executives charged with maintaining profit and productivity levels. Rising fuel and materials costs, changing standards of human relations that add to costs, and consumerism that makes quality and service more expensive are but a few of the major forces pushing more profit improvement programs to the fore. And it is in these problem areas that MBO has much to offer.

Better Management Control

During the 1980s, increased fire will be directed at traditional kinds of autocratic control. Concern about participation in decisions already is increasing, and when they are not worrying about this, employees will become even more concerned about due process, which takes time and money. Under these circumstances, self-control by the subordinate will become a challenge of the workplace. Self-control can be the tightest and most effective form of control, which is a plus for management by objectives because MBO generates self-control among those who, under the process, have made commitments to somebody else for their performance.

Tying Pay Closer to Performance

Relating output to input forces a recognition that the boss should be able to judge whether or not the company is getting back its costs in the form of useful achievement. For many, this implies a kind of incentive compensation that ties pay to results. A recent study by the Conference Board found that 30 percent of consumer products companies, 20 percent of financial firms and utilities, and nearly half of the retailers in the survey sample had inaugurated MBO plans linked to compensation.

Clearer Definitions of Strategic Objectives

During the past decade, general managers have responded to the rapid rate of change by more orderly planning at a strategic level. The ever earlier arrival of the future disaster that formerly hovered so long on the horizon has produced a kind of management by anticipation. Dependence upon momentum and faith and optimism that the good things of the past will continue forever has been shaken in many companies. Thus, in major firms, the rise of the corporate strategic planning group and demands for detailed business planning in advance of budget and resource allocation is easily observable.

These planning efforts have produced more sophisticated forecasting that requires use of all available quantitative data and analysis of that data through sophisticated analytical methods. But there is a very real danger that such planning will deteriorate into just a planning exercise. There is equivalent danger that the planning documents may blur into political white papers to prove a specific point of the moment.

MBO in the Corporate Hierarchy

The extent to which MBO will probably be used during the coming decade by various levels of management can be summarized as follows:

Boards of Directors

Unless current behavior of boards is changed by education or perhaps legal pressures, it is reasonable to expect that boards will continue to act by responding to problems and proposals rather than by initiating objectives for their firms. Most boards don't deal with strategic objectives in an affirmative way. They just react to what managements present. But when they do show occasional bursts of diligence, this effort emerges as an irritating and often damaging meddling into operations. Thus, having avoided the true role of directors by abdication, they compensate by spurts of attention to things that usually are none of their business.

General Managers

Most large company general managers will depend heavily upon MBO to manage profit centers and divisions. Most of the objectives will consist of financial or other tangible and measurable outputs; the intangible goals will receive considerably less attention in the program details. For the typical small firm, however, a seat-of-the-pants approach to objectives will prevail, leading inexorably to failure. Small-firm applications of MBO will center mostly at the operating level, with increased production and selling objectives dominating these programs. Smaller firms do not seem ready to change their usual practice of depending on their accountants to define budgetary goals, which they then rely on as indicators of directional changes.

Operating Managers

MBO has become an established, almost orthodox doctrine at operating management levels in manufacturing and selling. It is reasonably safe to predict that MBO will be as common as accounting in conducting the business of making and selling products by the end of the coming decade. The process will be so natural that many of its more formal elements will have disappeared. Sales force management can clearly define sales quotas, control ratios for expense control, new product launches, credit and problem account goals, and sales training objectives. Operating plant management has already slipped naturally into an MBO mode with engineered standards, statistical quality levels, standard costs, and the growth of operations research and computerized management systems.

Corporate Staff Positions

Staff departments should be engaged in long-range strategic goal setting, but, in fact, they tend to be obsessed with short-run, operational, and measurable goal setting that often does not fit the needs. However, engineering, marketing, and the controller departments have embraced MBO enthusiastically and will probably continue to do so. But certain other staff departments—such as personnel administration, labor relations, legal, purchasing, and research—have long track records of being indifferent, if not hostile, to defining any goals. Nonetheless, the major change in MBO generally in the 1980s will occur exactly in the corporate staff areas. The major shift wil be from staff department involvement in operating MBO toward a serious effort in strategic goal setting.[3]

Strategic Goals for Staff

For years, many have defined the traditional line-staff relationship in traditional organizational theory as absolute. The eighties, in fact, probably will see its final disappearance as staff departments tend to operate more as strategic management units.

A case in point is General Electric, where so-called strategic business units (SBU) have been in operation for many years. Already widely copied by others, the SBU may well be the forerunner of what staff departments will become, though it is not the organizational form that is important but its output—strategic goals and assessments of the present situation, trends, missions, and strategies.

This is significant because much of the resistance of present staff departments to MBO has stemmed from their reluctance to engage in, if not to downright avoid, strategic thinking.[4]

Personnel departments (with the exception of training) have generally failed to anticipate and have lacked strategic responses to new needs and requirements. It is not surprising then that OSHA, EEO, and ERISA (all of which are human-resource related) have overtaken personnel departments of most firms and found them facing backward, resisting not only advance strategic planning but even setting today's objectives.

Research departments also have been a major disappointment in some firms. Engaged in costly and pretentious projects, they have been best at adding costs rather than value, inventions, or improvements. But in companies where R&D has been headed by strategic thinkers and planners rather than responders to intellectual meanderings and urges, MBO has taken hold.

Computer departments, including MIS and data processing, have generally not been effective strategic goal setters either but have followed instead the leads of computer manufacturers and software suppliers. As a result, many firms have wandered aimlessly over the map of computer technology. During the eighties, however, more disciplined statements of strategic goals for these tools will have to emerge.

Additional Expectations

MBO thus can be expected to permeate top and middle management mainly as a control system, as a strategic planning tool, and for applied management science. Yet this won't fully satisfy most people at work, for there remains a whole backlog of expectations about MBO that have not been fulfilled—the expectations that MBO would bring about improvements in applied behavioral sciences in the workplace. Here are some examples:

1. Expectations that MBO would universally produce participative management have not been met. High hopes raised by McGregor and Likert that MBO would evolve into participative management have been only partly realized. While it is true that MBO permits and even encourages participative management, it is equally possible to operate MBO as a top-down directive kind of management. This is a source of discomfort to many who hoped that MBO would bring about an equalization of power between those in charge and those in subordinate positions.

2. Nor has the expectation that MBO would produce group management made much progress. Research shows that a solid MBO program probably equates to Likert's "System 4," but an ideal System 4, which calls for group management, simply doesn't emerge from a proficient MBO system.[5] Thus, chances for group management seem no brighter for the 1980s than in the 1960s or 1970s. It simply takes too much time, seems to be an extravagance, and creates apprehension and tension in managers who must make such a style of management work for them. At the higher levels of management, special corporate committees, management committees, and, of course, boards of directors are well established in larger firms. In smaller firms, the board is viewed as something to be managed, and committee management at lower levels is relatively unheard of.

3. A tendency to make MBO an exchange of pieces of paper rather than a face-to-face managerial system is widespread. The practice has the dual effect of creating more paper and reducing the personalized style of management in which real people deal with one another on the basis of individual differences. As a result, people feel overworked, swamped in paper, and powerless to have real influence over the decisions that affect them.

The future growth of applied behavioral science in MBO and other managerial processes in the 1980s will be a function of the amount and quality of managerial training that is invested. Not only will more managers require more training in applied behavioral science, but the quality of that training must be substantially enhanced.

Much behavioral science training is unrelated to work, management, and organizational problems. And until trainers stop asking people to do arcane exercises like assembling magnetic blocks into horses or playing other glorified parlor games and get around to applying behavioral science to the real problems of the organization, it is expected that nothing much will occur with respect to behavior change on the job.

Notes

Chapter 1.   The Simple World of MBO and How It Became So Sophisticated

1. Richard Mansell, "Management by Objectives Bibliography," mimeographed (Waterloo, Ontario: University of Waterloo, 1977), p. 55.
2. C. West Churchman, *The Systems Approach* (New York: Delacorte Press, 1968), pp. 238–240.
3. Alfred D. Chandler, Jr. and Steven Salsbury, *Pierre S. du Pont and the Making of the Modern Corporation* (New York: Harper & Row, 1971), p. 499.
4. Alfred P. Sloan, *My Years with General Motors* (Garden City, N.Y.: Doubleday & Co., 1963).
5. John S. Tarrant, *Drucker: The Man Who Invented the Corporate Society* (Boston: Cahner's Books International, 1976), p. 77
6. William H. Rodgers, *Think: A Biography of Watson and IBM* (New York: New American Library, 1970), p. 37.
7. H. Larson, E. Knowlton, and D. Popple, *History of Standard Oil [New Horizons 1927–1950]* (New York: Harper & Row, 1971), p. 22.
8. Alfred D. Chandler, Jr., *Strategy and Structure* (Cambridge, Mass.: M.I.T. Press, 1962).
9. Peter F. Drucker, *The Concept of the Corporation* (New York: John Day Co., 1946), chap. 2.
10. *Report of the Temporary National Economic Committee* (Washington, D.C.: U.S. Government Printing Office, 1973).
11. Peter F. Drucker, *The Practice of Management* (New York: Harper & Row, 1954).
12. Churchman, *The Systems Approach.*
13. George S. Odiorne, *Management by Objectives: A System of Managerial Leadership* (Belmont, Calif.: Fearon Pitman Publishers, 1965).
14. William H. Whyte, Jr., *The Organization Man* (New York: Simon & Schuster, 1956).
15. Virgil K. Rowland, *Standards of Managerial Performance* (New York: Harper & Row, 1959).
16. Edward C. Schleh, *Successful Executive Action* (Englewood Cliffs, N.J.: Prentice-Hall, 1955). Probably the first full book exposition of MBO. Schleh wrote on MBO in "Make Your Executive Merit Rating Realistic," *Personnel* 29, no. 6 (May 1953): 480–483.
17. *How Am I Doing?* (Minneapolis: General Mills, 1955).

18. Walter S. Wikstrom, *Managing with and by Objectives,* National Industrial Conference Board, Studies in Personnel Policy no. 212 (New York, 1968).

19. Edwin A. Locke has published numerous articles in such journals as the *Journal of Applied Psychology.* Most of his twenty-one reports were published between 1965 and 1970 when MBO was becoming most widespread.

20. Henry L. Tosi and Stephen J. Carroll. Tosi's first research report appeared in *Management of Personnel,* 1965, no. 4. Tosi was a frequent coauthor with S. Carroll, and their work was reported in *Academy of Management Journal* 11 (1968); *MSU Business Topics* (Spring 1979); *California Management Review* 12, no. 4 (Summer 1970); and *Management Review* 58, no. 9 (September 1969).

21. Harry Levinson, "Management by Whose Objectives?" *Harvard Business Review* 48, no. 4 (July–August 1970): 125–134.

22. "Should Teachers Say No to MBO?" *Briefing News* (Washington, D.C.: National Education Association, 1976).

23. H. E. Wrapp, "Management by Objectives or Wheel and Deal," *Steel* 160 (May 1967).

Chapter 2.   MBO as a Style for Managers

1. Hedrick Smith, "Steering a Middle Course," *New York Times,* 24 January 1978, sec. 1, p. 1, noted the calculated and uninspirational style of the executive branch under President Carter.

2. The shape of the new approach is best described by C. West Churchman, *The Systems Approach* (New York: Delacorte Press, 1968).

3. The extent of this new human development movement for the eighties is spelled out by George S. Odiorne, *Personnel Administration by Objectives* (Homewood, Ill.: Richard D. Irwin, 1971).

4. Howard Carlisle, *Management: A Contingency Approach* (Chicago: Science Research Associates, 1977).

5. David McClelland, *The Achieving Society* (Princeton, N.J.: D. Van Nostrand Co., 1961).

6. Richard Beckhard, *Organization Development Strategies and Models* (Reading, Mass.: Addison-Wesley, 1969).

7. Thomas H. Naylor and M. James Mansfield, "The Design of Computer Based Planning and Modelling Systems," *Long Range Planning* 10, no. 1 (February 1977): 16–25.

8. Carlisle, *Management: A Contingency Approach.*

Chapter 3.   Stemming the Decline of Risk Taking and Innovation

1. Joseph Schumpeter, *Capitalism, Socialism, and Democracy,* 2d ed. (New York: Harper & Row, 1943). An excellent beginning for people wishing to become acquainted with the philosophy and work of this germinal thinker.

2. Adolph Berle and Gardiner Means, *The Modern Corporation and Private Property* (New York: Macmillan Co., 1937).

3. Oswald Knauth was the first major corporate executive to come out in print and make the then breathtaking admission that old-style capitalism was dead. Prior to *Managerial Enterprise: Its Growth and Methods of Operation* (New York: W. W. Norton, 1948), such statements had been limited to muckrakers.
4. Carl Polanyi, *The Great Transformation* (Boston: Beacon Press, 1944). Here Polanyi referred to the collapse of the market economy as an accomplished fact.
5. Douglas McGregor, *The Human Side of Enterprise* (New York: McGraw-Hill Book Co., 1960).

Chapter 4. Looking at Your Organization as a System

1. Erwin Laszlo, *The Systems View of the World* (New York: George Braziler, 1972).
2. George S. Odiorne, *Management and the Activity Trap* (New York: Harper & Row, 1974).
3. Robert Merton, ed., *Sociology Today: Problems and Prospects* (New York: Basic Books, 1959). Merton is generally agreed to be the originator of the goals displacement concept in bureaucracies.
4. Norman R. F. Maier et al., *Supervisory Subordinate Communication in Management* (New York: American Management Association, Research Study #52, 1961).
5. Peter F. Drucker, *The Practice of Management* (New York: Harper & Row, 1954).

Chapter 5. The System of Management by Objectives

1. Rensis Likert, *New Patterns of Management* (New York: McGraw-Hill Book Co., 1961).
2. Norman R. F. Maier et al., *Supervisory Subordinate Communication in Management* (New York: American Management Association, Research Study #52, 1961).

(Notes do not appear in Chapters 6 and 7.)

Chapter 8. Measuring Organization Performance

1. Charles P. Edmonds III and John H. Hand, "What Are the Real Long Run Objectives of Business?" *Business Horizons* 19, no. 6 (December 1976): 75–81.
2. Richard M. Steers, "Problems in Measurement of Organization Effectiveness," *Administrative Science Quarterly* 20 (1975): 546–558.
3. James David Thompson, *Organizations in Action* (New York: McGraw-Hill Book Co., 1967).
4. J. H. Barrett, *Individual Goals and Organization Objectives* (Ann Arbor, Mich.: Institute for Social Research, University of Michigan, 1970).
5. Robert Anthony, *Managerial Accounting,* 5th ed. (Homewood, Ill.: Richard D. Irwin, 1976).
6. George R. Berman, "Constructing and Using a Company Cost Index," *Business Quarterly* 41, no. 2 (Summer 1976): 50–53.

Chapter 9. What Successful Goal Setters Do

1. Thomas P. Kleber, "Forty Common Goal Setting Errors," *Human Resource Management* 11, no. 3 (Fall 1972): 10–13.
2. Dale D. McConkey, "Twenty Ways to Kill Management by Objectives," *Management Review* 61, no. 10 (October 1972): 4–13.
3. George S. Odiorne, *Management by Objectives: A System of Managerial Leadership* (Belmont, Calif.: Fearon Pitman Publishers, 1965).

Chapter 10.   Management's Vital Signs: The Indicators We Live By

1. G. Sommerhoff, "The Abstract Characteristics of Living Systems," in *Systems Thinking*, ed. F. E. Emery (Baltimore, Md.: Penguin Books, 1969). See also R. G. Murdick, "M.I.S. for MBO," *Journal of Systems Management* 28, no. 3 (March 1977).
2. J. J. Todd, "Management Control Systems: A Key Link Between Strategy, Structure, and Employee Performance," *Organizational Dynamics* 5, no. 4 (Spring 1977).
3. Rex V. Brown, *Research and the Credibility of Estimates* (Cambridge, Mass.: Harvard University Press, 1969).

Chapter 11.   Setting Routine and Emergency Goals

1. Peter F. Drucker, *The Practice of Management* (New York: Harper & Row, 1954).
2. F. D. Barrett, "The MBO Time Trip," *Business Quarterly* 37, no. 3 (Autumn 1972): 42–51.
3. John Argenti, *Corporate Collapse: The Causes and Symptoms* (New York: Halsted Press, 1976).

Chapter 12.   Problem Solving by Objectives

1. Herbert Simon, *The New Science of Management Decisions* (New York: Harper & Row, 1960).
2. Charles H. Kepner and Benjamin B. Tregoe, *The Rational Manager* (New York: McGraw-Hill Book Co., 1960).
3. This chapter has been adapted from George S. Odiorne, *Management Decisions by Objectives* (Englewood Cliffs, N.J.: Prentice-Hall, 1969).

Chapter 13.   Setting Creative Goals

1. George S. Odiorne, *How Managers Make Things Happen* (Englewood Cliffs, N.J.: Prentice-Hall, 1961).
2. For a more complete discussion of this topic, see Margaret Mead, *Cultural Patterns and Technological Change* (New York: Mentor Books, 1955). See also a useful recent study, Bernard W. Taylor III and K. Roscoe Davis, "Implementing an Action Program

via Organizational Change," *Journal of Economics and Business* 28, no. 3 (Spring 1976): 203–208.

4. Joseph Juran, *Managerial Breakthrough* (New York: McGraw-Hill Book Co., 1961).

Chapter 14. Setting Personal Development Goals

1. R. A. Pitts, "Unshackle Your Comers," *Harvard Business Review* 55, no. 3 (May 1977).

2. Robert N. McMurry, "Validating the Patterned Interview," *Personnel* 23, no. 4 January 1947): 263–272.

3. Ronald J. Burke and Tamara Weier, "Readying the Sexes for Women in Management," *Business Horizons* 20, no. 3 (June 1977): 30–35.

4. For a full statement of the opposing viewpoint, see Frederic Margolis, "A Survey of Methods in the Human Potential Movement," *Training and Development Journal* 31, no. 2 (February 1977): 38–42.

5. J. Sterling Livingston, "The Myth of the Well-Educated Executive," *Harvard Business Review* 49, no. 1 (January–February 1971): 79–89.

6. George S. Odiorne, *Training by Objectives: An Economic Approach to Management Training* (New York: Macmillan Co., 1971).

Chapter 15. Selection by Objectives

1. Hugo Munsterberg, *Psychology of Industrial Efficiency* (Boston: Houghton Mifflin, 1913).

2. M. Joseph Dooher and Elizabeth Martin, *Selection of Management Personnel,* vol. 1 (New York: American Management Association, 1957).

3. William H. Whyte, Jr., *The Organization Man* (New York: Simon & Schuster, 1956). See also B. Schlei and D. Grossman, *Employment Discrimination Law* (Washington, D.C.: BNA Books, 1976).

4. Howard C. Lockwood, "Critical Problems in Achieving Equal Employment Opportunity," *Personnel Psychology* 19 (Spring 1966): 3–10. See also A. G. Bayroff, "Test Technology and Equal Employment Opportunity," *Personnel Psychology* 19 (Spring 1966): 35–39.

5. John S. Fielden, "The Right Young People for Business," *Harvard Business Review* 44 (March–April 1966): 76–83. See also G. Benson and J. Chason, "Entry Level Positions," *Journal of College Placement* 37, no. 1 (1976).

6. George S. Odiorne, *Personnel Administration by Objectives* (Homewood, Ill.: Richard D. Irwin, 1971). See also Edward C. Schleh, *Management by Results* (New York: McGraw-Hill Book Co., 1961).

7. Marvin D. Dunnette and Wayne K. Kirchner, *Psychology Applied to Industry* (New York: Appleton-Century-Crofts, 1965).

8. Robert Kahn et al., *Discrimination without Prejudice* (Ann Arbor, Mich.: Institute for Social Research, Survey Research Center, University of Michigan, 1964).

9. Vance Packard, *The Pyramid Climbers* (New York: McGraw-Hill Book Co., 1962), pp. 279–285. See also Martin Gross, *The Brain Watchers* (New York: Random House, 1962).

10. Harry Levinson, "The Pschologist in Industry," *Harvard Business Review* 37 (September–October 1959): 93–99.

11. Mason Haire, "Psychological Problems Relevant to Business and Industry," *Psychological Bulletin* 56, no. 3 (May 1959): 174–175.

12. Anne Anastasi, *Psychological Testing* (New York: Macmillan Co., 1954), pp. 8–18.

13. Clark Hull, *Aptitude Testing* (New York: World Book Co., 1928), pp. 16–19.

14. Robert M. Guion, *Personnel Testing* (New York: McGraw-Hill Book Co., 1965), pp. 469–471.

15. Hull, *Aptitude Testing.*

16. Five widely used inventories are: (1) California Psychological Inventory, (2) Gordon Personal Profile, (3) Guilford-Zimmerman Temperament Survey, (4) Minnesota Multiphasic Personality Inventory, and (5) Thurston Temperament Schedule.

17. As Guion, in *Personnel Testing,* has commented concerning personality measurement, "The available measures have generally been developed for clinical and counseling purposes rather than for selection, they are too subjective, and the evidence of their value is too weak."

18. Robert N. McMurry, "Validating the Patterned Interview," *Personnel* 23, no. 4 (January 1947): 263–272.

19. W. Lloyd Warner and James C. Abegglen, *Occupational Mobility in American Business and Industry* (Minneapolis: University of Minnesota Press, 1955), pp. 95–97.

20. Frederick R. Kappel, "From the World of College to the World of Work," *Bell Telephone Magazine* (Spring 1962).

21. Warner and Abegglen, *Occupational Mobility in American Business and Industry.*

22. J. Sterling Livingston, "The Myth of the Well Educated Executive," *Harvard Business Review* 49, no. 1 (January–February 1971): 79–89.

23. Philip Marvin, *The Right Man for the Right Job* (New York: Dow-Jones, Irwin, 1973).

24. Abraham Maslow, *Motivation and Personality* (New York: Harper & Row, 1954).

Chapter 16. Relating Salary Administration to MBO

1. Thomas H. Patten, Jr., *PAY: Employee Compensation and Incentive Plans* (New York: Free Press, 1977).

2. Adolph A. Berle and Gardiner C. Means, *The Modern Corporation and Private Property,* 2d ed. (New York: Macmillan Co., 1940).

3. Edward E. Lawler III, *Pay and Organizational Effectiveness: A Psychological View* (New York: McGraw-Hill Book Co., 1971).

4. H. H. Meyer, "The Pay for Performance Dilemma," *Organizational Dynamics* 3, no. 3 (Winter 1975).

5. Ernest C. Miller, "Top and Middle Management Compensation," *Compensation Review* 8, no. 4 (1976): 33–46.

Chapter 17. Zero-Based Budgeting and MBO

1. Allen Austin, *Zero Base Budgeting: Organizational Impact and Effects* (New York: AMACOM, 1977).

2. Peter A. Pyhrr, *Zero Base Budgeting* (New York: John Wiley & Sons, 1973).

3. G. Mimmier and R. Hermanson, "A Look at Zero Base Budgeting: The Georgia Experience," *Atlanta Economic Journal* 26, no. 4 (July–August 1976).

4. Peter A. Pyhrr, "Zero Base Budgeting," *Harvard Business Review* 48, no. 6 (November–December 1970): 111–121.

5. U.S. Senate, Subcommittee on Intergovernmental Relations, Committee on Government Operations, *Compendium of Materials on Zero Base Budgeting in the States* (January 1977).

Chapter 18. Discipline by Objectives

1. Henry Ford II, *The Human Environment and Business* (New York: Weybright & Talley, 1970).

2. Reed Richardson, *Collective Bargaining by Objectives* (Englewood Cliffs, N.J.: Prentice-Hall, 1977).

3. Douglas McGregor, *The Human Side of Enterprise* (New York: McGraw-Hill Book Co., 1960).

4. B. F. Skinner, *Beyond Freedom and Dignity* (New York: Alfred A. Knopf, 1971).

5. John Gardner, *Excellence* (New York: Harper & Row, 1961). Gardner refers to this as the "democratic dilemma."

6. George P. Morris, *Progressive Discipline* (Ann Arbor, Mich.: Bureau of Industrial Relations, University of Michigan, 1959).

7. Dallas Jones, *Industrial Discipline* (Ann Arbor, Mich.: Bureau of Industrial Relations, University of Michigan, 1961).

Chapter 19. The Problem of the Annual Performance Review

1. B. F. Skinner, *The Behavior of Organisms: An Experimental Analysis* (New York: Appleton-Century-Crofts, 1938) is a basic study. More current is Skinner's *Contingencies of Reinforcement: A Theoretical Analysis* (New York: Appleton-Century-Crofts, 1969).

2. Charles Hughes, *Goal Setting: Key to Individual and Organizational Effectiveness* (New York: American Management Association, 1965).

3. Marion Kellogg, *What to Do About Performance Appraisals* (New York: American Management Association, 1965).

4. Douglas McGregor, *The Human Side of Enterprise* (New York: McGraw-Hill Book Co., 1960).

5. Gary P. Latham and Gary A. Yukl, "A Review of Research on the Application of Goal Setting in Organizations," *Academy of Management Journal* 18, no. 4 (December 1975): 824–845.

6. McGregor, *The Human Side of Enterprise.*

7. Edward A. Locke of the University of Maryland authored numerous articles reporting his research on the limitations under which MBO works and goal setting as a behavior-shaping influence.

8. T. R. Manley, "Personal Value Systems of Managers and the Operative Goals of Organization" (Ph.D. diss., Rensaellaer Polytechnic Institute, 1972).
9. R. E. Lefton et al., *Effective Motivation Through Performance Appraisal* (New York: John Wiley & Sons, 1977).

Chapter 20.   Six Factors in Assessing Potential

1. Norman R. F. Maier, *The Appraisal Interview* (New York: John Wiley & Sons, 1958).
2. Richard M. Steers, "Effects of Need Achievement on the Job Performance–Job Attitude Relationship," *Journal of Applied Psychology* 60 (1975).
3. Eric Vetter, *Manpower Planning for High Talent Manpower* (Ann Arbor, Mich.: Bureau of Industrial Relations, University of Michigan, 1968).
4. Robert M. Guion, *Personnel Testing* (New York: McGraw-Hill Book Co., 1965).

Chapter 21.   The Politics of Implementing MBO

1. Dale McConkey, "Implementation, the Guts of MBO," *Advanced Management* 37 (July 1972).
2. Robert N. McMurry, "The Case for Benevolent Autocracy," *Harvard Business Review* 36, no. 1 (January–February 1958): 82–90.
3. Aaron Lowin, "Participative Decision Making: A Model, Literature Critique, and Prescription for Research," *Organization Behavior and Human Performance* 3, no. 1 (February 1968): 68–106.
4. John C. Aplin, "The Impact of Superior's Attitude on the MBO Process" (Ph.D. diss., University of Iowa, 1975).
5. Gerard F. Carvalho, "Installing Management by Objectives: A New Perspective on Organization Change," *Human Resource Management* 11, no. 1 (Spring 1972): 23–31.
6. C. E. Lindblom, "The Science of Muddling Through," *Public Administration Review* 19 (1959).
7. Frederic V. Malek, "Managing for Results in the Federal Government," *Business Horizons* 17, no. 2 (April 1974): 23–28.
8. Arthur C. Beck and Ellis D. Hillmar, *Making MBO/R Work* (Reading, Mass.: Addison-Wesley Publishing Co., 1976).
9. Neville Eastman, "MBO in R & O," *Business Management* (Great Britain) 100, no. 2 (February 1970): 28–31.
10. Peter F. Drucker, *The Practice of Management* (New York: Harper & Row, 1954).

Chapter 22.   How Much Subordinate Participation in Goal Setting?

1. Gary P. Latham and Gary A. Yukl, "A Review of Research on the Application of Goal Setting in Organizations," *Academy of Management Journal* 18, no. 4 (December 1975): 824–845.

2. Rensis Likert, *New Patterns in Management* (New York: McGraw-Hill Book Co., 1961).

3. Douglas McGregor, *The Human Side of Enterprise* (New York: McGraw-Hill Book Co., 1960).

4. Gerald Gurin, Joseph Veroff, and Sheila Feld, *Americans View Their Mental Health* (New York: Basic Books, 1961).

5. Victor H. Vroom and Philip W. Yetton, *Leadership and Decision Making* (Pittsburgh, Pa.: University of Pittsburgh Press, 1973).

6. Latham and Yukl list sixty-three research reports on applications of goal setting which bear out the *situationality* of goal-setting methods.

7. George S. Odiorne, "Participative Management—A Game," *Personnel Administration by Objectives* (Homewood, Ill.: Richard D. Irwin, 1971), chap. 22.

8. Robert F. Mager, *Goal Analysis* (Belmont, Calif.: Fearon Pitman Publishers, 1972).

Chapter 23. *MBO as an Antidote to Future Shock*

1. J. A. Cornelissen, "Corporate Strategy in the Eighties," *Long Range Planning* 10, no. 5 (October 1977): 2–6.

2. Liam Fahey and William R. King, "Environmental Scanning for Corporate Planning," *Business Horizons* 20, no. 4 (August 1977): 61–75.

3. Harold W. Henry, "Formal Planning in Major U.S. Corporations," *Long Range Planning* 10, no. 5 (October 1977): 40–45.

4. H. S. D. Cole, "Accuracy in the Long Run—Where Are We Now?" *Omega* 5 (November 1977): 529–542.

5. George S. Odiorne, *Management and the Activity Trap* (New York: Harper & Row, 1974).

Chapter 24. *MBO—Systematic or Mechanistic?*
Nine Cases with Nine Precepts

1. C. West Churchman, *The Systems Approach* (New York: Delacorte Press, 1968).

2. This emerges from F. D. Barrett, "Everyman's Guide to MBO," *Business Quarterly* 38, no. 2 (Summer 1973): 65–82. See also P. J. Chartrand, "From MBO to Business Planning," *Canadian Personnel Journal* 18, no. 4 (September 1971): 15–22.

3. M. L. Carter, "Effects of Management by Objectives System in Public Two Year Community Colleges" (Ed.D. diss., Ball State University, 1976).

4. George S. Odiorne, *Management Training by Objectives* (New York: Macmillan Co., 1970).

5. George S. Odiorne, "Selection by Objectives," *Management by Objectives* (London) 3, no. 2 (1971).

6. Heinz Weihrich, "A Study of the Integration of Management by Objectives with Key Managerial Activities and the Relationship to Selected Effectiveness Measures" (Ph.D. diss., University of California at Berkeley, 1973).

(Notes do not appear in Chapter 25.)

Chapter 26.   MBO in the 1980s: Will It Survive?

1. Dale McConkey, "How to Succeed and Fail with MBO," *Business Quarterly* 37, no. 4 (Winter 1972): 57–61.

2. Fred Luthans and Jerry Selentin, "MBO in Hospitals: A Step Toward Accountability," *Personnel Administrator* 21, no. 7 (October 1976): 42–45. See also Fred E. Schuster and Alva F. Kindall, "MBO—Where Do We Stand Today?" *Human Resource Management* 13, no. 1 (Spring 1974): 8–11. See also "Thirteen Most Popular Management Techniques," *Administrative Management* 34, no. 6 (June 1973): 26–29.

3. Thomas P. Kleber, "The Hardest Areas to Manage by Objectives," *Management by Objectives* 2, no. 2 (1972): 41–43. See also Dale D. McConkey, "20 Ways to Kill MBO," *Management Review* 61, no. 10 (October 1972): 4–13.

4. J. Bologna, "MBO's Precursor—Strategic Planning," *Management by Objectives* 6, no. 4 (July 1976).

5. Bruce A. Kirchoff, "Is MBO System Three?" *Management by Objectives* 2, no. 4 (1973): 12–15.

Index

continued

continued